With a sovereign gesture, Andrés Burbano puts Latin America and the Global South on the agenda of media archaeological research, at the same time opening up a perspective for them as exciting and indispensable agents in the deep-time interplay between the sciences, technology, and the arts. In his case studies, past, presences, and possible futures meet to form fascinating surprise generators.

—**Siegfried Zielinski**, Professor Emeritus of Media Theory, Universität der Künste, Berlin, and author of *Deep Time of the Media: Toward an Archaeology of Hearing and Seeing by Technical Means*

With five case studies, Burbano introduces a world of Latin American innovations that could potentially alter existing histories of media. Unifying historical research with experimental design, this book is required reading for scholars and students of art, media, and design practices and histories.

—**María Fernández**, Associate Professor of Art History, Cornell University, Ithaca, and author of *Cosmopolitanism in Mexican Visual Culture*

Different Engines offers fascinating insights into the history of Latin American media technology. Beyond this, Burbano proposes a promising new research approach that not only brings together ideas from STS, art history, media archaeology, and postcolonial studies, but introduces experimental interaction with historical media as an indispensable epistemological method.

—**Margit Rosen**, Head of Collections, Archives & Research at the Zentrum für Kunst und Medien, Karlsruhe (ZKM), and editor of *A Little-Known Story About a Movement, a Magazine, and the Computer's Arrival in Art: New Tendencies and Bit International, 1961–1973*

Different Engines: Media Technologies from Latin America constitutes the first genuine historical ontology of media artifacts from the much-ignored experience of the Global South. Whether focusing on early experimentations with analog sound and image or examining contemporary involvement with computerized media, what the author finds in these revealing Latin American cases is a lot of anticipatory, creative, and alternative technological paths that defy the conventional accounts and criteria of successful innovation. With *Different Engines*, Burbano emerges as the premiere decolonial and pluriversal media archaeologist in the world at present. His "experimental reconstitutions" of past experiences should become an obligatory passage point for those wishing to engage in similar reconstructions with other media or in other parts of the South. This eminently readable book will be of great value to those interested in science and technology studies, media studies, design, and cultural, decolonial and Latin American Studies.

—**Arturo Escobar**, Professor Emeritus of Anthropology, University of North Carolina, Chapel Hill, and author of *Designs for the Pluriverse: Radical Interdependence, Autonomy, and the Making of Worlds*

Different Engines

Different Engines investigates the emergence of technologies in Latin America to create images, sounds, video games, and physical interactions. The book contributes to the construction of a historiographical and theoretical framework for understanding the work of creators who have been geographically and historically marginalized through the study of five exemplary and yet relatively unknown artifacts built by engineers, scientists, artists, and innovators. It offers a broad and detailed view of the complex and sometimes unlikely conditions under which technological innovation is possible and of the problematic logics under which these innovations may come to be devalued as historically irrelevant. Through its focus on media technologies, the book presents the interactions between technological and artistic creativity, working towards a wider understanding of the shifts in both fields that have shaped current perceptions, practices, and design principles while bringing into view the personal, social, and geopolitical singularities embodied by particular devices. It will be an engaging and insightful read for scholars, researchers, and students across a wide range of disciplines, such as media studies, art and design, architecture, cultural history, and the digital humanities.

Andrés Burbano is Professor in the Arts and Humanities School at the Open University of Catalunya (Barcelona, Spain) and Visiting Lecturer at Donau-Universität (Krems, Austria). He holds a Ph.D. in Media Arts and Technology from the University of California at Santa Barbara (California, EEUU) and has developed most of his academic career in the School of Architecture and Design at Universidad de los Andes (Bogotá, Colombia). Burbano works as a researcher, curator, and interdisciplinary artist. His research projects focus on media history and media archaeology in Latin America and the Global South, 3D modeling of archaeological sites, and computational technologies' historical and cultural impact. Burbano has been appointed as ACM SIGGRAPH 2024 Chair.

Research in Design, Technology and Society

Series Editors: Daniel Cardoso Llach (*Carnegie Mellon University, USA*) and Terry Knight (*Massachusetts Institute of Technology, USA*)

The Routledge Research in Design, Technology and Society series offers new critical perspectives and creative insights into the roles of technological systems and discourses in the design and production of our built environment. As computation, software, simulations, digital fabrication, robotics, 'big data,' artificial intelligence and machine learning configure new imaginaries of designing and making across fields, the series approaches these subjects critically from enriched socio-material, technical and historical perspectives – revealing how conceptions of creativity, materiality and labor have shifted and continue to shift in conjunction with technological change.

Computer Architectures
Constructing the Common Ground
Edited by Theodora Vardouli and Olga Touloumi

Data Publics
Public Plurality in an Era of Data Determinacy
Edited by Peter Mörtenböck and Helge Mooshammer

The Digital Bespoke?
Promises and Pitfalls of Mass Customization
Ginger Coons

The Architectural Imagination at the Digital Turn
Nathalie Bredella

Different Engines
Media Technologies From Latin America
Andrés Burbano

For more information about the series, please visit: https://www.routledge.com/Routledge-Research-in-Design-Technology-and-Society/book-series/RRDTS

Different Engines
Media Technologies From
Latin America

Andrés Burbano

LONDON AND NEW YORK

Cover image credit: PCB schematic of the Wiring input-output board, 2003. Courtesy of Hernando Barragán

First published 2023
by Routledge
4 Park Square, Milton Park, Abingdon, Oxon OX14 4RN

and by Routledge
605 Third Avenue, New York, NY 10158

Routledge is an imprint of the Taylor & Francis Group, an informa business

© 2023 Andrés Burbano

The right of Andrés Burbano to be identified as author of this work has been asserted in accordance with sections 77 and 78 of the Copyright, Designs and Patents Act 1988.

All rights reserved. No part of this book may be reprinted or reproduced or utilised in any form or by any electronic, mechanical, or other means, now known or hereafter invented, including photocopying and recording, or in any information storage or retrieval system, without permission in writing from the publishers.

Trademark notice: Product or corporate names may be trademarks or registered trademarks, and are used only for identification and explanation without intent to infringe.

British Library Cataloguing-in-Publication Data
A catalogue record for this book is available from the British Library

ISBN: 978-1-032-00111-1 (hbk)
ISBN: 978-1-032-00116-6 (pbk)
ISBN: 978-1-003-17278-9 (ebk)

DOI: 10.4324/9781003172789

Typeset in Sabon
by Apex CoVantage, LLC

To my daughter, Amelia, and her quest for the golden glue to stick together her mind and heart.

Contents

Acknowledgements	x
Introduction	1

PART I
Backtracking — 15

1	Bioacoustics and Photography, Brazil, 1832	17
2	The Color Wheel of Television History, Mexico, 1939	43
3	COMDASUAR: A Very Personal Computer, Chile, 1978	78

PART II
Sidetracking — 113

4	Lua: The Scripting Side of the Moon, Brazil, 1993	115
5	Wiring: Tangible Interaction, Intangible History, Italy, Colombia, 2003	147
	Conclusions	181
	Index	201

Acknowledgements

Words are insufficient to express my profound gratitude for the individuals and communities who have made this publication possible; every author behind a book is just a visible node of an extensive grid of friendship, creativity, debate, and intellectual exchange. The following lines aim to make accountable that knowledge is at the heart of the word "acknowledgment."

To begin with, I am extremely grateful to my family, María Clara Bernal and Amelia Burbano, for their love and unlimited support. Writing a book could be described in numerous ways, but it is first and foremost a feat of love in its fierier nature. With the memory of my parents in mind, I also want to thank my close and distant family in the south of Colombia, particularly my sister Ivonne Burbano.

I would like to extend my profound appreciation to the professors who were part of my doctoral committee in the Media Arts and Technology program at the University of California Santa Barbara: George Legrady, Marko Peljhan, Curtis Roads, Lisa Jevbratt, and W. Patrick McCray; my doctoral dissertation is the first component of this book's content. Additionally, I would like to highlight the valuable collaboration of former MAT fellows Pablo Colapinto, Marco Pinter, and Javier Villegas.

The primary intellectual references for my work come from Media Archeology, Science and Technology Studies, and Latin American Studies. This project would not have been possible without the authors who have been my critical guidelines: Siegfried Zielinski, Erkki Huhtamo, Emanuel Adler, Hernán Thomas, Eden Medina, María Fernández, and Arturo Escobar. Some are personal friends, and others I know through their ideas and publications. In the following lines. I want to express my gratitude to the people and organizations who were crucial for the unfolding of each of the chapters that make this book:

Chapter 1: Boris Kossoy, Jacques Vielliard (RIP), Guillermo Santos, Pierre Puentes, and the Instituto Moreira Salles in Brazil.
Chapter 2: Guillermo González Camarena Jr. (RIP), Arturo González Camarena, Paul Coan, Juan José Diaz Infante Casasús, Leonardo Aranda, and the Centro Multimedia in Mexico.

Chapter 3: José Vicente Asuar (RIP), Ignacio Nieto, Andrés Cabrera, Federico Schumacher, Claudio Asuar, and the Revista Musical Chilena.

Chapter 4: Roberto Ierusalimschy, Luiz Henrique de Figueiredo, Waldemar Celes, Fabiana de Barros, Caroline Menezes, Analivia Cordeiro, Margit Rosen, and the ZKM | Zentrum für Kunst und Medien in Germany.

Chapter 5: Hernando Barragán, Casey Reas, Lauren Lee McCarthy, Andrés Colubri, Myriel Milićević, Michal Rinot, Karmen Franinović, Camilo Ayala, and María Amalia García.

I am also very grateful to the publications around the globe that offered me the opportunity to disseminate parts of the research that constitute the corpus of this book; they are *Neural, Artnodes, Leonardo, Aural, Ars USP,* and many others. I express my deepest gratitude to the SIGGRAPH and ISEA communities, which allowed me to share, expose, and discuss some of the ideas materialized in the following pages. Thanks to the Media Art Histories conference steering committee members: Francesca Franco, Chris Salter, Inge Hinterwaldner, and Machiko Kusahara, among others. I must also mention authors like Esteban García, Alessandro Ludovico, Everardo Reyes, and Gabriela Aceves, who inspired me with their sister publications.

The generosity of the diverse institutions that hosted me through these years has been treasured. Therefore, I acknowledge the help of my friend and colleague Angus Forbes, who invited me to the University of California Santa Cruz, where I had the chance to share part of my research and further develop some of the last chapters. I would also thank Oliver Grau, Wendy Coones, and the students exposed to some of the book's content at the Donau-Universität in Krems, Austria. And more recently, to Myriel Milićević and the creative students who were part of the *Zoophonie* workshop at the Potsdam Fachhochschule in Germany. Additionally, I want to express my appreciation to my new team at the Universitat Oberta de Catalunya, mainly Joan Fuster and Pau Alsina. Finally, special thanks go to Professor Silvia Restrepo; without her support, this publication couldn't be a reality. Consequently, I should acknowledge the Vice Presidency of Research and Creation's Publication Fund at Universidad de los Andes in Bogotá, Colombia, for its financial support in the last stages of the book.

Naturally, I want to sincerely recognize the outstanding work of the editors behind the Routledge *Research in Design, Technology, and Society* book series, Terry W. Knight and Daniel Cardoso Llach. This book collection is fascinating and a much-needed platform to articulate diverse intellectual reflections, which is difficult to find elsewhere. I also want to thank the rest of the Routledge team, Trudy Varcianna, Francesca Ford, Caroline Church, and Varun Gopal.

And last but not least, I recognize the invaluable assistance of my friend and mentor Tupac Cruz for his decades of friendship; we started our common path in the '90s by listening to the music of Sonic Youth and Pavement xii *Acknowledgements*

and also playing in our own band Los Telúricos; now he is a master of style correction and editing. Tupac has made an outstanding contribution to the process of writing and reviewing the more than 80,000 words in the English language that build this publication. Even though English is not my mother tongue, I feel I inhabit these words now.

Introduction

In the final pages of his *Deep Time of the Media*, Siegfried Zielinski sketches a set of abstract visual portraits of geographical locations, like Riga, Budapest, and Saint Petersburg, to summon a cluster of stories that point towards what he describes as a shift in direction for media archaeology, a "shift of geographical attention: from the North to the South, from the West to the East."[1] When I first came across this captivating intellectual proposal, I asked myself what could be the place of Latin America in this reanimated cartography. Although as a matter of principle it was clear that the field of media archaeology was open to every effort to redraw and reinterpret the slipstreams of technological emergence, it seemed difficult to imagine Latin America as playing a relevant role in the foundational processes of contemporary media. Being from Latin America myself, I wondered why this kind of question had never been prominent in my intellectual environment.

I still had a clear memory of what it was like in the early 1990s, when I was an undergraduate film student in Bogotá, fascinated by the work of media pioneers like Shigeko Kubota and Nam June Paik. At the time, media technologies like digital video were the subject of feverish bouts of discussion and speculation among my peers, based for the most part on the fact that it was extremely difficult to actually get to use, say, a Commodore Amiga 2000 to compose video effects. If there were media archaeological vestiges to be found in my own backyard, how come I had never caught a glimpse of them or heard about them? And if they were indeed there, weren't they likely to be exceptions? In all likelihood, ventures undertaken by people who, although coming from or even based in Latin America, were culturally and economically closer to the Global North. Although these doubts were grounded on my own experiences, it was just as easy for me to shift to another layer of experience and consider how easily and profusely media technologies had been embraced by different cultural agents in Latin America. Zielinski's research clearly warranted the assumption that the absence of a technological industry did not entail an absence of engagement with technology and that this engagement spanned the continuum between conception, design, implementation, and use. I began to look for traces, and

DOI: 10.4324/9781003172789-1

2 Introduction

after a while, I decided to draft my own map in order to visualize relevant potential case studies in the history of media technology and media art in Latin America, correlating local developments with their mainstream historical counterparts in the Global North. I soon found myself confronted by an eclectic collection of cases that clearly suggested that this field of inquiry could be much more extensive and complex than anything I might have anticipated.

Although my inquiries were sparked by the possibility of unearthing neglected artifacts from the past, my work was also driven by a practical commitment to media as a field where research and creativity can (and at times must) collaborate. Indeed, as I began to examine my historical case studies, I realized that they had much to tell me about contemporary media technologies – in fact, these old artifacts could often be read as *alternative* media technologies, in more than one sense: in the sense that they suggested an alternate development of technologies that we know today as standardized commercial products and in the sense that, for this very reason, they clearly resonated with contemporary efforts to produce alternative media technologies and practices capable of contesting the claim to dominance and homogeneous outputs of those commodities.

It seems clear to me now that contemporary media technologies cannot be fully comprehended if we are not prepared to scan and rescan their recent and deep historical trails. Over the past couple of decades, media scholars have done much to show that these trails often lead in unexpected directions, away from the centers of political and cultural dominance where technologies are standardized into industrially produced commodities. The premise of this book is that those historical traces can be analyzed, reinterpreted, and experimented on within a frame that is relevant to contemporary discourses on media, design, and technology, and that in doing so, it is possible to articulate a broader and richer account of the emergence of now-familiar media and to gain thereby a deeper understanding of what they are – and perhaps most importantly, what they can be.

One thing that I have learned from my case studies is that the history of media technologies in Latin America cannot be written in a strictly chronological key since it is populated by events that, although located in the past, haven't actually *happened* yet. This singular temporality suggests that the most important task is not that of simply inscribing these events in the global historical record, where they will most likely play the part of oddities or anomalies. To do justice to these events is rather to engage in a different kind of historiography, one whose main focus is to allow us to deal with what technologies are for us now and what they can be for us in the future. For this reason, I see the study of different territories as linked to a theoretical exercise that seeks to tap into the parallel, unrealized, but virtual unfolding of alternative technologies.

For this book, I have chosen to develop detailed accounts of five case studies that open the way for a critical assessment of the reasons why certain

Introduction   3

versions of media technologies developed into what may now be called a technological mainstream that is both geographically and culturally biased. In different ways, these case studies all present us with a unique kind of narrative: they show us what it has been like for people in Latin America to engage in unique forms of uncanny invention. I use the word "invention" grudgingly, knowing full well that it may already bias our attention towards the kind of event that we are told makes up the history of technology: discoveries, first times, strikes of luck, and lightning bolts of genius. Although my case studies do often present us with individuals and groups who could easily be cast in the role of the isolated and misunderstood inventor, that is not the kind of narrative that I think will allow us to really unpack invention as a concept that plays out in a wide range of forms. I will examine the emergence of five media-technological systems – a system of photography, a system of color television, a computer system for music composition, a programming language, and a platform for physical computing – each of which demonstrates a different way in which invention can take place within a singular process of interaction between personal, cultural, social, economic, and geopolitical trajectories. Inevitably, each of the five devices examined will count as an index to an ecosystem whose complexity can only be summarily conveyed. Although it seems obvious enough to say that we cannot account for media technologies created in Latin America without a degree of familiarity with the cultural framework within which they have emerged, discourses on technology are often unwilling to stray too far from a conceptual construct that seems to take it for granted that, ultimately, culture is not a central factor in the development of technology. However, an emphasis on the cultural determinants of technological invention can often lead scholars to overlook the concrete technical constituents and decisions that ultimately make media technologies what they are. In this book, I have tried to strike a balance between these two approaches in order to offer a sufficiently complete account of the multiplicity of factors that contribute to the emergence of a new artifact.

The case studies analyzed in this book are all, although in different ways, instances of technological creativity: they show us how technological systems are created, but they are also specifically concerned with technologies *for creating*. With that in mind, this book aims to contribute to the construction of a historiographical and theoretical framework that may allow us to understand the work of creators who have been geographically and historically marginalized. I will thus consider the complex (and sometimes unlikely) conditions under which technological change is possible and some of the problematic logics under which these inventions have come to be devalued as historically irrelevant. In parallel, I will try to contribute towards a wider understanding of the major technological shifts that have shaped current perceptions, practices, and design principles, while bringing into view the personal, social, and geopolitical singularities embodied by particular devices.

4 *Introduction*

My argument will be that the five media technologies examined here can be read in a close dialogue with ongoing discussions in the fields of media history, media art history, and media archaeology, and my aim in doing so will be twofold. On the one hand, I mean to contribute to the creation of a more nuanced understanding of the historical development of media technologies in Latin America and the Global South; on the other, I would also focus on a theoretical and future-oriented understanding of the interactions between the technical and the creative. In that sense, I do not understand media technologies simply as tools that can be used for art. Instead, I aim above all to examine how creative practices can shape technical systems at their point of emergence and to take a close look at the creative processes that underlie the conception and assemblage of different apparatuses. The fact that the creative processes described in my case studies are linked to marginalized locations and individuals who worked in relative isolation from the mainstream allows us to see aspects of technological creativity that are probably less conspicuous in industrialized or institutionalized environments. My hope is thus to shed light on the specific cultural, economic, geopolitical, and personal constellations through which a marginal history of media technologies can be outlined as a promising field of study.

In each of the following chapters, I will be taking a very close look at the technical features of the projects described here in order to craft a new understanding of the relationship between technological creativity and artistic creativity, and of the socio-technical dynamics within which they are embedded. In this regard, I will argue that it may be better to abandon preconceived notions about technological inventiveness, and I will build on the idea that media technologies can have specifically unique strands of idiomatic development. In that sense, I consider my detailed inquiries into the singular development of a television device, or of a programming language, as meaningful to our overall understanding of what these technologies are from an ontological point of view, just as the study of a dialect can be regarded as accounting for what a given natural language is. The analogy with linguistic constructions is not incidental since language has been one of the first aspects of Latin American societies to be examined as instancing the complexities and pitfalls of regarding identity as an ontological given.[2] Ongoing conversations in the contemporary history of science have considerably expanded our understanding of the ways in which processes of modernization and colonization played a part in shaping all levels of Latin American societies while generating unique and often ignored strategies of resistance.[3] The monolithic understanding of Latin America's relation to successive waves of oppressors and exploiters is often quick to brand technology as one of the enemy's most prominent weapons, and this may be one of the reasons why the idea of writing a history of Latin American technologies can make some readers uncomfortable. Although I share the discomfort, I argue that a reflection about the role of technologies, and of media technologies in particular, may allow us to find novel ways of

Introduction 5

negotiating and reframing inherited discursive and practical assumptions about Latin America.

Inspired by postdevelopment studies, media technologies cannot be simply framed as foreign to Latin American societies, and it might even be said that when they are examined under the right lens, these societies actually exemplify the sense in which technologies as a whole need not be conceived as inherently linked to Western forms of economic and political power. If we make an effort to reconceptualize technology in light of case studies such as the ones in this book, we will see that past and present hierarchical structures have never been as definitive and irreversible as they seem to those who benefit from them. My stake is thus that it is time to develop modes of analysis that shift away from an understanding of media technologies based on the kind of success that is measured in terms of standardization and mass production, and it is my hope that the case studies discussed in this book can inspire analogously independent and locally sensitive research projects by individuals and institutions. The first of my case studies dates back to the late nineteenth century, and the last is a project that, in a sense, is still underway. In response to this broad historical spectrum, I have attempted to embrace a malleable argumentative strategy that yields a complex picture out of in-depth accounts of very particular historical configurations.

The case studies are arranged in chronological order, and the book is split in two parts: Part I Backtracking discusses two analog systems and one example of early digital computation, and Part II Sidetracking deals with two systems that can be described as digital in the contemporary sense. Although I do not mean to present an overarching and continuous narrative, my hope is that when they are read in sequence, these studies shed a light on the shifts brought on by the passage from analog media into media based on computational processes. The chapters in Part II Sidetracking specifically work towards an understanding of computation that is informed by the media-archaeological notions of deep time and topos study, which also bring into view the role of cultural creativity in the development of the digital sphere. By taking a close look at the way in which technological systems were conceived and built, often by hand, by particular individuals, the book seeks to make these socially and geographically embedded processes visible as embodied in concrete and singular artifacts.

In addition to laying out a small set of chronologically ordered key events in a parallel history of media technologies, the book sketches a theory of media shaped by its case studies. Together, the five case studies delineate a historical ontology of artifacts that determine possibilities for creative activity within specific cultural settings and complex intercultural matrices, contributing to a broad understanding of design as a socio-technical field by paying particular attention to the possibilities for use – or the affordances – implicit in each artifact. The alternative stories outlined by the five case studies move through the fissures of dominant narratives about invention and innovation, revealing unexpected locations of change, reimagining

6 Introduction

geographies, and setting forth new cartographic lines that configure broader maps, allowing us to navigate the true diversity of technical innovation and technologically mediated creativity and dispelling a vision of uniformity and teleology that is often driven by political and economic interests. Through an understanding of these five individual devices informed by a grasp of the geopolitical, social, and personal conditions of their coming into being, the book aims to articulate a sense of technologically mediated creativity as a cultural and social field whose past, present, and future are ripe with unexplored potentialities.

In the following pages, I will be taking a closer look at the way in which the five media technologies came into being at different temporal and geographical locations. The three chapters that make up Part I Backtracking explore three historical examples that can be described as marginal inventions of media technologies that we now regard as old acquaintances: photography, color television, and computer music software and hardware. These case studies allow us to understand that processes of technological innovation have been part of Latin American history for a long while and that a deep time perspective may uncover valuable lessons about how technologies can be understood and used. In part, these chapters also mean to redress a tendency on the part of Latin American historical discourses to disregard the role of technology, a tendency that is echoed in the fact that debates within cultural criticism and social movements in Latin America tend to view the links between creativity and technology as suspicious and as inevitably reinforcing colonial and neoliberal structures of domination. The first three chapters of the book compile materials that suggest an alternative understanding of what media technologies have been and can be within marginalized and peripheral geographies.

In a way, Part I Backtracking will be set against the shifting background of Latin America's long twentieth century, beginning with the incipient stages of Brazil's transformation into a postcolonial nation state in the early nineteenth century. The first chapter carefully reconstructs the conditions under which Hércules Florence, a Frenchman who immigrated to Brazil in the early 1820s developed a photographic translation of the printing press in order to reproduce a notational system that he had designed to transcribe the sound patterns of Amazonian fauna. As the chapter will show, Florence achieved a unique field of interaction between image, sound, and printing technologies, determining photography as a device-type that does not have the camera obscura at its core and that does not rely on the picture as the conceptual paradigm for what is to be reproduced. In that sense, the cameraless photography practiced by Florence amounts to an alternative paradigm in light of which it is possible to reinterpret the official history of photography, shedding new light on the role of European pioneers like Bayard and Talbot.

The second chapter traces the early stages of the introduction of color into television, arguably the most influential of media during the post–World War II period. As the chapter shows, the history of color television is critically aligned with the geopolitical restructurings brought on by the Cold War in successive stages, visible in the way in which the globe came to be divided through the use of different color television systems and the intertwined development of competing space programs and electronic imaging technologies. The chapter offers a glimpse of this complex historical moment through the work of Guillermo González Camarena, a Mexican self-taught engineer and musician who designed and attempted to mass-produce and market an adapter system that could be used to convert black-and-white television systems into color devices. As I will show, postrevolutionary Mexico attempted to create a synthetic account of the nation as a postcolonial state, and in this context, the search for an autonomy of resources was closely linked to the creation of a coherent national culture. This gave rise to an enduring cultural climate that crucially inflected the embrace of media technologies by artists and cultural agents from the 1920s and onwards. González Camarena uniquely exemplifies the hybrid figure of an engineer, artist, and entrepreneur, who, throughout his life, channeled the vision of a postcolonial state infused with a mixture of references to Mexico's precolonial past and living native cultures with an acute sense of modernity framed by a vision of industrial development as a national concern. González Camarena's color television system, which was for a while believed to have been the basis for the color television systems used by NASA in the Apollo and Voyager missions, is shown to be informed by a project for technological nationhood driven by Mexico's efforts to consolidate as a coherent state.

The third chapter tells the story of the development of a music-making microcomputer in Chile during the late 1970s. The chapter outlines Chile's rich history of informatics and computation, and its unique tradition of avant-garde musical composition, in order to craft a detailed account of the activities of José Vicente Asuar, a composer, engineer, and university professor who, in 1978, designed and built a device that he called the Asuar Digital Analog Computer, or COMDASUAR. Chile's socio-political conditions in the early 1970s fostered a wide range of innovative institutional and social spaces that made room for avant-garde artists, scholars, and social scientists to practically engage with the idea of technology as a tool for liberation. The COMDASUAR embodies a very particular range of concerns that drew its creator away from the institutional-technical space of avant-garde composition in university laboratories and towards the personal computer as a design paradigm that could make new approaches to sound and composition available to a wider variety of users who could now engage with advanced musical techniques in their own domestic or workspace. The chapter argues that Asuar's visionary anticipation of the personal computer as a design paradigm is in part set against the abrupt closure of this vital space of interaction between popular culture and experimental thought and practice brought on by Pinochet's coup d'état in 1973.

Although the cases of Florence, González Camarena, and Asuar are ripe with historical riddles and fascinating byways, my approach to these first

8   Introduction

three case studies is not simply historical. Rather, my interpretive strategy entails a constant search for alternative conceptual models through which to think about the particular way in which these technologies undermine the distinction between what is historically significant and what is historically successful. In the case of media technologies, this distinction grounds a narrative that links the process of invention to later processes of industrial production, commercialization, and standardization. I argue that these narratives do not allow for an accurate account of the kind of *significance* that these cases bring into view. The first three case studies show us how the emergence of a media technology has often been embedded within a space of creativity that went beyond that of problem-solving within previously established industrial and commercial frameworks. Figures like Florence, González Camarena, and Asuar demonstrate, in different ways, a unique articulation of what we would now tend to regard as isolated professional skills, some artistic, some scientific, some technical, and a few in-between. The people who developed these technologies and the context within which they carried out their work could both be said to operate within a hybrid field where science and technology interacted with necessities and visions that had not been delimited by an established professional or cultural space, merging the social roles of the inventor, the teacher, the artist, the engineer. Although it would be anachronistic to describe these individuals as designers, my conceptual framework focuses on the conception and emergence of devices whose linkage with human creative activities can be conceptualized under a broad understanding of design.

This approach has also led me to the idea that, if we regard these media technologies as designs, it may be useful to examine whether their potentialities allow for contemporary practical explorations since it may be said to be proper to the ontology of a design to allow for further developments beyond the conditions under which it emerged. To understand a media technology as a design, in that sense, is to look behind and beyond its position as a historical artifact and to articulate its conditions of emergence in such a way as to grasp its functionality in an open way. In this, I have been inspired by the work of contemporary artists like Leslie García, Tania Candiani, Iván Puig from Mexico, and Jorge Barco and the collective Atractor from Colombia, who have relied on the media archaeological framework to craft a vision of a non-industrial and non-standardized experience of media technologies. This kind of media practice based on historical research challenges the notion that Latin American societies can only aspire to the position of consumers with respect to the products of media technology corporations, and I have tried to open up a practical dimension for my work in order to contribute to what I regard as a crucial complement to my scholarly research.

The conceptual guideline for this layer of my project is the notion of a "resignification of technology," coined by the Argentinean theorist Hernán Thomas. In his own work, Thomas is interested in the way in which technologies are ontologically determined by their inscription and potential

Introduction 9

reinscription within different cultural systems, and in that sense, my take on resignification differs from his. In the context of my argument, the resignification of technology can only be properly understood through a hybrid interpretive approach that establishes a dynamic conversation between history, theory, aesthetics, and practice – with an emphasis on the last.

My own practical engagement with the work of Florence, González Camarena, and Asuar began as a series of projects that were originally conceived in order to test the technical consistency of the historical documentation available for the devices that they created. My first aim was simply to construct functioning models based on their designs to determine and understand how they worked. As I did this, however, I found that these reconstructions could also bring up the unexplored potentialities of the media technologies that they had created. Gradually, my work on these projects developed into a mixture of historical and experimental practice, which then led me to confront theoretical questions about the roles of intentionality and functionality in the consolidation of mainstream technologies, and about the unexpected ramifications of a renewed engagement with discarded or undeveloped, marginalized alternatives to this mainstream. This process has led me to regard practice as a key component in the resignification of media archeological devices and to interpret practice as the localized and transformative actualization of potentialities in relation to a given technological structure. It is in this sense that I conceptualize my experimental reconstructions as resignifications, and I have used this procedure in the first three chapters of the book in order to base my analyses on a living and embodied relationship with the technologies created by Florence, González Camarena, and Asuar.[4] Ultimately, this line of thinking lends support to the claim that it is not possible to understand what these devices *were* without a protensive experience of what they *could be*, and I argue that this way of understanding the idiosyncratic temporality of media technologies is something that can be better understood in light of their emergence in contexts like Latin America.

In Part II Sidetracking, I turn my attention to two case studies located closer to our own technological daily lives and to a geopolitical framework that has been considerably rearranged by the ideologies of globalization and neoliberalism. In the two chapters that make up Part II Sidetracking, I will explore how Latin American creators have contributed their voice to recent efforts to reconfigure the landscape of digital media technologies through their work in programming and interaction design. We will also get a sense of how the shift from analog to digital technologies played out in Latin American societies around the last turn of the century in cultural settings that welcomed the arrival of digital technologies while experiencing the ambiguous promises of an increasingly deterritorialized world. These two chapters offer a critical perspective on the assumption that digital media technologies are inherently global and democratic, although they also show how the network paradigm and the emergence of open-source culture have

10 Introduction

enabled forms of interaction that clearly destabilize inherited geographical paradigms and question simplistic accounts of the digital divide.

The inclusion of case studies that are relatively contemporary also allows us to understand how technological innovation and the artistic use of media technologies interact under current conditions and to register the shifts in the structures of geopolitical cultural domination enabled by digital technologies and network culture. More specifically, the two last case studies advance an approach to computation through the lens of media studies and, thus, work towards an understanding of the computer as a media technology that is able to create positive feedback loops in specific socio-cultural environments that determine new forms of locality. The computer will be understood first and foremost as a reprogrammable machine that is able to embody the identity of various media while also transforming other things into media, and I will argue that these processes of transformation bring into play, in a range of nonhierarchical feedback dynamics, all the layers of the computer as a device, from the logical to the tactile. The fact that some of these transformative possibilities were first explored by Latin American engineers, scientists, mathematicians, and designers, warrants the claim that marginalized geographical regions have played a crucial role in productively pluralizing the development of contemporary mainstream technologies.

The first of these two case studies of recent development is the book's sole success story – and it is a global success story at that. It is also the most abstract and elusive of the artifacts to be analyzed, one that in fact tested my own ability to understand what determines the identity and mode of existence of artifacts in general. Lua is a programming language created by a group led by two computer scientists and a mathematician working for a laboratory at the Pontifical Catholic University in Rio de Janeiro: Roberto Ierusalimschy, Waldemar Celes, and Luiz Henrique de Figueiredo. It is a light multiparadigm scripting language that has garnered global recognition for its simplicity, flexibility, and portability, features that account for its wide use in a growing variety of computing contexts, from video game development to graphics plug-ins, and from mobile apps to embedded applications. The language was created in the early 1990s to serve the specific technical needs of engineers and other scientists working for Petrobras, Brazil's state-owned oil company, and its history is in fact deeply rooted in that country's earlier efforts to achieve a degree of technological autonomy by establishing a home-grown computing industry. As the chapter shows, Lua's unexpected global spread is the result of a unique alignment of local and global historical contingencies, and it was crucially enabled by the decision to release the language under an open-source license. The chapter examines these contingencies to show how, in this case, the restrictions under which technology can be developed in a Latin American context can be said to drive a change of paradigm with potentially global repercussions. It also reflects on the extent to which an artifact like Lua can be regarded as significantly bound to its place of origin and examines more generally the possibility of understanding abstract constructs like programming languages as culturally determined.

The fifth and final chapter analyses the critical contribution to the consolidation of physical computing as a field of practice by a Colombian engineer and designer Hernando Barragán. In 2003, while he was a student at the Interaction Design Institute in Ivrea, Italy, Barragán conceived Wiring, a platform that builds on Processing and that can be regarded as the immediate forerunner to popular physical computing and electronics prototyping kits like Arduino and Fritzing.[5] The Wiring platform comprises a single-board microcontroller, a printed circuit board (PCB), and a programming language that is informed, like Lua, by the philosophy of open-source. Barragán, who as an undergraduate experienced a unique surge of excitement around the convergence of digital technologies and artistic practice in Bogotá in the early 1990s, based his design on premises that were clearly centered on affordability, accessibility, and malleability, in a direct attempt to overcome the limitations of existing boards like the Basic Stamp and the Nylon. Inspired by a foundational understanding of code as an artistic medium, Barragán envisioned an easier way of programming microcontrollers, reading sensors, and controlling actuators, in order to allow artists and designers to experiment with embodied computing creatively and at a low cost. The chapter sheds new light on the historical origins and theoretical implications of physical computing by locating its emergence within a tradition that reread the basic epistemological premises of modern design through a Southern lens, referring to the theoretical and pedagogical work of Gui Bonsiepe and Tomás Maldonado. These theorists of design, who met at the Ulm School of Design and went on to forge vital links between the school's ideas and South American realities, critically theorized the introduction of computing tools into the practice of design and the shift from objects to interfaces, arguing for the interface as a design paradigm capable of promoting new forms of creative use. The chapter argues that Barragán's work can be said to have spearheaded a second shift, from interfaces to object-interfaces, driven by the desire to make the intricacies of hardware open, tangible, and manipulable, opening the way for what can be described as new kinds of users.

These five case studies have led me to develop a synthetic disciplinary framework that has allowed me to integrate and comparatively assess previous contributions to the field, laying out a set of questions that makes it possible to outline a comprehensive and systematic approach to the study of media technologies from Latin America. I have embraced a syncretic conceptual framework, drawing from different fields and establishing a dialogue between the discourses of media archaeology, media art history, contemporary media history, design, historical epistemology, science and technology studies, decoloniality, and Latin American studies. My hope in doing this is to seek out a new way to define the historicity of the technologies studied on a case-by-case basis. This is particularly important given

12 *Introduction*

the risk of approaching the material with unexplicit preconceptions, a risk that is surprisingly strong when it comes to media technologies. How much am I assuming by simply naming my objects of study "a system of photography" or "a music computer," and by so doing, reading them in light of device types that, however recent, seem quite naturalized by now? In order to guard my analysis from these risks, I have developed an argumentative strategy that connects analytical and comparative angles of interpretation to envision a new way of looking at the role of technologies in cultures that are typically regarded as recipients, rather than creators of it.

My research situates Latin America within contemporary discussions of media archaeology and media history, and simultaneously rehearses a redrawing of the boundaries and premises of these fields through the study of marginalized technological traditions, bringing into the conversation the work of scholars like Arturo Escobar, Hernán Thomas, David Edgerton, Emanuel Adler, Judith Sutz, and Susana Quintanilla, who have made substantial contributions to the history and philosophy of technology in Latin America. The intersections between media, art, technology, and science have been the subject of intense, imaginative, and sharp work in Latin America for the past few decades, led by writers like Beatriz Sarlo, María Fernández and Eduardo Kac. As postcolonial and decolonial studies have strengthened and widened their research spectra, a growing number of peers have already laid out a promising and exciting array of projects, some of which overlap with my own. In that sense, I have been fortunate to be able to draw from the work of colleagues like Yury Takhteyev, Eden Medina, Anita Say Chan, Gabriela Aceves, Alejandra Bronfman, Eduardo Herrera, and Joanna Page. Like many of these authors, I have found that the stories that we are trying to tell call for a keen balancing act between detail and overview, more so knowing that many of our readers are not familiar with the particular configurations and nuances of Latin American social and cultural realities. Thus, rather than attempting to establish general trends in the development of media technologies in Latin America, this book presents its analyses under the figure of the archipelago, inspired by the work of Edouard Glissant.[6] The particular case studies scatter like islands to configure an open territory through their detailed singularity, and the task of navigating the known waters and of finding connections between them is something that I hope will inspire further research. By following Glissant's premise, I intend to show that this history should not be understood as a complement or appendix to established narratives but as an endeavor that may well trigger a reassessment of historiographical methods and structures.

Notes

1 Siegfried Zielinski, *Deep Time of the Media* (Cambridge: MIT Press, 2008), 255–280.
2 Walter Mignolo, *Idea of Latin America* (Malden, MA; Oxford, 2021), 149–162.

Introduction 13

3 Mauricio Nieto Olarte, *Exploration, Religion and Empire in the Sixteenth Century Ibero-Atlantic World: A New Perspective on the History of Modern Science* (Amsterdam, 2021), 271–280.
4 Experimental reconstruction is a specific type of research practice in archaeology that has been more recently also adopted by historians of science and (even more recently) computational design/media scholars (e.g., experimental reconstructions of computer-aided design systems).
5 "Processing is used to create projected stage designs for dance and music performances; to generate images for music videos and film; to export images for posters, magazines, and books; and to create interactive installations in galleries, in museums, and on the street. But the most important thing about Processing and culture is not high-profile results – it's how the software has engaged a new generation of visual artists to consider programming as an essential part of their creative practice." Processing.org.
6 Glissant, *Treatise on the Whole-World.* 141–147

Bibliography

Glissant, Édouard. *Treatise on the Whole-World*, translated by Celia Britton. Liverpool: Liverpool University Press, 2020.
Mignolo, Walter. *Idea of Latin America*. Malden, MA; Oxford: Blackwell Publishing, 2021.
Nieto, Mauricio. *Exploration, Religion and Empire in the Sixteenth Century Ibero-Atlantic World: A New Perspective on the History of Modern Science*. Amsterdam: Amsterdam University Press, 2021.
Zielinski, Siegfried. *Deep Time of the Media*. Cambridge: MIT Press, 2008.

Part I

Backtracking

1 Bioacoustics and Photography, Brazil, 1832

Introduction

If it seems obvious to say that the emergence of photography was a historical event, it is not entirely clear just what kind of an event it was. When we name an event, we are establishing a simple way of speaking about something complex; the value of the simplification is to give us an orientation within a multiplicity of converging and diverging streams, which, seen from a distance, can be said to congeal into the arrival of something new: a shift or a rupture. Undoubtedly, the arrival of photography introduced one such rupture in the space of images, the arrival of a new kind of visual artifact, and the fact that most key developments seem to have taken place somewhere between 1800 and 1840 make the image of a rupture even more compelling. According to Vilém Flusser, after this event, the space of images would be irrevocably divided in two: "traditional images," produced by eye-hand coordination processes, and "technical images," produced by apparatuses.[1] But this distinction, with which we feel wholly familiar, is not as transparent or definitive, from a historical point of view, as it may seem to us; in other words, the event of which this distinction is a repercussion is not itself a simple division of the space of images into two fields. We may approach a nuanced understanding of the emergence of this distinction between traditional and technical images if we consider some unexplored moments in the early historical configuration of photography, when photography was not yet what we now understand as a relatively standardized set of technological frameworks, something to which we can assign an identity of sorts. As Gilbert Simondon has pointed out, "technical objects" become "themselves" through a process of stabilization of potentialities that are hardly cohesive at first. This process, according to Simondon, must be viewed as "internal," that is, as a process of self-individuation not informed by external conditions or requirements and, thus, as independent of the uses to which the technical object will later become linked.[2] If we place ourselves at the stage that Simondon defines as the "primitive distribution" of possibilities that would later converge in the technical object "photography," we will likewise find ourselves in a zone of indetermination, where the

DOI: 10.4324/9781003172789-3

18 *Backtracking*

distinction between "technical" and "traditional" images is yet to congeal: in this not-yet of photography as a technology we may find images that can be described as handmade even though they were produced by an apparatus. What we get a glimpse of, if we do this, is a complex, perhaps even disorienting, sense of what the emergence of photography might have been.

The zone of indetermination that I have just described is very much the habitat of the photographic experiments conducted around 1832, in Brazil, by the Frenchman Hércules Florence. Indeed, the images that resulted from these experiments exemplify the contradictory condition of being something like technically produced traditional images. What accounts for the indeterminate status of these photographs for us is the fact that they were not produced using the camera obscura. Instead, they were handmade images reproduced technically by means of photochemical processes, without using a lens and a camera to create an inverted projection and, thus, capture an image of the external world. Since the camera was culturally interpreted as standing in for a viewer of this outside, the photograph, as the result of this process of introjection and fixation, was understood as analogous to a view, an interpretation further driven by efforts to establish an analogy between what the camera did and what a painter did. The fact that Florence's system of photography did not make use of a camera, which could lead us to question whether the images that he produced were photographs at all, might actually be said to determine the significance of his contribution to the history of photography. To see why this might be so, it is enough to place Florence's images side by side with those produced in the 1920s by avant-garde artists like Man Ray and László Moholy-Nagy, for whom the work in the darkroom and the manipulation of negative and film stock were just as, if not more, important than the use of the photographic camera. If we place Florence's images alongside these rayograms and luminograms, we can say that the avant-gardists were not resorting to an aberrant or abusive approach to photography as a technology but rather latching onto a divergent, unrealized process of individuation of photography as a camera-less technology. Thus understood, the aesthetic dimension of their work is grounded not in an experimental disregard for the normative use of a technology but in their attention to the potentialities that such a normative use often obscures and which nonetheless can be said to determine what the technology is.[3] At the source of this process, we find, alongside others, the work of Florence, who, in fact, may have been the first to use the word *photographie* (in his case, in French) to describe what he was doing. Regardless of whether this was the first use of the term or not, what calls for thought is the fact that Florence used it in an adequately literal way, for his was, quite strictly, a system for *writing with light*: indeed, Florence originally conceived of his system as a way of reproducing what he had produced using yet another system of his own invention, a code for graphically transcribing animal sounds, such as birdsong, which he called *zoophony* (Figure 1.1).

Figure 1.1 Zoophonie. Score of *Tropeiro* bird song as described in *A Zoophonia de Hercule Florence*, J. Vielliard.

Source: Reproduction by Andrés Burbano and Guillermo Santos using the photographic techniques implemented by Florence in 1832, 2012

The way in which Florence's system was conceived and used leads us to wonder about the potentialities that were captured, and those that were not, as photography took on the standardized form of a picture-taking device. Arguably, it is only in light of this standardized form that a device that did not rely on the camera obscura to capture a view of nature may be read as one whose possibilities only partially align with those of what we call photography. Although we acknowledge the possibility of a camera-less photography in light of the work of artists whose images register the silhouettes of objects or the traces of movements, we hesitate to extend the concept to include images such as those produced by Florence, which today we might describe instead as chemically produced photocopies of texts or drawings. But this may well lead us to wonder why it is that we find a picture of a text to be something less, or something other, than a photograph. If such a picture is produced by photochemical means, but without using a camera, why should we regard the result as anything but photographic? These questions become more pointed if we bear in mind that what Florence originally intended to reproduce photographically were not just any graphic images but images to be read as representations of the natural world – although they were not representations of the way it looked but of the way it sounded. The following pages will attempt to reconstruct the singularity

20 *Backtracking*

of this twinned invention of photography and zoophony, and draw some conclusions about why they are not part of what we officially understand as "the emergence of photography."[4]

From *Zoophonie* to *Photographie*

Hércules Florence was born in 1804 in Nice, France. At the age of 19, inspired by the idea of exploring the New World, he relocated to Brazil. Although Brazil had recently achieved independence (in 1822) from Portugal, it was not yet a republic but an empire (it would remain one until 1889).[5] A few important changes had already taken place before independence, when the Portuguese court, pressured by the Napoleonic wars in Europe, decided in 1808 to relocate to Rio de Janeiro, which would function as the provisional capital of the Portuguese Empire.[6] This decision would have enormous consequences in the development of Brazilian society and cultural life. Before 1808, while Brazil was still a colony of Portugal, the possession of books was strictly forbidden, with the exception of the church.[7] When Florence arrived, the circulation of printed matter was still a new source of vitality for the country's scientifically and intellectually driven inhabitants. Indeed, Florence got his first job working in a bookstore and directly experienced the excitement around the newly growing book market between Europe and Brazil, a position that he could take exceptional advantage of by virtue of being a native speaker of French.[8] Florence remained closely attentive to the book business his entire life, and for this reason, he was arguably able to access cutting-edge scientific literature. He began working with photosensitive compounds, for instance, after reading the works of Jöns Jacob Berzelius and Johann Wilhelm Ritter, who were at the avant-garde of "chemical thought" in Europe.[9] In this context, we need not assume that Florence would have regarded himself as an amateur and passive receiver of information, rather than as part of a network of researchers and innovators who relied on printed materials to exchange ideas and to develop them collectively. To publish the account of an experiment or the blueprint of a device was a fundamental component of this form of networked activity, and it was as an effort to participate in this graphic community, as we may call it, that Florence developed his work on photography.[10]

*

Although the wealth of natural resources to be found in Brazil was not a secret in Europe, the presence of European scientists was under strict control under Portuguese rule, which is why the German naturalist and explorer Alexander von Humboldt was not allowed to visit Brazilian territories while he was exploring South America between 1799 and 1804.[11] The new configuration of Brazilian diplomacy after independence made room for a wave of scientific expeditions to Brazil led by European and American scientists

Bioacoustics and Photography, Brazil, 1832   21

who were looking to make up for lost time. These expeditions were typically sponsored by colonial powers, both old and new, predominantly the United Kingdom, but also France, Austria, Germany, Russia, and the United States.[12] After some months working in the bookshop, Florence joined one of these expeditions, led by the General Consul of Russia in the Empire of Brazil, Gregory Langsdorff. Before leading the expedition, Langsdorff, who was originally from Prussia, had circumnavigated the globe and been part of a series of expeditions that took him to Siberia, Alaska, and eventually to California, where he became involved in the study of the indigenous communities and the Franciscan missions. In 1821, Langsdorff began explorations in Brazil, and in 1825, he decided to lead an expedition on behalf of the Russian Empire to the interior of the country. Langsdorff recruited the newly arrived Florence to replace one of his original draftsmen, a well-known German visual artist by the name of Johann Moritz Rugendas, with whom he had some squabbles as they prepared to set out. The expedition, with Florence as part of the team, finally set out in 1826 from Porto Feliz, on the shores of the Tietê River.[13]

The Langsdorff expedition changed Florence's life, not only because of the intense degree of dedication and the new experiences brought on by expeditionary work but also because he was one of the few members of the expedition who survived in good health. The second draftsman, Aimé-Adrien Taunay, the son of a prestigious painter, died trying to swim across the Guaporé River, and Langsdorff himself became extremely ill and was forced to return to Europe in bad physical and mental condition. Thus, Florence, who at first became involved with the expedition by chance, unexpectedly became its sole living memory, as can be seen in the notebooks, diaries, drawings, paintings, and musical scores that describe or picture materials relevant to botany, zoology, ethnography, architecture, and several other scientific and artistic disciplines. Florence produced abundant quantities of visual material and writings, and throughout the rest of his life, he continued to elaborate on them, occasionally publishing the results in the form of written accounts or series of drawings and paintings.[14]

*

In 1830, one year after the end of the expedition, Florence settled in the small city of Campinas, in the province of São Paulo, where he would remain for the rest of his life. According to Boris Kossoy, the leading Brazilian biographer of Florence, he was looking to publish a fragment of a notebook written during the course of the expedition, titled *Mémoire sur la possibilité de décrire les sons et les articulations des voix des animaux* (Report on the Possibility of Describing the Sounds and Articulations of Animal Voices). Florence described the content of this fragment as "the result of some observations I made while traveling with Mr. Langsdorff . . ., when I had the opportunity to notice how much sounds vary among animals according to

22 *Backtracking*

the species," adding that his meditations had been prompted by the overwhelming diversity of the sound-configurations that he would encounter as the expedition made its way, "when animals that I did not know before presented me with a new voice, as those of many others belonging to a region now left behind no longer resonated in my ears."[15]

What he had attempted to do in response to this fleeting variety was to design a method that would allow him to produce a graphic record of the structure and characteristic tonal features of those sounds by means of musical notation. Although his knowledge of musical notation was rather rudimentary, Florence took advantage of this limitation and stretched the notational capabilities of traditional musical script by implementing an alternative use of the score symbols. In his view, the proposed method was an important and original contribution to the study of nature, not only because he had perfected the use of traditional musical notation to transcribe the songs and voices of birds and other animals (this had been done for centuries) but because it opened the path for a new field of scientific research, which he called *zoophonie*:

> What I am undertaking is therefore not only to know the basis for transcribing the voices of animals but to propose to researchers and scientists a field of study and findings as comprehensive as each branch of the natural sciences. I would say that this field offers something more pleasant and more stimulating to our curiosity, for in the same way that Mineralogy is the study of inanimate nature, and Zoology a study of active nature, this ["Zoophonie"] would be the study of speaking Nature [de la Nature parlante].[16]

Florence's use of the concepts of voice and speech need not be regarded as metaphorical, bearing in mind that in the expeditionary context within which he developed his method the key task was that of the identification of species. Indeed, Florence saw his transcriptions as materials that should be placed alongside the "collections of animals" stored in museums and the widely circulated "drawings" accounting for all possible visual aspects of the diversity of animal life.[17] As Lorraine Daston and Peter Galison have shown, the first half of the nineteenth century witnessed a sustained debate about the ways in which the characteristics of a species could be rendered into an image, where the complex criteria determining the selection and interpretation of specimens and strategies of visual and textual rendering were being rewritten under efforts to consolidate the complex and heterogeneous value of objectivity, a value that was still regarded as embodied in the perceptual and manual skills of observers and artists.[18] Although those criteria were being pragmatically tested in the image-making practices linked to scientific-political endeavors, like the *Real Expedición Botánica del Nuevo Reino de Granada* (Royal Botanical Expedition of the Kingdom of New Granada), 1783–1816, the notion that sounds could merit consideration in this context was hardly a given.[19] Previous efforts to produce musical transcriptions of birdsong had been regarded as dubious from that point of view since its compelling musical qualities could make it easy for listeners to disregard relevant features, some of which, moreover, could not be adequately captured by traditional notation.[20] As J. Bruyninckx has shown, the process of shaping an objective listener of birdsong did not congeal until the early twentieth century, when fieldwork, previously the province of amateurs, was embraced by scientific ornithologists, and it was precisely at that time that efforts to create more nuanced systems of graphic notation began to proliferate.[21] Florence's method can be described as an early instance of this complex struggle for objectivity, to the extent that it was not conceived as a way of capturing the beauty of animal voices but of recording their correlations with the experience of a shifting territory, which we may interpret as an early understanding of what we would now call a soundscape. Indeed, Florence's premise was that "the voices of animals are in harmony with the places where one may hear them"[22] so that his own record of the voices of birds and other animals was also a record of his journey through the rivers that crucially determine the geographical structure of the regions explored by the Langsdorff expedition. Arguably, Florence's experiences as a foreigner in the perceptually overloaded tropical environment were quite different from those of European and North American bird lovers, and his interest in their voices was not socially coded within a space of leisure and contemplation. As he sharply remarked, his use of musical notation was not based on the assumption that animal voices were in any sense musical, which meant that the musical notation of durations was of no use and had to be replaced by a system based on the quarter second as unit. To some degree, this might explain why, according to Jacques Vielliard, a Brazilian bioacoustics scholar who translated Florence's document from French to Portuguese, Florence "was the first to make clear that the acoustic signal of animal communication is specific," and in that sense, his monograph can be described as a foundational document for the scientific discipline that is known today as bioacoustics.[23] Indeed, Florence sketched an understanding of the natural soundscape as a field of scientific inquiry and understood that the encoding or capturing of this layer of information, which would make it possible to visualize its ephemeral structures, was a key source of data, anticipating the work of later biologists and sound recordists, such as Ludwig Koch.[24]

*

In spite of his conviction as to its value, Florence had a difficult time trying to make his project available to the graphic community, finding no way to publish his work in Campinas. Indeed, given the relatively recent availability of the printing press in the Brazilian territories, the technology was hard to access everywhere. Before 1808, the possession and use of a printing press in Brazil had been prohibited and heavily penalized by the Portuguese,

24 Backtracking

which meant that all available printed materials came from overseas.[25] In fact, one of the first printing presses to operate legally in Brazilian territory, manufactured in Britain, arrived in 1808 in the same fleet as João VI of Portugal, the regent prince who would end the prohibition. Once it was lifted, the few extant printing presses did not have the capacity to satisfy the needs of the new empire. Moreover, they were mainly located in Rio de Janeiro, which, since 1822, functioned as the capital of the new Brazilian Empire. For the most part, these presses were used by newspaper publishers, and their owners were typically engaged in political interests.[26] When Florence

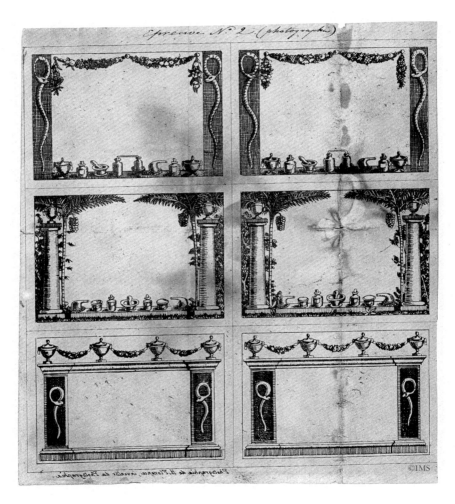

Figure 1.2 Epréuve No 2 *photographie*. Set of labels for pharmaceutical bottles made by Florence using gold(III) chloride (c. 1833).

Source: Courtesy of Instituto Moreira Salles, Rio de Janeiro

decided to settle down in Campinas around 1829, there was no printing press in the entire province of São Paulo, a circumstance that he would even thematize, in 1830, in a sarcastic cartoon, where an allegorical stand-in for civilization hands over a printing press to Campinas as a gift.[27]

In response to these limitations, Florence set out to work on possible ways of building a device of his own for mass printing, and it was along this path that he began to experiment with photosensitive chemicals. At this point, Florence's project can be described as laying out a field of overlapping cognitive, perceptual, and pragmatic challenges and possibilities, a field shaped and traversed by two ideas in creative co-implication: the idea of a *zoophonie* or, as we might now say, zoophonography, understood as a way to graphically register the range and configurations of sounds proper to animal life; and the idea of a *photographie*, understood as a way to reproduce this system of graphic symbols through the use of photosensitive chemicals (Figure 1.2). If we take note of the singular way in which this field was constituted, we come to see how it is that it makes as much sense to say that Florence invented photography as it does to say that he didn't. Although he was just looking for a way to work around the unavailability of an established technology (the printing press), the content of the material that he was eager to publish was not entirely incidental to his project: it is, we might say, as though having his own system of sound notation was what drove Florence to develop his own system of image reproduction. This technological idiosyncrasy, as we might call it, determines the sense in which his work can be understood as an invention.

Photographie: What Was It?

The year 1839 is often described as the birth year of photography as a usable technology, when Daguerre formally announced the invention of the daguerreotype. That same year, the São Paulo newspaper *A Phenix* published a letter from Florence claiming to have developed a photographic system of his own without any previous knowledge of the invention of the work being done in France. The text of the letter might seem confusing, for Florence seems to switch from discussing his role as possible inventor of photography to an apparently disconnected discussion of another technology, which he called *polygraphie*, an economic color printing system on which he had worked for several years. Rather than a sign of incoherence, we can consider this, in fact, as indexing a sharp reflexive process, on Florence's part, regarding his invention. Indeed, if we consider *photographie* and *polygraphie* as components of the same technical field, it becomes clear that through his experiments, Florence was consistently working at harnessing photochemical processes for use in a system that could take on some of the functions of the printing press.[28]

What we know about Florence's device and process confirms the idea that his guiding technological parameters were graphic. The blueprints that he

26 *Backtracking*

drew for the equipment that he used to produce his photographs show a structure of wooden supports where sensitized paper was placed and covered with pieces of glass previously impregnated with a mix of lampblack and Arabic gum in order to print the negative: it was, by all accounts, a simple and effective system for writing and drawing with light and, in that sense, a fully sufficient photographic system. In his notebooks, Florence also described the way in which he would work on the negative by hand, using a burin over a glass plate to engrave images and texts. First, he would cover the glass with a layer of the black gum; second, he would copy the figure to be reproduced onto a piece of tracing paper, which was then placed in reverse over the glass plate after being rubbed on with white lead. The tracing was then transferred onto the plate with a burin, and the black layer was then engraved also with a burin, after placing a black cloth over the glass plate (darker than the black layer of the glass itself) to facilitate engraving. The image was then recorded in the opposite direction, meaning that "the lines in the print are the result of the absence of the black layer" removed by the burin, which would finally be printed in the right direction by producing a contact copy on sensitized paper under the action of light.[29]

An effort to describe Florence as an inventor of photography in what is now its standardized form will undoubtedly be mighty accounting for the insufficiencies of his system, which one would be compelled to interpret as partial failures. In a sense, what I have called the self-sufficiency of his system seems to make the absence of the camera even more patent, as though it signaled the closure of all efforts to integrate these two chains of technological image processing. One may well argue, as Kossoy convincingly does, that the insufficiencies of his camera-less photographic system are not a reflection of the inventor's inability to successfully develop all aspects of his device but rather a reflection of the limitations imposed upon him by his geographical location.[30] Indeed, as Kossoy shows, Florence was certainly aware of the fact that his circumstances did not allow him to develop his ideas to their full capacity, and specifically, he clearly acknowledged that he had not been able to come up with a functional way of capturing images of the outside world through the camera obscura.[31] There is no doubt that Florence was aware of the potential of using the camera obscura in connection with photosensitive chemicals, and there are surviving sketches describing his tests with that device. As he tells it, he built a camera obscura by adapting an old painter's palette and a lens from a pair of glasses and ran into difficulties shared by many of his contemporaries who were working along similar lines:

> The object that is represented in the camera obscura was a closed window, being visible the frames, the roof of a neighboring house, and part of the sky. I left this for four hours and went to check. . . . [A]fter removing the paper, I found the window fixed, but showing clear what should be dark and dark what should be clear. . . . The action of light drew the

objects in the camera obscura, setting only the larger shapes with high contrasts, and with the defect that clear was dark, and vice versa.[32]

Thus, Florence was only able to obtain a high-contrast negative on sensitized paper, and although he later came up with a procedure that he thought would allow him to transform that image into a positive, there is no evidence that he ever succeeded in doing this or even of his actually testing it:

> But if the image, meanwhile, could be fixed on the glass, all you need to do is perform that first operation, and then place the prepared paper and expose it under the sunlight, and then the image will acquire its true way.[33]

It seems natural to say, in light of these failed efforts, that Florence's photography lacked one of the key components of the medium as it is traditionally understood, in other words, that Florence invented only a part of photography. But this description would be anachronistic, based as it is on a retroactive determination of what photography was supposed, or destined, to be. It seems more prudent and accurate, then, to say that Florence invented photography in a different sense, and the sense of this difference must be located in the fact that Florence's photographic experiments were not directly linked to his failed efforts to capture what I have called a view of the world through the camera obscura. In other words, Florence was after a photographic apparatus that was not dominated by the paradigm of the picture as a visual artifact but rather dominated by the paradigm of a graphically structured sign and, thus, a system for the reproduction of graphic images through the action of light on photosensitive paper (Figure 1.3).

We see this clearly in a notebook entry from 1837, bearing the title "Ami des arts," where Florence wrote a summary of his previous research subdivided into a dozen topics, which included the "discovery" of "photography, or printing with sunlight" alongside his "research on the fixation of images in the camera obscura."[34] This undoubtedly tantalizing document may well be the first instance of the term "photography" being used to refer to something akin to what is now so called. However, it is clear that Florence drew a sharp distinction between what he called photography and the process by which images projected into the camera obscura could be fixed: indeed, he saw this fixing as one possible application of photography, rather than seeing the two processes as subsidiary components of an encompassing apparatus. As he described it, the field of experimentation that Florence understood as "photographic" hinged on his efforts to produce a "[n]ew way to print writings and drawings, simpler and expeditious than in the art impressions known until today,"[35] which entails that it was first and foremost conceived (if not conceptualized) as a technology for the reproduction of graphically coded information. Since the system was paradigmatically framed as a procedure for the reproduction of graphic information on paper, its products seem to us to inevitably gravitate around the concept of

28 Backtracking

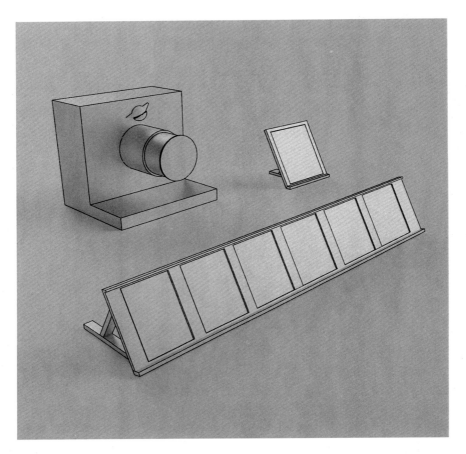

Figure 1.3 Tridimensional models of the technical equipment described by Florence in his *photographie* experiments; models based on his drawing from 1837, as presented in *A descoberta isolada da fotografia no Brasil*, B. Kossoy.

Source: 3D models in Blender by Pierre Puentes

a copy since our current technological landscape leads us to assume that a reproduction of a view is inherently different from a reproduction of a text. However, the graphic space that preoccupied Florence was not dominated by the paradigm of printed texts but rather dominated by potential interactions between textual and non-textual graphemes, of the kind needed to present his method of zoophony. Florence not only developed his photographic system in order to deal with the unavailability of printing technology, he also clearly continued to focus on this possibility, achieving photographic reproductions of quite a few drawings and texts by means of chemical reactions driven by light, using both gold and silver salts. The kind of images that he printed, including labels for pharmaceutical products, labels for wine bottles, labels for unidentified products, and a Masonic diploma, demonstrate that his paradigmatic image-space could be populated by all manner of inhabitants, as the needs of commodity trading seem to overlap with those of scientific representation.

Moreover, his descriptions of the device and of the way it was used to make prints lead us to think that the manipulation of the negative was the expressive center of Florence's photographic process, which indicates to what extent his images were, in Flusser's terminology, "traditional." If we compare it to contemporary procedures of mass printing, his light-based method for mass printing seems, on the one hand, delicate and non-machinic, and on the other, a singular technological extension of the acts of writing and drawing by hand.[36] What Florence uniquely formulated, in other words, was the possibility of synthesizing the behavior of photo-sensitive chemicals with the mechanics of manual graphism. Although this was clearly motivated by the original need to reproduce a specific kind of image, namely a graphic rendering of sound configurations, which called for a certain degree of diagrammatic flexibility, the fact that it was used in the practice of product labelling captures the open range of action to which the device was clearly suited: a certain number of copies of a certain kind of image could now be produced without the need for heavy and cumbersome printing machinery, using only wood, glass, chemicals, and sunlight.

A Parallel Genealogy

In the first pages of his book on the Langsdorff expedition, *Viagem Fluvial do Tietê ao Amazonas* (A River Journey from the Tiete to the Amazon), Florence recounts his arrival to the city of Santos, their first stop, which he describes as the homeland of Alexandre de Gusmão, a seventeenth century scholar "who, according to several people, had invented aerostatic balloons." Interestingly, Florence presents de Gusmão in terms that might be applied to him as well, as "a genius [who] had the misfortune of being born in a Portuguese colony, for which reason he was ignored."[37] Florence's claims are in fact inaccurate, for it was Bartolomeu de Gusmão, Alexandre's brother, also born in Santos, who pioneered a lighter-than-air ship design in the seventeenth century.[38] Nonetheless, his remarks index an awareness of the fate of an inventor who was working in a location far removed from the centers of techno-scientific discourse and practice, a fate that Florence would later attribute to himself by describing himself as an "inventor in exile."[39] There is no doubt that Florence's understanding of his own projects, achievements, and disappointments was informed by this sense of being in the wrong place. He thought that an inventor working under such conditions would inevitably face anonymity and indifference, given his limited means and inability to share his work through the relevant channels. Correspondingly, Florence nourished an image of Europe as a place where inventors could find fertile ground to plant and harvest the results of their work.

30 *Backtracking*

This obviously idealized image of Europe is sharply out of tune with what actually took place during the early stages of the development of photography. When Daguerre took the bulk of the credit for the invention of photography, his figure eclipsed the work of people like Nicéphore Niépce, who arguably authored most of the important technical contributions.[40] There is also the very emblematic case of Hippolyte Bayard, who, like Florence, invented his own photographic process (known as direct positive printing) and presented his results to the public before Daguerre, only to fall into anonymity for quite a long time after negotiating a concession of the patent to Daguerre. In an act of protest against the inordinate amount of attention received by Daguerre in disregard for his own contributions, in 1840, Bayard produced what could arguably be described as the earliest photographic masterpiece, the very first photograph in a contemporary sense: *Self-Portrait as a Drowned Man*, a staged scene of himself after having committed suicide due to the lack of recognition for his work as inventor of photography.[41] Bayard's picture captures the same kind of tension that Florence voiced in his letter to *A Phenix* after the announcement of Daguerre's discovery in 1839; both documents alert us to the fact that the attribution of an invention to an author could have a very strong effect on the people who were collectively engaged in the development of technologies and on the fate of these technologies. Indeed, Bayard's story strongly suggests that Florence was wrong in thinking that his fate would have been different if he had been in Europe.

That being said, the category of the inventor in exile does capture something of Florence's particular path, and that of analogous figures, a point that is argued more than once in the texts compiled by Kossoy in the valuable text *L'inventeur en exile*. According to Kossoy, the common trait of all inventors in exile is a lack of means. Accordingly, he outlines the relevant features of Florence's particular context, describing Brazil in general, and Campinas in particular, as preeminently rural and agricultural societies, and detailing the limitations in means of production that he encountered while he was working on his inventions. Nonetheless, these limitations need not be interpreted as keeping an inventor from realizing an idea or exploring a possibility, for they are just as likely to be the very sources of these ideas and possibilities. As Flusser points out in "Exile and Creativity," the situation of exile can be seen "as a challenge to creative activity" and "a breeding ground . . . for the new."[42] It seems fair to say that this was the case for Florence, and in that sense, it is inaccurate to describe his position as unfortunate, even if that is how he himself experienced it. His, we might say, was just a different kind of fortune, and it places his work in a different kind of history.

To get a sense of what this other history of photography might be like, it is enough to consider the extent to which the history of photography has been written under the guidelines set by the genealogy of the camera obscura, a device that had been around for centuries by the time that the first photography patents appeared, being extensively used by painters and draftsmen since the Renaissance in the European context.[43] Our sense of what photography is, and of how it developed, turns more complex when we examine the genealogy of photography from the point of view of the use of controlled photochemical reactions, a field of experimentation that was closely linked to the consolidation of chemistry as a modern science in Europe. As we have seen, such photochemical reactions are at the heart of Florence's photographic experiments, and they clearly belong within a genealogy of projects that did not focus on the use of a camera obscura during the early days of photography. As an example, the procedures described by the German polymath Johann Heinrich Schulze clearly anticipate Florence's discoveries by almost one century, and they can be compared to those of his successor on two counts: they both worked with the photographic negative, and in both cases, the result of the process was symbolically coded information: something written with light (and so literally, photo-graphed) rather than captured as an optical image.[44] Thus, when Schulze was exploring the photochemical reactions of phosphorus and silver, he produced a written text through the darkening of chemicals on a glass plate, naming what he thus obtained a darkphorus, a bearer of darkness, in opposition to phosphorus, a bearer of light.[45] As Kittler suggestively describes it, "Schulze did not want to store the contingent nature of the real (in Lacan's sense of the word) in a technical medium, but rather he wanted to introduce the symbolic, namely a written code, into nature."[46] Although he was working within a different episteme, Florence's objective can be described along similar lines: to get natural processes to encode messages structured by a system of conventional signs – although Florence's graphic system, in turn, was an effort to understand animal sound itself as configured and, in that sense, as potentially symbolic. As Kittler provocatively postulates, following the thought of Joséf Maria Eder, who authored one of the first historical accounts of photography as a technology, this may have been the original thrust of photographic experimentation.[47] According to this postulation, Schulze would have been the initiator of a parallel technological tradition based, as Kittler remarks, on a strict adherence to the etymology of the word "photography," which is exactly what Florence did.[48] Since this is clearly not how the historical identity of photography as a technical medium eventually took shape, we are left with the sense of a parallel genealogy of photography, one that developed, as it unquestionably did, along the margins of its process of standardization. Although it makes no sense to call for a completely new historiographical framework for photography, the cases of Schulze and Florence can clearly be said to belong to such a parallel lineage, which focused on camera-less experimentation with chemical reactions.

*

Within this particular lineage, Florence may yet stand out as having paid particular attention to the potentialities of gold, whose photosensitive

32 *Backtracking*

properties were hardly explored elsewhere. He started to experiment in this field somewhere around 1832, after some conversations with a pharmacist acquaintance, Joaquim Correa de Mello, and the fact that he was able to conduct these experiments at all, given his geographical location, should not be taken for granted. To obtain adequate materials and chemical products was no easy task, even in Europe, during the early nineteenth century. The most important chemical components required to sensitize the paper were silver nitrate and gold(III) chloride. In addition to this, one needed to procure Arabic gum and lampblack in order to produce a negative on a glass plate. Some of these materials, although rare, would become available in Brazil thanks to a decree titled Opening the Ports to Friendly Nations, which aimed to link Brazilian ports to European markets.[49] This decree was the topic of one of João VI's first announcements upon reaching Brazilian soil, and its precise purpose was to secure the support and protection of the United Kingdom as the Portuguese court relocated to Rio de Janeiro.[50] The repercussions of the decree were soon felt, among them the emergence of a small but significant market of pharmaceutical and chemical products. Thus, thanks to his connection with Correa de Melo, Florence had access to chemicals, materials, and valuable practical experience on how to use them.[51]

The fact that Florence took a special interest in the photosensitive properties of gold chloride is another instance where the singularity of his work has been obscured by an effort to interpret his achievements in light of standardized photography. It is arguably for this reason that Kossoy and other scholars after him have focused on the fact that Florence did, at some point, also use a silver nitrate, as they were hoping to find proof of the proximity between his experiments and those of his European contemporaries. And yet, if we step aside from this framework, it can be argued that out of the surviving results of his experiments, the most interesting ones were those produced by using gold salts.[52] As Kossoy himself recounts, when he examined Florence's written reports, he had some doubts about the very possibility of gold chloride having photosensitive properties, until a series of tests conducted at the Rochester Institute of Technology in the 1970s corroborated the technical consistency of the materials found in Florence's notebooks.[53] And yet, it is one thing to ascertain that a media technology is plausible and another to have a clear sense of its concrete possibilities. For this reason, I decided to engage in a reconstruction of Florence's system that would allow me to determine the potentialities of his suggestive use of gold chloride, bearing in mind that the photosensitive properties of this compound, and the specificity of its behavior as a photographic medium, were not in view.

According to available documents, gold chloride may have been used in the past, although only as an additive, to alter the tone of a print and endow it with sepia-like effects with reddish and purplish hues,[54] but there is no account of it being used as the key component of a photographic process. Moreover, not all varieties of the compound are photosensitive, and

Florence did not single out the exact kind that he used. After some research, I established that Florence must have used gold(III) chloride (Au_2Cl_6), which I was then able to obtain from different sources and in different concentrations. A first run of tests, conducted in Santa Barbara, California, allowed me to ascertain that the compound was indeed photosensitive and to discover a peculiar feature of its behavior: it could be stored In a translucent container and exposed to light without losing its properties, reacting only when it was spread over the paper after exposure. It was critical to work only with papers that were 100% acid-free, to prevent the chemical reaction from continuing after exposure and fixation.

I then moved on to a second round of experiments, conducted in Bogotá, Colombia, in collaboration with photographer Guillermo Santos, an expert on ancient photographic techniques. The point of these experiments was to assess the capacity of gold(III) chloride to be used in a controlled manner and according to early photographic techniques.[55] We proceeded to run tests using gold(III) chloride in three different concentrations: 0.2 %, 1.0 %, and 2.0%. Our purpose was to work through the whole sequence, from exposure to processing, and up to fixing the image. However, we soon realized that something that had seemed to us like a relatively unimportant issue, namely that of finding a way to get the chemical reaction to stop after exposure, turned out to be extremely important. A look at Florence's notes allowed me to see that he also had run into this critical challenge after he had been experimenting for some time: he needed to find a way to stop the chemical reaction in due time, and he eventually found a way to achieve this by using ammonia, which plays the critical function of removing the gold chloride that hasn't been exposed at a given moment. Without this chemical, it is impossible to obtain adequate photographic results, as the reaction carries on and eventually results in an entirely dark image. During his own tests, Florence even tried using urine to achieve this, which indeed caused the desired effect due to the concentration of ammonia in urine.[56]

As I have noted, in his photographic experiments, Florence produced contact copies, rather than printing images captured through the camera obscura. To replicate his procedure, we needed to produce large negatives, which were designed digitally and printed on Pictorico OHP transparency film, with black-and-yellow layers (the latter meant to block ultraviolet light). For an image to print, we chose a sequence of zoophonic scores drawn by Florence during the Langsdorff expedition, wishing to address that meaningful moment when he envisioned the emergence of a scientific field of study: the science of the voice of nature. We printed the scores using two different kinds of exposure: first, we tried a 90-minute exposure to direct sunlight (Figure 1.4), and second, we used a UV table to expose the negatives after soaking the paper in gold chloride for 240 minutes. In this way, we were able to use Florence's technique to print the entire sequence of scores, and the results closely resembled the purple-like liquid *photographies* that he had produced in 1833, some of which have been preserved.

Figure 1.4 Exposure. The photographic images created carefully reproducing Florence's *photographie* techniques using gold(III) chloride and ammonia. Mariana Sánchez and Andrés Burbano, Bogotá, 2021.

Source: Photo by Mariana Sánchez, 3D model in Blender by Pierre Puentes

Our experiment was an effort to reinstate, or reload, this linkage between sound and image, between technologies of audio recording and visual reproduction, which originally drove Florence to translate the technology of the printing press into the realm of light.

The visual results obtained through the monochrome process devised by Florence are strikingly beautiful, especially because the sensitized parts of the paper that do not turn completely dark take on a light, reddish-purple tint.

Figure 1.5 Direct sunlight exposure. Using paper sensitized with gold(III) chloride and negatives printed on Pictorico Pro OHP. Andrés Burbano, Bogotá, 2012.

Source: Photo by Andrés Burbano

The shifts in hue register the uneven spread of the chemical over the surface of the paper, endowing the images with an organic feel. Whether these effects are intended or unintended, adequate or inadequate to the use for which the device was conceived or tested, is something that cannot be settled, or even considered, if we read them in the light of assumptions derived from our familiarity with a given technological system. Although it seems unsatisfactory to claim that Florence achieved something like accidentally aesthetic results, it may well be that it is only in the realm of aesthetics that his achievements can be assessed. What seems clear is that both of Florence's twinned inventions, *zoophonie* and *photographie*, belong to a space in which the symbolic and the technological are linked to embodied action. This linkage, in turn, refers to traditional figures like the observer of nature and the craftsman, whose ability to shift between registers by coordinating the work of their senses and the work of their hands constituted a singular media space that would soon be overtaken by the advance of mechanization. Since that space of negotiation between the body and its extensions is something that media technologies continually redraw, it seems plausible to argue that systems like Florence's are not simply earlier, rudimentary stages of systems now in place: both *zoophonie* and *photographie*, in the sense in which Florence understood them, constitute plausible dimensions for contemporary media practices (Figure 1.5).

Conclusion

I have argued that Florence's photographs occupy an intermediate space between technical and traditional images, to the extent that his system was designed with a view to the technical reproducibility of images produced by hand. The same may be said of another set of images experimentally realized without the use of the camera obscura, the photogenic drawings that the British scientist and inventor Henry Fox Talbot was working on around 1834, produced by placing actual objects over previously sensitized paper to obtain a negative. Although the next year Fox Talbot was able to couple his use of sensitized paper with a camera obscura, it is enough to look at these photogenic drawings to become convinced of the degree of elaboration and complexity of signification that can be found in images produced by camera-less photography. Unlike Florence, Fox Talbot did not focus on the technical reproduction of graphic signs, and his later turn to the camera as a capturing device suggests that he was working under what I have called a picture paradigm. Nonetheless, Talbot used the term "drawing" to capture, metaphorically, the idea that the print itself was drawn by what he would later describe as the "pencil of nature."[57] In contrast, the experiments conducted by Florence between 1832 and 1833 were based, quite literally, on drawings and handwritten texts, and to that extent, he was right to conceptualize his process, non-metaphorically, as a form of writing or drawing with light (Figure 1.6). By using a glass negative, Florence was able to obtain several copies from the same negative and was, thus, able to solve his original challenge: that of reproducibility, which Walter Benjamin identified as one of the most important contributions of photography

Figure 1.6 Photographic negative. *Photographie* of a *Zoophonie* score. Negative printed on Pictorico Pro OHP. It is the score of *Jáo* bird song as described in *A Zoophonia de Hercule Florence*, J. Vielliard.

Source: Reproduction by Andrés Burbano and Guillermo Santos, 2012

Bioacoustics and Photography, Brazil, 1832   37

to the development of the visual media world.[58] Although this may sound like a simple enough achievement nowadays, and one that had been and would later be solved again in different ways, one need only bear in mind that daguerreotypes were unique images, as unique as paintings.[59] Although adhering to diverging paradigms, both Fox Talbot and Florence were placing their experiments at the point of contact between reproducibility and nature, looking for a space of scientific and aesthetic experimentation that was not mediated by the optical paradigm of the view, which uncritically prevailed through artifactual analogues, like the window, the mirror, and the picture.

The results of my experimental reconstruction of Florence's apparatus, based on a commitment to his own description of the technical process, give weight to the notion that it is possible, and meaningful, to reactivate the possibility of working with image technologies that have been lost, particularly if this allows us to get a sense of their aesthetic potentialities. In the case of Florence's system, it seems clear that the use of gold chloride can still be regarded as a point of departure for creative work, more so if the singularity of its tonal and textural possibilities is explored without relying on the picture as a photographic paradigm. Indeed, the very project of a photographic *zoophonie* seems very much relevant to a range of contemporary artistic practices that dwell in the interstitial regions between the aesthetic and the scientific, like the communities articulated around the concepts of art-science and research-creation, which often work along these lines. The emergence of these intellectual projects within communities such as those that publish their work in journals like *Leonardo* and *Artnodes* can be regarded as an answer to the two-cultures problem.

As embodiment and the production of alternative epistemic practices have gained relevance as concerns within the field of contemporary art, attention to media technologies that retain a link to the perceptual, notational, and manual skills of an individual is clearly motivated. This, in turn, allows us to envision a new kind of historical practice based on a practical approach to the concept of resignification. Under this approach, an artifact is understood as fully resignified when it is reactivated; to reactivate, as we understand it, is not simply to use an old device for a new purpose but to invest it with a new historical meaning by treating it as a point of departure. In that sense, media technologies like Florence's *photographie* have the odd fortune of having remained inactivated in their time, which makes it clearer that their temporality is linked to their potential actualization in the present. Consider, for instance, a younger generation of image-makers who, in response to the immediacy and pervasiveness of the digital image, and by paying a new kind of attention to photochemical photographic processes, are fostering changes in different areas of the field of visual production. Iconic laboratories like Kodak have resumed the production of film stock, and brands like Lomography are marketing plastic replicas of old analog cameras. Some art

38 Backtracking

schools have also started to include in their curricula courses where students explore archaic processes like cyanotype. Visual artists like Annie Lopez are developing a sophisticated body of work, experimenting with new forms of visual experience based on the interactions between ammonium citrate and potassium ferricyanide. This variety of efforts at the resignification of outdated technologies injects a fruitful plurality into image-making practices, highlighting the fact that media, and not content alone, is a factor in the production of meaning.

Notes

1 Vilém Flusser, *Towards a Philosophy of Photography* (London: Reaktion Books, 2000), 14–30.

2 "[T]he technical object progresses through an internal redistribution of functions into compatible units, replacing what is random or antagonistic in the primitive distribution; specialization does not take place *from function to function*, but rather *from synergy to synergy*; it is the synergic group of functions, rather than the single function, which constitutes the true sub-set in the technical object." Gilbert Simondon, *Du mode d'éxistence des objets techniques* (Paris: Aubier, 1989), 34.

3 Brazilian artist Eduardo Kac has drafted a provocative timeline showing the rich history and prehistory of Brazilian electronic and technological art, and he assigns Florence a key role in that unexplored genealogy. See Eduardo Kac, *Luz & Letra. Ensaios de arte, literatura e comunicação* (Rio de Janeiro: Editora Contra Capa, 2004), 380. One may mention here the work of Brazilian avantgarde photographer Geraldo de Barros, who, in the 1940s, produced a series of astonishing works titled *Fotoformas*, obtained, in many cases, by manipulating the negative and even drawing on it with a burin. It is clear that the richness of this artist's visual discourse stems from the articulation of the capabilities of both "technical" and "traditional images." For a broader range of studies on the region where the figures of the artists and of the inventor intersects, see Dieter Daniels and Barbara U. Schmidt (eds.), *Artists as Inventors, Inventors as Artists* (Ostfildern: Hatje Cantz, 2008), 56–60.

4 Although the literature is still rare, there are two fundamental books on Florence's work as photographer/zoophonist: the first is Boris Kossoy's groundbreaking monograph, originally published in 1977 and recently translated into English (*Hercule Florence 1833: A descoberta isolada da fotografia no Brasil* [São Paulo: Facultade de Comunicacao Social Anhembi, 1977]; *The Pioneering Photographic Work of Hercule Florence* [London: Routledge, 2018]). Kossoy later restructured his study for a Spanish edition (*Hercule Florence. El descubrimiento de la fotografía en Brasil* [Mexico City: INAH, 2004]) and ultimately produced a revised Portuguese version which includes images of most of the key primary sources used in his research (*Hercule Florence: A descoberta isolada da fotografia no Brasil* [São Paulo: Edusp, 2006]). Kossoy's book is a priceless source, since during the 1970s, he had access to materials that would later be lost and of which he made photographic documentation. The second key source is Jacques Vielliard's *A zoophonia de Hercule Florence* (Cuiabá: Editora da Universidade de Mato Grosso, 1993), which includes a Portuguese translation and commentary on Florence's short treatise on bioacoustics.

5 Clarence Henry Haring, *Empire in Brazil. A New World Experiment with Monarchy* (Cambridge, MA: Harvard University Press, 1969).

Bioacoustics and Photography, Brazil, 1832 39

6 Francis A. Dutra, *A Guide to the History of Brazil, 1500–1822* (Santa Barbara: ABC-Clio, 1980), 524–554.

7 Nelson Werneck Sodre, *História da imprensa no Brasil* (Rio de Janeiro: MAUAD, 1998), 9–15, 109.

8 Kossoy, *A Descoberta Isolada*, 39.

9 See Vielliard, *A zoophonia*, 39.

10 On the circulation of books between the Old and the New World, and the configuration of a knowledge network as a condition of possibility for thought and experimentation on photography in both continents, see Pierre Bonhomme, "Le patrimoine au present," in *Les multiples inventions de la photographie. Actes des colloques de la Direction du Patrimoine. Cerisy-la-Salle* (Paris: Ministère de la Culture et de la Communication des Grands Travaux et du Bicentenaire, 1988).

11 Kossoy, *A descoberta isolada*, 40–41.

12 Dutra, *A Guide*, 467.

13 On the Langsdorff expedition, see: D. Bertels and B. Komissarov (eds.), *A expedição científica Langsdorff ao Brasil 1821–1829. Catálogo completo do material existente nos arquivos da União Soviética* (Brasilia: Ministerio da Educação e Cultura, 1981); Boris Komissarov, *Expedição Langsdorff – Acervo e fontes históricas* (Brasilia: UNESP, 1994); Salvador Monteiro and Leonel Kaz, *Expedição Langsdorff ao Brasil, 1821–1829: 2 vols.* (Rio de Janeiro: Edicoes Alumbramento, 1988).

14 See Hércules Florence, *Viagem fluvial do Tiete ao Amazonas* (São Paulo: Assis Chateaubriand: Museu de Arte de São Paulo, 1977). Most of the original materials of the Langsdorff expedition are archived in San Petersburg, where they resurfaced around 1930 after being lost for a few decades; a few additional materials are located in public libraries in Germany and Brazil. See Bertels and Komissarov, *Catálogo completo*.

15 Vielliard, *A zoophonia de Hercule Florence*, 19. Translation by Sandra Mesa and Andrés Burbano.

16 Vielliard, *A zoophonia de Hercule Florence*, 19.

17 Vieillard, *A zoophonia*, 21.

18 See L. Daston and P. Galison. *Objectivity* (New York: Zone Books, 2010), 63–98.

19 For an account of the political dimension of the expedition, see M. Nieto, *Remedios para el Imperio. Historia natural y apropación del Nuevo Mundo* (Bogotá: ICANH, 2000).

20 As an example, in a 1773 report on his "Experiments and Observations on the Singing of Birds," D. Barrington noted that "the intervals used by birds are commonly so minute, that we cannot judge at all of them from the more gross intervals into which we divide our musical octave." Quoted in P. Marler, "Science and Birdsong: The Good Old Days," in *Nature's Music. The Science of Birdsong*, edited by P. Marler and H. Slabbekoorn (Amsterdam: Elsevier, 2004), 3.

21 Bruyninckx, *Listening in the Field. Recording and the Science of Birdsong* (Cambridge, Mass.: The MIT Press, 2018), 25.

22 Vieillard, *A zoofonia*, 22.

23 Vieillard, *A zoophonia de Hercule Florence*, 13–14.

24 See J. Bruyninckx, "Sound Sterile: Making Scientific Field Recordings in Ornithology," in *The Oxford Handbook of Sound Studies*, edited by Pinch and Bijsterveld (New York: Oxford University Press 2012), 127–149.

25 Sodre, *História da imprensa*, 60–78. This lack of means for the production of mechanically printed materials contrasts with the situation in the Spanish colonies in South America, where printing presses had been available and extensively used since the 1600s.

40 Backtracking

26 Juarez Bahia, *Jornal e Historia Tecnica* (Rio de Jsneiro: Imprensa Nacional, 1964), 37–39.
27 Kossoy, *A descoberta isolada*, 87–89.
28 Kossoy, *A descoberta isolada*, 69–82.
29 Kossoy, *A descoberta isolada*, 358–393, 183–184.
30 Boris Kossoy, "Hercule Florence, l'inventeur en exil," in *Les multiples inventions de la photographie*, 73–80.
31 Kossoy, *A descoberta isolada*, 73–80. Weston Naef had already expressed some misgivings about Florence's achievements after examining the dimensions and design of the camera obscura as drawn by Florence in his memoirs. See Weston Naef, "Hercules Florence, Inventor do (sic) Photographia," *Artforum* (February 1976): 57–60.
32 Kossoy, *A descoberta isolada*, 393.
33 Kossoy, *A descoberta isolada*, 393.
34 Kossoy, *A descoberta isolada*, 358.
35 Kossoy, *A descoberta isolada*, 372.
36 Similar techniques were used later on in France by painters like Camille Corot; they were known as *cliché verre* or "photographic etchings." See Gerald W. Ward, *Materials and Techniques in Art* (Oxford: Oxford University Press, 1980), 109.
37 Florence, *Viagem fluvial*, 35.
38 See Afonso de Taunay, *Bartolomeu de Gusmão, inventor do aeróstato: a vida e a obra do primeiro inventor americano* (São Paulo: Edições Leia, 1942).
39 See Kossoy, "Hercule Florence, l'inventeur en exil," 73–80.
40 Rosemblum, *A World History of Photography*, 14–37.
41 Rosemblum, *A World History of Photography*, 32–33.
42 Vilém Flusser, "Exile and Creativity," in *The Freedom of the Migrant. Objections to Nationalism* (Urbana: University of Illinois Press, 2003), 81–86. Flusser knew quite well what he was talking about, for he was himself an exile after being "expelled" (as he prefers to describe it) from Europe to Brazil after World War II.
43 Friedrich Kittler, *Optical Media* (Cambridge: Polity, 2010), 47–49.
44 Curt W. Ceram, *Archaeology of the Cinema* (New York: Harcourt, Brace & World Inc, 1965), 73–85.
45 Kittler, *Optical Media*, 121.
46 Kittler, *Optical Media*, 122.
47 Josef Maria Eder, *History of Photography* (New York: Dover, 1980), 62–70.
48 Kittler, *Optical Media*, 122.
49 Boris Fausto, *A Concise History of Brazil* (Cambridge: Cambridge University Press, 1999), 64.
50 Patrick Wilcken, *Empire Adrift* (London: Bloomsbury Paperbacks, 2005), 125.
51 José de Campos, "Joaquim Correia de Mello," *Revista do Museu Paulista* 4 (1900): 165–190. Correa de Melo, who was younger than Florence, had acquired his legal accreditation as pharmacist in Rio de Janeiro and would later become a respected botanist and researcher in the field of biology.
52 Kossoy, *A descoberta isolada*, 369.
53 Kossoy, *A descoberta isolada*, 237.
54 J. Barnier, *Coming into Focus: A Step-By-Step Guide to Alternative Photographic Printing Processes* (San Francisco: Chronicle Books, 2000), 125.
55 I was fortunate to find a photo lab in Bogotá that focused exclusively on experimentation with older techniques like cyanotype, platinum and palladium, and others; the lab was equipped with professional dryers, ovens, a range of lights, UV tables, and so on, allowing us to proceed systematically.

Bibliography

56 Kossoy, *A Descoberta Isolada*, 239–240.
57 Eder, *History of Photography*, 317–318.
58 Walter Benjamin, *The Work of Art in the Age of Its Technological Reproducibility, and Other Writings on Media* (Cambridge, MA: Belknap Press, 2008), 294–295.
59 Naomi Rosemblum. *A World History of Photography* (New York: Abbeville Press, 1997), 17–45. Beyond his contact copies of objects, fabrics, and textures, Fox Talbot's most important contribution to the history of photography is the procedure he devised in order to obtain a photographic negative out of which multiple positive copies could be produced in the dark room. Later on, Fox Talbot would be able to connect the use of the camera obscura and the creation of multiple copies from one photographic negative. Indeed, Talbot decisively shaped the process from the camera obscura to the darkroom, which is why several historians consider him "the true father of photography." See Eder, *History of Photography*, 317–324.

Bibliography

Barnier, John. *Coming into Focus: A Step-by-Step Guide to Alternative Photographic Printing Processes*. San Francisco: Chronicle Books, 2000.
Benjamin, Walter. *The Work of Art in the Age of Its Technological Reproducibility, and Other Writings on Media*. Cambridge: Belknap Press, 2008.
Bertels, D. E. and Boris Komissarov (eds.). *A expedição científica Langsdorff ao Brasil 1821–1829. Catálogo completo do material existente nos arquivos da União Soviética*. Brasilia: Ministerio da Educação e Cultura, 1981.
Bonhomme, Pierre. "Le patrimoine au présent." In *Les multiples inventions de la photographie. Actes des colloques de la Direction du Patrimoine. Cerisy-la-Salle.* Paris: Ministère de la Culture de la Communication des Grands Travaux et du Bicentenaire, 1988.
Bruyninckx, Joeri. "Sound Sterile: Making Scientific Field Recordings in Ornithology". In *The Oxford Handbook of Sound Studies*, edited by Trevor Pinch and Karin Bjisterveld. New York: Oxford University Press, 2012, 127–149.
———. *Listening in the Field: Recording and the Science of Birdsong*. Cambridge: MIT Press, 2018.
Campos, José de. "Joaquim Correia de Mello." *Revista do Museu Paulista* 4 (1900): 165–190.
Ceram, Curt W. *Archaeology of the Cinema*. New York: Harcourt Brace, 1965.
Daniels, Dieter and Barbara U. Schmidt (eds.). *Artists as Inventors, Inventors as Artists*. Ostfildern: Hatje Cantz, 2008.
Daston, Lorraine and Peter Galison. *Objectivity*. New York: Zone Books, 2010.
Dutra, Francis A. *A Guide to the History of Brazil, 1500–1822*. Santa Barbara: ABC-Clio, 1980.
Eder, Josef Maria. *History of Photography*. New York: Dover, 1980.
Fausto, Boris. *A Concise History of Brazil*. Cambridge: Cambridge University Press, 1999.
Florence, Hercules. *Viagem fluvial do Tietê ao Amazonas*. São Paulo: Assis Chateaubriand: Museu de Arte de São Paulo, 1977.
Flusser, Vilém. *Towards a Philosophy of Photography*. London: Reaktion Books, 2000.

42 Backtracking

———. "Exile and Creativity." In *The Freedom of the Migrant: Objections to Nationalism*. Urbana: University of Illinois Press, 2003, 81–86.

Haring, Clarence Henry. *Empire in Brazil: A New World Experiment with Monarchy*. Cambridge: Harvard University Press, 1969.

Juarez Bahia, Benedito. *Jornal, história e técnica*. Rio de Janeiro: Imprensa Nacional, 1964.

Kac, Eduardo. *Luz & letra: Ensaios de arte, literatura e comunicação*. Rio de Janeiro: Editora Contra Capa, 2004.

Kittler, Friedrich. *Optical Media*. Cambridge: Polity, 2010.

Komissarov, Boris. *Expedição Langsdorff: Acervo e fontes históricas*. Brasilia: UNESP, 1994.

Kossoy, Boris. *Hercules Florence 1833: A descoberta isolada da fotografia no Brasil*. São Paulo: Facultade de Comunicacao Social Anhembi, 1977.

———. "Hercule Florence, l'inventeur en exil." In *Les Multiples inventions de la photographie*. Cerisy-la-Salle: Ministère de la Culture de la Communication des Grands Travaux et du Bicentenaire, 1988, 73–80.

———. *Hercule Florence: El descubrimiento de la fotografía en Brasil*. Mexico City: INAH, 2004.

———. *Hercules Florence: A descoberta isolada da fotografia no Brasil*. São Paulo: Edusp, 2006.

———. *The Pioneering Photographic Work of Hercule Florence*. London: Routledge, 2018.

Marler, Peter. "Science and Birdsong: The Good Old Days." In *Nature's Music: The Science of Birdsong*, edited by Peter Marler and Hans Slabbekoorn. Amsterdam: Elsevier, 2004, 1–28.

Monteiro, Salvador and Leonel Kaz. *Expedição Langsdorff ao Brasil, 1821–1829: 2 vols*. Rio de Janeiro: Edições Alumbramento, 1988.

Naef, Weston. "Hercules Florence, Inventor do [sic] Photographia." *Artforum*, February 1976, 57–60.

Nieto, Mauricio. *Remedios para el Imperio: Historia natural y apropiación del Nuevo Mundo*. Bogotá: ICANH, 2000.

Rosenblum, Naomi. *A World History of Photography*. New York: Abbeville, 2019.

Simondon, Gilbert. *Du mode d'existence des objets techniques*. Paris: Aubier, 1989.

Sodré, Nelson Werneck. *História da imprensa no Brasil*. Rio de Janeiro: MAUAD, 1998.

Taunay, Afonso de. *Bartolomeu de Gusmão, inventor do aeróstato: a vida e a obra do primeiro inventor americano*. São Paulo: Edições Leia, 1942.

Vielliard, Jacques. *A zoophonia de Hercules Florence*. Cuiabá: Editora da Universidade de Mato Grosso, 1993.

Ward, Gerald W. *Materials and Techniques in Art*. Oxford: Oxford University Press, 1980.

Wilcken, Patrick. *Empire Adrift*. London: Bloomsbury, 2005.

2 The Color Wheel of Television History, Mexico, 1939

Introduction

An event registered as a historical leap can often be understood in retrospect as the cumulative effect of a myriad small steps. The landing of humans on the moon is one such event, and this chapter concerns what may at first seem like a very minute step. Arguably, if the moon landing is counted as a unique symbolic event in the global cultural history of the twentieth century, it is not merely due to its undeniable status as a techno-scientific accomplishment but also as a result of its mode of being rendered. Indeed, it may be said that the moon landing was *conceived and produced as* a historical event, one that, perhaps paradigmatically, was constructed through a complex array of media strategies, all of which could be said to converge in the figure of the live television broadcast. This is at least a crucial component of its later transmission as a cultural artifact: as an eventful stream of signals traveling back to Earth from space.

It should not be surprising to learn that this extremely successful media-based construction could only have been achieved by overcoming serious technical limitations.[1] According to Paul Coan, who served as NASA's Manned Spaceflight Center Television Subsystem Manager for the Apollo missions, the decision to include television equipment – in addition to photo and film cameras – was carefully weighed against the implications of loading any additional piece of gear onto the vessels. The transmission of television images from space had to be embedded in a complex system of telemetry that relayed different kinds of data, and only part of the bandwidth used by this system could be allotted to the broadcast signal. Accordingly, images had to be captured and broadcast through a slow-scan, low-resolution, and slow-update system.[2] Standard television equipment could not be used, and Coan's team tried out three different systems, both black-and-white and color, specially designed for the missions. Although the iconic Apollo 11 moonwalks were captured with a black-and-white camera, the Apollo 10 mission had previously broadcast color images from the moon's orbit, and color television cameras were used in all subsequent Apollo missions.[3]

DOI: 10.4324/9781003172789-4

44   *Backtracking*

The use of color was a desideratum not only for the sake of documentary accuracy but also as a way of amplifying the cultural effect that these images were expected to have by being conveyed through live transmission. In other words, color was valued as a means for the construction of this unique event as a lived experience, an intense and massive perceptual encounter enabled by media, and the decision to use it brought on a unique set of technological implications. Although one might presume that NASA could rely on the cutting edge of technological research to work through these implications, this was not the case at all. In fact, the color television cameras used in the Apollo missions were based on a technological premise that had been discarded more than a decade earlier.[4] Thus, these awe-inspiring images, expected to signify the beginning of a new age for the human species, were produced through an outdated technology, itself based on an artifact that takes us all the way back to the nineteenth century: the color filter wheel.

This relatively simple mechanical device, which long predated television as a possibility, had been incorporated as a key component of various television systems at the time when the technology was being developed in the 1920s. More specifically, early television systems were based on a scanning disk design patented in 1884 by the German inventor and designer Paul Nipkow. Schematically, the device was a disk bearing equally distanced holes distributed in a spiral shape; each of these holes would capture a fragment of an image, whose values could then be converted into an electric signal and transmitted. A synchronized disk on the other end of the line would then reconvert the incoming signals into images, fragment by fragment. This type of system came to be known as electromechanical since the image was captured and reproduced by a mechanical device – the wheel – and transmitted as a stream of electric signals.[5]

The possibility of adding color filters to this mechanical component in order to capture and reproduce color values was also explored since early on. The use of filters to decompose and recompose color dates back at least to the theoretical work of the German scientist Hermann von Helmholtz. A student of psychophysics, Helmholtz built on the work of Thomas Young to postulate his trichromatic theory of color vision, arguing that the color spectrum as perceived by humans was the result of diverse combinations of three basic wavelengths corresponding to the colors blue, green, and red.[6] The Scottish polymath James Clerk Maxwell later made substantial contributions to our understanding of the practical potential of this theory and was even involved in the production of one of the first color photographs with the photographer Thomas Sutton, in 1861. The image was produced by taking three black-and-white pictures of the same static model through red, green, and blue filters, and superimposing the results by printing the separate images on glass and projecting them onto the same screen through the corresponding filters. The same principle was at work when color filters were added to the mechanical scanning wheel of early television systems, which came to be known as field-sequential because the values for

The Color Wheel of Television History, Mexico, 1939   45

the separate colors were captured, transmitted, and displayed in a rapid sequence, to be synthesized by the neurophysiological perceptual apparatus of a human observer. Their contender, all-electronic systems, were known as additive because they created color through the simultaneous use of the colors. The dispute between these two types of technical solution was a key factor in the development and implementation of color television up until the early 1950s.[7]

From the late 1920s to the mid-1930s, the industry developed consistently, and its advance clearly pointed in the direction of a widespread media technology that would prolong the incursion of communication devices into domestic spaces initiated by the telephone and the radio. In a basic sense, television took up the models established by the radio, with the receiver as the core consumer product and the production studio and broadcasting station as key structural components. The 1930s witnessed an explosion of early television broadcasts in many parts of the world; in the United States alone, three different companies – CBS, NBC, and General Electric – were involved in attempts to establish regular broadcasting as the decade advanced.[8] Some of those early transmissions, like the broadcast of the Berlin Olympic Games in 1936, had already unmasked the technology's strong potential for symbolizing political power both within and beyond national borders.[9] Accordingly, countries with geopolitical aspirations – the United States, the United Kingdom, Germany, and the Soviet Union – were key players in pushing forward the development and commercialization of television. This rapid spread, however, took place in the absence of a technical consensus.

In the United States, the situation evolved into a highly competitive race between two companies, CBS and RCA, which respectively advocated for electromechanical and all-electronic systems as candidates for a standard.[10] What ensued was a protracted negotiation between industrial, commercial, and political interests, in the absence of strictly technological reasons for favoring one system-type over the other. In 1940, the FCC created the National Television System Committee (NTSC), which a year later set a transmission standard for black-and-white television, recommending the use of 30 frames per second with 525 lines in 4:3 aspect ratio (and FM for the sound signal). In 1950, the committee met again to deal with color and, for a brief time, favored a standard based on an electromechanical system sponsored by CBS and based on a design by the Hungarian-American engineer Peter Goldmark. At this point, the color filter wheel was close to becoming a central component of a standard system, and its impact on the American imagination was captured in the front page of the December 1950 issue of *Time* magazine, where a black-and-white portrait of CBS president Frank Stanton could be seen partially rendered into color through the action of a superimposed filter wheel.[11] However, RCA successfully advocated against the implementation of this electromechanical standard, accurately arguing that it would lead to compatibility issues with existing

46 *Backtracking*

equipment, until eventually the FCC settled for an all-electronic standard in 1953. This new standard, hence known simply as NTSC, had the crucial advantage of being compatible with existing black-and-white television sets since the color information was added to the signal in a color subcarrier. The frame rate was 29.9 frames per second, with 525 lines per frame, of which 486 scan lines were visible. The FCC's decision thus marked the end of the color wheel's potential role as the core component of a major media technology and pushed Goldmark's design to the margins of the technological mainstream.

By the time that NASA began to look for a way to broadcast in color from space, the wheel may have already obsolesced into a thing of the past, but Coan's team came across it in their search for alternatives to the bulky and energy-consuming all-electronic devices in existence.[12] The constraints imposed by the functionality of space vessels suddenly brought the wheel into a new domain of relevance, and so a technological premise that had been defeated in a struggle for standardization now proved optimal under different, extraterrestrial conditions. This fact alone should be of interest to media archeologists since it shows just how unstable our definitions of advanced technologies can be and patently undermines linear readings of technological history. However, if we follow the particular trail of events that led to the resurrection of the color filter wheel, we will find ourselves following some unexpected meanders that will lead us even further afield from established narratives.

The Reverse-Spinning Wheel of Technology Transfer

In 2009, a Mexican online news portal published a story with the bombastic headline "TV NASA: Made in Mexico."[13] In the report, Arturo González Camarena, the son of a Mexican inventor named Guillermo González Camarena (1917–1965), claimed that his father had played a crucial role in the design of the color television system used by NASA in the Apollo missions. Arturo argued that in the early 1940s, his father had patented a system for color television based on the color filter wheel and that this very system had been adapted for use in the moon mission broadcasts. This report caught my attention, and soon after, I interviewed Arturo and his brother Guillermo Jr., who stood by their claims. They even went a little further: their father's design, they now told me, had also been used in the Voyager missions.[14]

These assertions may not have garnered much attention if they had not been confirmed by Coan himself, who, in an interview for Mexican television, seemed to acknowledge the link between his team's work and González Camarena's invention (Figure 2.1):

> We found this camera that Mr. Camarena had put together, this technology, so we were able to build a smaller camera, and . . . there was a lot of quick work back then. . . . Well, I wish I had known Camarena,

The Color Wheel of Television History, Mexico, 1939 47

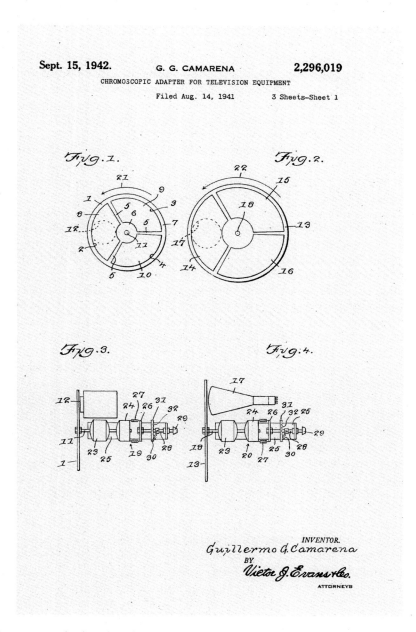

Figure 2.1 Wheel with red, green, and blue filters of the *Chromoscopic Adapter for Television Equipment*. There was a filter wheel in front of the camera and another in front of the television set. US patent by Guillermo González Camarena, 1941.

Source: Google Patents, Public Domain

48   *Backtracking*

I never did meet him, I never knew him. But I can tell you that the technology that he developed was a very good one, a very simple one – simple in the sense of not being complicated, like the NTSC – and it provided better, high-quality images. We still use it today, there are some . . . for example, some medical television cameras that use Camarena's type of technology. It is a very good system to use, it has many uses for many different things, and we will continue to use it even though we are going to much more sophisticated technologies in the future.[15]

Understandably, this video fragment was quickly interpreted in Mexico as an unequivocal validation of the brothers' claims, attesting to what seemed to be a highly unusual case of technology transfer from the Global South to the Global North.

Technology transfer is a fairly common process among countries or regions with relatively similar economic conditions, and it is typically mediated by institutional agents with links to academia, industry, business, and government organizations.[16] Under a standard account, processes of technology transfer rely on fairly established frameworks of interconnection, which are unlikely to exist between countries like the United States and Mexico, even if they are neighbors. In such cases, the assumed norm is rather the purchase of technological products developed and produced in the Global North by countries of the Global South. These technological products are sold to be used in previously specified ways, and their transfer may well be a factor in a process of economic domination, as when the purchase of new agricultural technologies forces farmers in the Global South to alter traditional ways of managing their land, leading to violent transformations in patterns of land ownership.[17] The unlikelihood of a transfer in the opposite direction, and under such particular circumstances, clearly signaled the need to take a closer look at the case.

Hoping for a more detailed account, in 2011, I contacted Paul Coan and requested an interview. When I asked him about González Camarena's presumed contribution to his team's work, his answer flatly contradicted his earlier statement:

I had forgotten the interview you referenced. I had not even seen the video until I accessed it after you referenced it, on YouTube. In the interview, my comments were made in regard to the type of color TV camera technology, and not to any specific work done by González Camarena. In fact, I had not known about his work until shortly before the interview, when I was given a paper describing his work. My comments were intended to acknowledge that the color wheel design was appropriate for certain applications, and that we were using this technology. However, to my knowledge, the specific design of the color video camera developed by NASA and its contractors was based on the CBS color system designed by Goldmark.[18]

The Color Wheel of Television History, Mexico, 1939 49

Coan's answer came as a bit of a shock since there seemed to be no indication in the previous interview that he was referring to a system that, while being based on the same principle as González Camarena's, was in no way derived from it. However, my early training in documentary production allowed me to see how Coan could have responded honestly in both cases: in the first interview, he had recently come to learn of González Camarena's work and was offering a positive assessment of it as being in all respects analogous to the system used by his team. We might think that he was led in that direction by the documentary team, who indeed were there to confirm a given hypothesis and were not inclined to probe deeper into his reply. Nonetheless, it seems fair to say that neither party was engaged in willful deceit or distortion of the facts – it's just that the facts in question are of a particular kind.

If we examine the date and the technical makeup of the system that González Camarena indeed patented, we realize that we are dealing with an example of a form of simultaneity that is often encountered in the histories of science, technology, and even thought. As mentioned above, CBS had based their proposed standard system on Goldmark's patent, and there is no reason to doubt that this same design served as the point of departure for NASA's later system.[19] It is worth noting that Goldmark actually protested against what he regarded as an infringement; he claimed that NASA had in fact contacted CBS as a possible contractor but that the two had failed to agree on a price.[20] NASA then contracted Westinghouse and a team there led by Stanley Lebar developed a system that, according to them, was analogous to but entirely different from Goldmark's. As Lebar described it in conversation with James O'Neal, Goldmark disputed the alleged difference between the two systems:

> "Peter Goldmark was trying to claim credit for the color system," Lebar said. "We had to fight him off continually. He said that anything that anyone did was infringing on his work. The color wheel was really all that we used. The frame rates he had used were totally incompatible with NTSC. It wasn't the same animal at all. He didn't have the technology available in the early 1950s that we were using."[21]

Although this seems to settle the question of whether González Camarena's design had any role in the early use of color television by NASA, it does not reduce the significance of the fact that, as Coan concedes, it had all the qualifications to do so. Now, although we could find contentment in the idea that his system *might well have* inspired NASA's, the particular mode of significance – and the ontological standing – of this unrealized possibility is something to which a media-archaeological gaze must pay close attention in the Latin American context. The excitement generated by Coan's comments in the Mexican media is symptomatic of the difficulties attached to the construction of narratives around local technical creators in Latin America, where failed possibilities and missed opportunities are sometimes

50 *Backtracking*

perversely fetishized at the expense of systematic research. In the case of González Camarena, this lack of academic engagement contrasts with the efforts by Jalisco's Museo de la Radio y la Televisión (MURTV) and with the work of Camarena's two sons, who have created a foundation named after their father and maintain a YouTube channel devoted to his work, compiling a useful trove of audiovisual material. But what should we make out of this material? What kind of narrative could do justice to facts that, on their own, seem condemned to inhabit a kind of limbo wherein the important and the irrelevant cannot be told apart? In the following sections, I will offer an account of González Camarena's work that I hope will allow us to grasp its status as an unrealized possibility in a new way.

Media as National Resource

Living in a world that is saturated by color screens, we have for the most part naturalized the production and perception of color in or through different technical media. However, native color technologies are relatively recent, and for some of us, it should not be too hard to recall that photography, cinema, television, and computer screens all started out as black-and-white or monochrome devices. Consequently, most color media devices can be understood as migrant technologies, and the arrival of color in different media must be analyzed as inscribed within a broader play of cultural forces. This process of migration to color has drawn different degrees of interest in the study of the history of different media, and until recently, scholars have had much more to say about the origins of color cinema than about television's migration to color, even though the cultural impact of the latter process was arguably just as strong, if not stronger. Television's migration to color was attempted in different settings, under different premises, and with different motivations in different localities, and the media-archaeological relevance of this plurality of sites is yet to be elaborated. In a sense, these different migrations were embodied by a diversity of color intensities, tonalities, and textures, archived only in the vague recollections of those who perceived them. The case of González Camarena fits within this spectrum, and it allows us to locate the phenomenon of technological migration within a historical, geographical, and even personal singularity.

González Camarena started working as a technological creator in the early 1930s, when he was still a teenager, and continued to do so until his untimely death in 1965, at the age of 48. These were decades of intense sociopolitical change, ripe with shifting tensions that arguably shaped his experiences and creations. In Mexico, the 1930s and 1940s are known as decades of "consolidation," during which the Mexican Revolution endeavored to "institutionalize" its achievements.[22] Later, during the 1950s and 1960s, the country was forced to adjust its nascent identity as a modern and autonomous postcolonial nation to the new layout of global pressures that entered the stage after WWII. Media technologies played important roles

The Color Wheel of Television History, Mexico, 1939   51

throughout these decades, in Mexico, as elsewhere. As industries old and new (press, radio, cinema, and television) struggled to dominate – and in a sense, create and recreate – the markets of information and mass culture, the idea of a technologically mediated national identity gained a foothold in some of the countries that came to be strategically labelled as developing nations within the new geopolitical parameters of the Cold War. Alongside the new forms of economic dominance promoted through institutions like the World Bank, new modalities of cultural imperialism quickly developed, and they often found in television their tool of choice. The new medium seemed to both enable and symbolize deterritorialized configurations of cultural, economic, and military alliances, and the idea of the Earth as a whole permeated a wide range of emerging cultural practices, from advertisement to ecology. Along with the consolidation of televised international sporting events, the experienced significance of the live broadcast of the moon landing in 1969 can be understood as a crucial node in the unfolding of this ideological inscription of a media technology: an extraterrestrial event being transmitted for a viewership that was construed as global, with the clear aim of symbolizing a new and ambiguous form of world power that portrayed the values of technological progress as universal while conspicuously exercising control over them.

We must note, however, that this inscription took place in a geographically differentiated manner and under variously determined local conditions. In the agitated cultural context that framed González Camarena's early self-understanding of his activities as a technical creator, new media technologies were experienced as a space for individual and collective creativity in ways that predated and informed the arrival of television. As Ruben Gallo has described it, the creative approach to technologies in postrevolutionary Mexico produced a second "technological revolution" brought on by "the cultural transformations triggered by new media in the years after the armed conflict of 1910 to 1920":

> The new revolutionaries were not soldiers or bandits but artists and writers; they did not fight with weapons but with cameras, typewriters, radios, and other mechanical instruments; and the goal was not to topple a dictator but to dethrone the nineteenth-century aesthetic ideals that continued to dominate art and literature in the early years of the century. This was a struggle to set words and images in freedom, to synchronize cultural production to the vertiginous speed of an incipient modernity.[23]

The arrival of wireless media sparked a process that led cultural agents to reconsider the very sense of what a modern national culture could be. As elsewhere, the experience of listening to disembodied speech on the radio had an enormous impact on Mexican writers and visual artists, and inspired a drastic reorientation of their aesthetic premises. A vivid example can be

52   Backtracking

found in Estridentismo, an avant-garde movement that envisioned radio as a critical tool in the configuration of a new perceptual and social reality. Estridentista writers like Manuel Maples Arce and Luis Quintanilla produced literary pieces to be performed at the new radio stations, often conceiving interventions that would now be regarded as radio art. They also collaborated in the design of advertising campaigns, signaling their understanding of radio as calling for a repositioning of creative practices within social space.[24] These writers and artists did not even wait for the technology to become established before they began to test its possibilities: in fact, the first radio broadcast in Mexico City, in 1923, was organized by the literary magazine *El Universal Ilustrado*, and it featured Maples Arce reading the poem "T.S.H.," named after the Spanish acronym for wireless telephony (*telefonía sin hilos*):

> Where might it be, the nest
> of this mechanical song?
> The insomniac antennae of memory
> collect wireless
> messages
> from some frayed goodbye.
> . . .
> Now it's the "Jazz-Band"
> from New York;
> the synchronized ports
> where vice blooms
> and the propulsion of the engines.
> Hertz, Marconi, Edison's madhouse!
> . . .
> The phonetic brain shuffles
> the accidental perspective
> of languages.
> Hallo![25]

These cultural phenomena shed light on a unique receptivity to a new media technology that was experienced as enabling democratic communication and innovative cultural expression, giving rise to a sense of interaction between the avant-garde and an emergent modern popular culture that was often driven by political and commercial agents.[26] Due to Mexico's unique historical development, these experiences were often framed and driven by the vision of a nation state that could be expressive of and responsive to these heterogeneous potentials.

Like many youngsters during this early wave of excitement, González Camarena first took an interest in electronic sound and its modes of transmission. He obtained a radio amateur license when he was still a teenager and worked as a technician for several radio stations. He joined an amateur league, the Liga Mexicana de Radioexperimentadores, created in 1932,

The Color Wheel of Television History, Mexico, 1939   53

to encourage and structure communication among the country's growing community of radio enthusiasts.[27] Through it, he gained access to technical literature based on which he was able to conduct practical experiments and start designing his own equipment. He also befriended a few musicians and composers who followed and encouraged his early experiments in sound transmission, one of whom was Luis Herrera de la Fuente (1916–2014), a performer, composer, and later, conductor of Mexico City's National Symphony Orchestra. The two met when the 17-year-old González Camarena was working as a studio technician in a government radio station where Herrera de la Fuente performed as a pianist. Over time, Herrera de la Fuente became an assistant of sorts for González Camarena – a "hand worker" (*trabajador manual*), as he puts it; the two spent many sleepless nights exploring the technological possibilities of sound and, later, image transmission.[28]

In 1931, an engineer named Javier Stavoli had already used a system based on the Nipkow disk to carry out the first (although irregular) television transmissions in Mexico.[29] Significantly, his experiments had been partially funded by a political party, the PNR, which was interested in exploring the medium's use for propaganda purposes. The sense that Mexico could and should build its own technological systems grew stronger in the second half of the 1930s, when President Lázaro Cardenas promoted the nationalization of oil and mineral resources. This bold move created an atmosphere of tension between Mexico and the United States, the United Kingdom, and the Netherlands, which led to the boycotting of Mexican goods. Lacking qualified technicians, Mexico was not in principle prepared to run its own refineries, but the government managed to keep them operational and productive. The rhetoric around the value of Mexico having its own resources experienced a peak during this period, and the date of the nationalization of oil is still celebrated today as a holiday.[30]

There was a clear and felt resonance between these efforts towards an autonomy of resources and technology and the project of cultural autochthony that had inspired the administrations and artistic movements of the postrevolutionary period. Things took a different turn during the transition from the 1930s to the early 1940s, when President Manuel Ávila Camacho drastically reconfigured the relationship between Mexico and the United States. The new orientation was symbolically confirmed when Mexico joined the allied nations in 1942; Mexico sourced supplies to the United States and sent troops to the Pacific front – a unit of Mexico's Air Force, Squadron 201 (also known as the Aztec Eagles), even joined in aerial combat in the South Pacific islands.[31] These efforts by a new generation of politicians to position Mexico as a modern nation in the global stage exemplify a unique conversation between the previously established values of cultural and economic rootedness and self-sufficiency, and a new set of geopolitical conditions. The sense of what being a postcolonial nation entailed was being redefined at considerable speed, and it was becoming clear that media technologies would play a crucial role. In such a context, the notion that such technologies could be designed and produced in Mexico and be expressive of its own

54 Backtracking

cultural values may well have been perceived as a condition for being an autonomous nation in modern times. Thus, a media technical creator like González Camarena would not have understood what he was doing in his home studio, at night and with the help of his musician friend, as a personal hobby, but as a contribution to a unique process of nation-building.

A Patent and a Song

González Camarena focused his attention on television around the late 1930s. He was still living and working in his parent's house in Mexico City, where he shared a working space with his elder brother, the painter Jorge González Camarena. Jorge had started his career coloring architectural drawings by his mentor, Dr. Atl, and by the 1930s, he had gained some visibility through his engagement with Muralismo, a movement that advocated for public art as a means for mobilizing and strengthening new social bonds. Many of Jorge's murals can be read as efforts to create a visually synthetic account of Mexican history through a postrevolutionary lens, and a few of them were conceived for some of Mexico City's iconic public cultural buildings, like the Museo de Antropología and the Palacio de Bellas Artes. Like his younger brother, Jorge envisioned technology as playing a part in this budding postcolonial national narrative, right alongside an affirmative reappropriation of the values of indigenous and popular cultures.[32] According to one of Guillermo's sons, it was Jorge who first encouraged him to present his experiments with color television to the public,[33] but his role as a spiritual companion can be said to go much further. In a way, the two brothers were working towards forms of communication whose main task would be to code, enable, and celebrate the formation of a modern Latin American nation.

González Camarena eventually made his experiments with color television public in 1939, and in August of 1940, he submitted a patent application to Mexico's agency for industrial property rights, which granted the patent a month later. In fact, what he patented was a specific device, described as a Chromoscopic Adapter for Television Equipment (Adaptador Cromoscópico para Aparatos de Televisión) (Figure 2.2 and Figure 2.3). According to the patent, this artifact would allow users to transform existing black-and-white television cameras and receivers into color television devices:

> *Esta invención se refiere a un sistema de adaptador sencillo y totalmente novedoso, que sirve para la transmisión y recepción por radio o "línea" de imágenes en colores, con solo adaptarlo a cualquiera de los actuales equipos de televisión a rayos catódicos.*

> This invention refers to a simple and entirely novel adapter system that can be used to transmit and receive color images by radio or wire, requiring only to be adapted to fit any current cathode-ray television device.[34]

The Color Wheel of Television History, Mexico, 1939 55

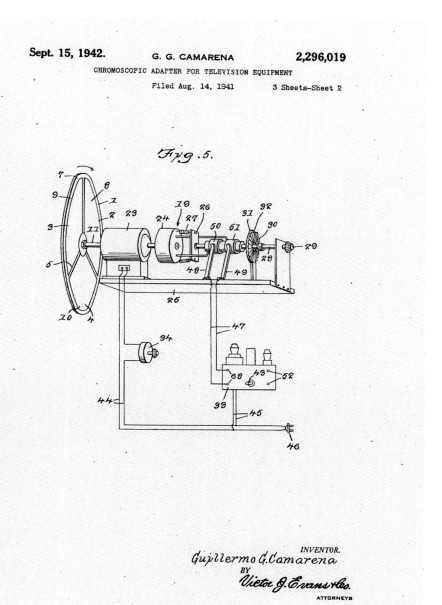

Figure 2.2 Mechanical components of the *Chromoscopic Adapter for Television Equipment*. US patent by Guillermo González Camarena, 1941.
Source: Google Patents, Public Domain

56 Backtracking

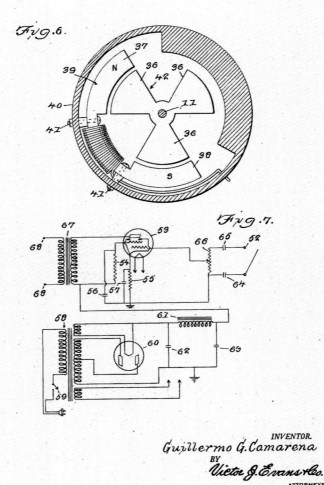

Figure 2.3 Electric circuits of the *Chromoscopic Adapter for Television Equipment.* US patent by Guillermo González Camarena, 1941.

Source: Google Patents, Public Domain

The Color Wheel of Television History, Mexico, 1939   57

As we already know, the adapter relied on color filter wheels to apply the colors red, green, and blue sequentially, one frame at a time, in both the camera and the receiver. The system also featured a module that synchronized the spinning wheels at both ends, and a set of electronic controllers that ensured that the red, green, and blue filters were in the same position in both devices at the same time.

One year later, González Camarena sought to obtain a patent for this system in the United States. The application was expensive, and he struggled to gather the necessary funding; a potential lender required him to mortgage his mother's house as collateral, and the government responded to his requests for support with indifference.[35] He eventually found someone who was willing to lend him the amount with no concern for financial gain, but finding the payback money was another taxing job since the acquisition of the patent was no guarantee of immediate returns. To cover this debt, González Camarena took an interesting turn: tapping back into his love of music, he decided to try his hand as a composer and wrote a popular song, *Río Colorado*. According to the Discography of American History Recording (DAHR), the earliest documented version of this song was performed around 1950 by Los Tres Diamantes, a Mexican male vocal trio backed by an instrumental ensemble. However, since the trio was formed in 1948, this was probably not the first version.[36] Another performance, this one by Los Hermanos Reyes y Teresita, from Jalisco, was released in 1970 as part of a golden hits compilation, which suggests that they may have recorded the song long before, at the time when they were hired by the XEW radio station in Mexico City, in 1941. Since, by 1970, it had earned the status of a hit from the old days, this was probably the version whose royalties allowed González Camarena to pay back his loan.

As I have noted, music and its recording, transmission, and playback were extremely important for González Camarena from the very start, and it may not be far-fetched to read this episode as another sign of his awareness of the productively porous interface between culture and technology at the time. Arguably, an experience of the generative mutation undergone by popular (or folk) musical forms when they are recorded or transmitted through technical media would have been a crucial component of his sense of what media technologies could achieve.[37] Going a bit further, the song's lyrics, with their references to moonlit crystals, a blushing sweetheart, and crimson clouds, remind us of the kind of cultural coding that surrounded the arrival of color as an element in the language of visual technical media, as in the use of saturated colors in landscape postcards or the films of Douglas Sirk to induce heightened degrees of emotional intensity and lyrical states of mind:

Hermosa claridad que resplandece,
en esta hermosa noche de ilusión.
Es la luna bella que aparece
besando los cristales del balcón,

58   *Backtracking*

mientras que las nubes en el cielo
ya se van tiñendo de carmín.

Beautiful glimmering clarity
in this beautiful night of illusion,
as the gorgeous rising moon
kisses the balcony windows
while the clouds in the sky
are dyed in growing crimson.[38]

Far from being an anecdotal sidestep, González Camarena's decision to resort to composing a commercial hit song in order to fund a patent application for a color television adapter could be said to illustrate the complex and unique field of action that we are trying to reconstruct *Rio Colorado* was written to be captured as a recorded performance, and in that sense, it was conceived as a *product*, just like the adapter. In other words, González Camarena was clearly attuned to the emergent connections between the spheres of culture, industry, and commerce, and he perceived himself as an agent engaging in the multidimensional space created by such connections. To write a song and to design an adapter were not simply isolated aspects of an eclectic personality: they were confluent tracks in the configuration of a new kind of social agent that could amalgamate the talents of the poet and the engineer without contradiction. Moreover, González Camarena expected to make a profit from the production and marketing of his adapter, rather than from the sale of the patent, which suggests that he also regarded entrepreneurship as a potential component of technical creativity and that he understood entrepreneurship as an integral component of a vision of technological autonomy as a national virtue.

This grasp of the field of possibilities was probably uncommon for a Mexican inventor, more so if we bear in mind that González Camarena envisioned the United States as a potential market. The US patent for his adapter was eventually granted in September 1942, only a few months before Goldmark obtained one for his own wheel-based system. Although the color filter wheel in Goldmark's design was more complex, the main difference between the two systems resides in their ground conception: Goldmark had designed an integrated device, and just for this reason, his system was not compatible with the black-and-white television equipment already in the market. As I have noted, the fact that electromechanical color television systems were developed and promoted by CBS as an all-or-nothing solution is one of the factors that led to their eventual disqualification as the potential standard. In that sense, González Camarena's design was a significantly different proposition.

Although it may strike us as odd, up until the 1950s, the idea of using adapters to transform black-and-white into color television sets was not only considered plausible but even implemented and commercialized in

The United States. At the time, a range of products with names like the Coloradaptor, the Airtronic Color Converter, and the Col-R-Tel entered the market, staking out the exact slot that González Camarena may well have imagined for his own device a decade earlier. The basic technical framework was quite similar and relied on the premise of using filters in the receiver to read and reproduce the color information from the signal. The Col-R-Tel, for instance, would take the color information from the NTSC signal and apply it sequentially to the picture tube in the black-and-white television set.[39] A vertical synchronizing pulse was used to control the motor's speed and thus keep the proper filter in place at the appropriate time. The existence of these adapters is symptomatic of a need that was rooted in the plausible behavior of consumers during this transitional time, when it could have made more sense to adapt an old device than to replace it with a new one. Most importantly, then as now, the commercial relevance of adapters, broadly understood, is linked to the inability or unwillingness on the part of industrial, commercial, and/or political agents to settle on a standard. Although in the early 1950s, the situation might still have favored a turn towards the adapter as an affordable way of updating a device, color adapters failed to take a hold. Their size was inconvenient, making them fit for use only on small monitors, and this was enough to offset the fact that they sold for 15% of the price of a new color television set. Had it reached the production stage, González Camarena's design may well have been an alternative – perhaps the first – although there is no reason to assume that this would have improved the chances of the color adapter as a device-type in the market. In any case, González Camarena was far from done with television.

GonCam Rising

In the second half of the 1940s and early 1950s, González Camarena's technical proficiency came to be well-known in Mexico. In 1945, the Ministry of Communications awarded him funds to carry out a study to establish reference units for electrical communication systems, and a year later, he made the first experimental color television broadcast from the headquarters of the Liga Mexicana de Radioexperimentadores in Mexico City. That same year, he began to launch meteorological balloons to lift radio equipment to the stratosphere in order to determine the reach of the signals.[40] As before, these endeavors were embedded in Mexico's ongoing and evolving efforts to craft a complex identity as a modern nation state. Right after WWII, the country elected its first civilian president of the postrevolutionary period, Miguel Alemán Valdés,[41] who, like his predecessors, was strongly committed to industrial development and created a commission to explore the global state of the art in television. Under this initiative, in 1947, González Camarena and the writer Salvador Novo traveled to the United States and Europe to become acquainted with innovations in television network engineering

60 *Backtracking*

for a report that examined the potential roles of the public and private sectors in the spread of communications technologies. Notably, this report still settled for black-and-white television as the technical basis for government-led efforts to establish a national network.

Alongside these advisory positions, González Camarena made good and steady progress as an entrepreneur. In 1948, he created GonCam, a company for the production of color television equipment based on his system, which by then had evolved from an adapter into a set of integrated devices. During the 1950s, he established connections with peers in the United States who recognized the technical ingenuity of his work; these included technicians like Lee De Forest, inventor of the Audion vacuum tube, and Alexander Poniatoff, the founder of AMPEX. More significantly, he met Norman Alexandroff, a radio broadcaster and president of Columbia College, who actually commissioned GonCam to produce color television equipment for the school's Chicago and Hollywood campuses. According to several sources, Alexandroff surveyed quite a few options before coming to the conclusion that GonCam's system was the best available.[42] In a sense, this purchase can be regarded as one of González Camarena's crucial achievements, at least from his own point of view; indeed, it can be described as a highly unusual export of state-of-the-art technological products from the Global South to the Global North, and it draws our attention to the fact that academic institutions were gradually creating the space for an alternative market for technological innovations (Figure 2.4).

In 1952, González Camarena went a step further and created his own television station, Channel 5 (XHGC-TV), a decision that is consistent with his understanding of media technologies as conduits for a national culture. In collaboration with Jorge, he designed the channel's logo, based on the premise of spelling out the word "television" in the ancient Nahuatl script, a system used in pre-Hispanic and early colonial times that mixed ideographic writing with phonetic logograms and syllabic signs. The Channel 5 logo assembled a set of glyphs that, as the brothers imagined, might have been used to ideographically represent television (Figure 2.5). In a brief video interview, Guillermo Jr. offers the following reading of the logo: an inverted divine eye at the top, set against a triangular background that stands for the temple of the air god Ehécatl, emits two light rays that are received by two upright regular eyes below.[43] Curious about the accuracy of this strange exercise in anachronistic semantics, I asked a couple of experts to venture a plausible reading of the logo. Professor Roberto Flores, of Mexico's National Institute of Anthropology and History, read the inverted eye as standing for the year (*xihuitl*) and agreed with Guillermo Jr.'s reading of the two lower circular glyphs as standing for the eye (*ixtli*); his reading for the assemblage was thus "vision in time." Professors Ángel González and Julie K. Wesp, from UC Riverside and NC State University, respectively, read all circular glyphs as standing for the eye (*ixtelotli*) and the two diagonal bands as standing for luminous rays (*itonalmeyotsitsiuan*); they also read

Figure 2.4 The color television camera built by Guillermo González Camarena and branded by his company GonCam, an implementation of his pioneering color system for color television broadcasting. Radio and TV Museum, Palacio de la Cultura y la Comunicación, Zapopan, Jalisco, Mexico.

Source: ProtoplasmaKid, Creative Commons license

the triangular background as a third glyph standing for the sky (*iluikak*). In that case, a plausible reading would be "eyes interconnected by luminous rays across the sky," not too far from Guillermo Jr.'s interpretation, except for the latter's distinction between "transmitter" and "receiver" eyes. In any case, the scholars all agreed that the glyphs used in the logo are too stylized to be matched with historical counterparts.[44] Although the inclusion of references to Mexico's pre-Hispanic cultures in commercial iconographies has an older and enduringly problematic history, it seems fair to think that the González Camarena brothers meant, above all, to express the same commitment to the possibility of synthesizing this ancient background with media technologies that informed so many of their previous activities. Whether naive or opportunistic, this kind of nationalistic techno-indigenism undoubtedly played an important role in shaping Mexico's cultural landscape in the second half of the twentieth century.

In 1955, González Camarena joined the owners of two other channels, Channels 2 and 4, to create Telesistema Mexicano, an early media conglomerate that would later morph into Televisa, currently the largest television company in Mexico and one of the most important television

62 Backtracking

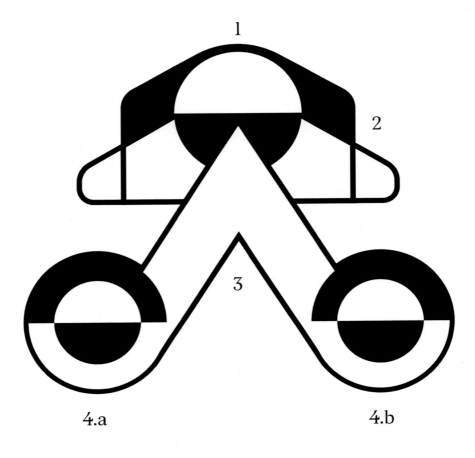

1. Image
2. Temple of Ehécatl
3. Rays of light
4. The eyes of the people

Figure 2.5 The Channel 5 logo assembled a set of prehispanic Mesoamerican glyphs that, as the brothers Guillermo and Jorge González Camarena imagined it, might have been used to represent the word "television" in ancient Nahuatl ideographically.

Source: Vector-based image version by Pierre Puentes

companies worldwide.[45] In 1960, Emilio Azcárraga, former owner of Channel 2 and founding president of Telesistema, commissioned Jorge to create a bas-relief facade for a new studio building. The work, titled *Frisos de la televisión* (Television friezes), covered the entire southern facade of the six-story building. For each story, Jorge composed an elongated strip populated by a mix of contemporary and pre-Hispanic motifs in silhouette. The play of shapes is reminiscent of traditional Mexican perforated paper techniques, and each stripe refers to a specific group of cultural activities. The ascent from the lower to the upper stories offered a portrait of modern Mexican culture as a whole, a kind of cultural utopia where all layers of human activity had a place, although under a fairly traditional hierarchy that placed bodily activities below and intellectual and creative activities above: sports, dance, theater and cinema, information and education, the arts and sciences. Crowning the whole composition was the old Channel 5 logo. To the right, Jorge depicted three studio workers, a cameraman, a studio coordinator, and a soundman holding a boom microphone, who could be read as capturing and broadcasting all these activities so that each frieze could be understood as representing a kind of program. Although the utopian synthesis of culture, technology, and knowledge was already a recurring theme in Mexican Muralism,[46] Jorge's work is a remarkable example by virtue of its stylistic restraint and graphic, almost design-based approach. Significantly, the work was inaugurated in a live television broadcast, where Jorge explicitly states that he had turned to a visual language inspired by folk and pre-Hispanic motifs in order to affirm the potential affinities between the new media cultures and these earlier and parallel cultural formations.[47]

Chromoscopic Forays into Near Space

Although the use of the color filter wheel in the Apollo missions may register as its moment of greatest cultural significance, it was in the 1970s, with the Voyager program, that this technological premise may be said to have reached its fullest potential. As before, the decision not to use all-electronic standard NTSC cameras in the Voyager probes was grounded on weight, size, and power constraints, measured against accuracy in color representation, but in the context of this program, the color filter wheel system was reframed to tap into a level of relevance that would not have come into view otherwise: television cameras were now conceived as research instruments and not simply as communication devices.[48] Color was explicitly framed as a research topic in the Voyager missions, and the filters were now inscribed within a system designed to allow scientists to "characterize the nature of the colored material in the clouds of Jupiter and Saturn, and identify the nature and sources of chromophores on Io and Titan,"[49] among other things. Accordingly, the functionality of the system was radically expanded through the use of a wider range of filters (now including ultraviolet, violet, orange, methane 1, sodium, and methane 2).[50] Thus, a color television system was now perceived as capable of capturing data and not only as a source of awe-inspiring imagery.

64 *Backtracking*

When I interviewed Bradford Smith, who led the Voyager Imaging Experiment, he portrayed the color filter wheel as a device that had already long been naturalized, as it were, as a tool for the visual scrutiny of outer space:

> I have no idea where the idea of using filter wheels came from, but they have been used on various space cameras and ground-based telescopes for as long as I have been involved in astronomy. For Voyager, we simply built on the experience of previous NASA planetary spacecraft.[51]

In that sense, the fate of the color filter wheel as a technological component was decisively altered by what may be called a change of milieu – from the terrestrial to the extraterrestrial.

There is surely something fantastic about this strange blossoming of the color filter wheel in space, which can be imaginatively portrayed as a mutation into a new lifeform. The scientific and symbolic affordances of color could be said to have merged in that device at that particular moment, as the very sense of what transmitting color from space was changed: color was now the carrier of information about complex physical and chemical systems – otherworldly atmospheres. This imaginative framework could allow us to envision a different kind of technical lineage for González Camarena's system, even while knowing full well that there is no historical connection between his work and NASA's systems. To understand this lineage, it may be necessary to fuse history and fiction, as Philip K. Dick did in his novel *The Man in the High Castle*, where the triumph of the Third Reich in WWII is read as the source of parallel forms of living and thinking whose resonance and dissonance with our own shed light on the instability of what we take for granted. The power of this kind of fiction is predicated on the role that the possible plays in the constitution of our cultural systems, for these parallel present-futures make us aware of the way in which unrealized possibilities are nonetheless a part of what these systems articulate.

The kind of fiction that I have in mind is better captured through practice than through discursive or narrative constructions, and in this particular case, it entails a certain kind of reconstruction. When STS scholar Hernán Thomas conceptualized the resignification of technologies, he was mainly referring to the socially mediated reinscription of technologies leading to modes of use other than those that they were invented for. Thus understood, resignification goes beyond adaptation or misuse, for it entails a relocation of the very meaning of a technology within a different cultural complex. In that sense, an act of resignification can be described as having ontological implications, if we consider technological artifacts as socially mediated realities.[52]

For media technologies, resignification is likely to function in a slightly different way since they have a specific manner of taking on a new meaning when they are activated in different historical and cultural contexts. To see how this might be so, it is not enough to simply repair or reconstruct a

The Color Wheel of Television History, Mexico, 1939   65

device and put it to work. When this is done simply in order to theatricalize the functioning of an old machine, its historical significance is taken for granted and quoted as a given. But acts of reconstruction and reactivation can be conceptualized, alternatively, as a way of mobilizing the original meaning of the technologies through a creative relocation, under the premise that they may have something unexpected to tell us – as I have shown, this is in a sense exactly what happened to the color filter wheel when it was resurrected by NASA. At the very least, a creative practice based on such exercises of resignification – which must inevitably take on the form of experiments – may allow us to perceive directly how uniform and inflexible our production and consumption of information and experiences through media have become, in spite of the putatively additive progress and wider availability of media technologies. Recently, Sigfried Zielinski has conceptualized a new field of practice, prospective archaeology, which takes these criteria into account. An exercise in prospective archeology engages in the reconstruction of media devices for the sake of allowing them to produce a kind of meaning that perhaps is neither new nor old. This is an interdisciplinary venture that conjoins the archeologist's commitment to historical accuracy with the creative practitioner's ear for surprises.[53]

One contingency that considerably hinders our understanding of early color television is the fact that it originally developed as a transmission technology, rather than as an inscription technology.[54] Television devices were engaged in the production and reception of broadcasts, vanishing streams of electromagnetic signals. AMPEX invented video recording in electromagnetic tape only in 1957, and even then, the compatibility between standards and formats prevented widespread video recording for quite some time. This means that, in a sense and unlike other media, we can have no direct experience of what television was like during its first decades of existence. This impossibility is particularly significant in the case of color television. Given the difficulty of describing in words the particular textures and fluctuations of color, the historiographical importance of a direct reactivation of early color television devices should not be underestimated. However, we could also regard this challenge as the point of departure for an exercise in prospective archaeology. This was the starting premise of my attempts to resignify González Camarena's Chromoscopic Adapter for Color Television.

My first aim was to shed light on the mode of production of color images in the old electromechanical cameras and to have a direct qualitative experience of the kind of color that can be obtained solely through the sequential activity of the filters. I first took three photographs of the same static model with a black-and-white camera, each through one of three color filters, and used a computer to apply the red, green, and blue color filters in a digitally controlled sequence. I tested two different sets of filters in the camera, one made of plastic and one made of dichroic glass. Although the plastic filters were resistant and affordable, they performed poorly in tests, yielding a restricted spectrum when the images captured through them were overlaid.

66 *Backtracking*

The dichroic color filters performed much better and proved to yield a wider dynamic range in the final color mix.

The next step was to run tests with the color wheel. I first designed one based on González Camarena's schematics, but I soon encountered difficulties when trying to run a motor at the rpm rate required to generate accurate and lasting color effects. The video frequency of the NTSC video made it difficult to synchronize the motor powering the color filter wheel, which would eventually run out of phase. I then obtained a color filter wheel of the kind used in DLP projectors[55] and found a microchip that allowed me to control it through a feedback loop to maintain a constant speed. With this setup, I obtained satisfactory results, enough to get a good sense of the wheel as a device. Most importantly, I now had a direct experience of the feel and look of the color images produced by the field-sequential system.

Having assembled a functional version of the system, I tried to think of a way of using it to imaginatively explore the unrealized possibility of the Chromoscopic Adapter's voyage into space. At first, I considered collaborating with some Latin American colleagues who are involved in space projects – like Juan José Díaz Infante, who launched the satellite Ulises from Mexico – but after learning about González Camarena's tests with meteorological balloons in the 1940s, I thought that this might be the appropriate vehicle. Not only would the use of balloons be affordable and relatively simple to learn, but it also allowed me to construct a historical-fictional event with more than one connection to González Camarena's work and, thus, to create something like a resonant chord out of realized and unrealized possibilities. Bearing in mind that the first satellites relied on radio signals to transmit telemetry data, the experiment could be conceived as a conceptual probe into a potentially alternative meaning of space exploration as a historical and geopolitical construct.

Given the reach of balloons, I conceived my mission as a near-space mission. Near space is a section of the earth's atmosphere that extends through the stratosphere, the mesosphere, and part of the thermosphere, from 12 to 62 miles above sea level. The basic idea was to send a weather balloon up into near space, as González Camarena had done, but loaded with cameras that would record color video images through a color filter system. Strictly speaking, then, mine would not be a television system but a video recording system that would capture images to be physically retrieved after the system's descent. After some tests, I established that the use of a sniping motor would destabilize the trajectory of the balloon to an unmanageable degree, so I had to come up with an alternative to the motor-powered filter wheel. The most practical solution was to work with three cameras, all recording in black-and-white but each through a different color filter. After launching the balloon and recovering it, I would overlay the videos shot with the three separate black-and-white cameras to obtain a composite color video.

To carry out the mission, I conceived a flying system composed of a weather balloon, a parachute, a radar reflector, and a payload container

The Color Wheel of Television History, Mexico, 1939 67

carrying five cameras; two of these cameras would shoot documentary color images (one Kodak Playfull Waterproof shooting video and one GoPro 2 camera taking still pictures with a time-lapse function), and the other three cameras (also Kodak Playfulls) would shoot black-and-white video through the filters. I used Keymont 500 helium-filled weather balloons that can reach an altitude close to 65,000 feet, up to the lower stratosphere. Since, in the vicinity of the stratosphere, the atmospheric pressure is lower, the helium would gradually expand the balloon until it reached bursting altitude, at which point the balloon would explode and the payload would begin its descent. The mechanically activated parachute would muffle the fall, and the radar detector would allow me to track the payload's path to its landing site. Additional components included hand warmers (to prevent the payload equipment from freezing) and extra batteries for the cameras. A GPS Spot was also used to track the position of the balloon every ten minutes. To predict the balloon's trajectory, I used the online software application Landing Predictor, designed by Habhub.[56] I then ran computer simulations for a month to calculate strategically the most appropriate place to launch from and to define the approximate area where the payload could be recovered.

I sent the system out on two missions, the first of which launched from Cuernavaca, Mexico, in May 2012, and the second from Carpinteria, California, in December 2012 (Figure 2.6). In Mexico, the balloon was filled with 10.2 cubic feet of helium, and in California, with 11.5 cubic feet. In the first mission, the burst altitude was 72,000 feet, which is considered low stratosphere; the time to burst was 70 minutes, the ascent rate was 18 feet per second, and the descent rate was 12 feet per second. The payload was recovered within three hours of launching. In California, the burst altitude was 65,000 feet, also low stratosphere; the time to burst was 90 minutes, the ascent rate was 19 feet per second, and the descent rate was 11 feet per second. This time, it took two days to recover the payload. In the first mission, the video system malfunctioned, and we were unable to obtain any images. In California, things fared better, and we were able to capture 6 hours of high-definition video and more than 400 pictures. All the recordings were then mixed using computational means to apply the field-sequential principle. Although my system differed considerably from González Camarena's, it still produced a color palette that was drastically different from that of CCD color cameras. The computational assemblage of the video shot by the three black-and-white cameras created a stunning color range, reminiscent of a technicolor movie but with low resolution. We could see the Earth's halo from the stratosphere, the sun, the moon, the Pacific Ocean, and the mountains of central California in colors that merged the old with the new: a joint artifact of archeology and science fiction, less than a document but more than a fancy.

Figure 2.6 Picture of the California mountains and coastline taken with a weather balloon launched from Carpinteria that reached an altitude of 22 kilometers (72,180 feet), exploring the lower stratosphere in the near outer space. The payload had a reconstruction of González Camarena's color camera.

Source: Photo by Andrés Burbano, 2012

Conclusions

This chapter began with a drive to depart from Earth in search of answers to a few questions about a little-known Mexican color television system; now it is time to heed Bruno Latour's recent invitation to fix our gaze back on our planet.[57] Television's migration to color arguably cemented its role as the most influential media technology of the postwar period, and the cultural repercussions were felt in myriad and well-known ways all over the globe. At the time, the logos of some of the leading TV studios and channels appropriated the rainbow and the color spectrum as signs of technological achievement, and some of them still use them.[58] To a great degree, many of our media habits are a result of this process, and they persist even after the technological framework that shaped them has been abandoned.

The setting of the NTSC standard was a landmark in this process and in the history of audiovisual technologies, but the system had its flaws, many of which soon became prominent in the United States. This prompted technicians in other parts of the globe to continue the search for alternative color television systems. Two strong contenders emerged in Western Europe, both based on the premise of using 50 fields and 25 frames to correct the issues with NTSC. European countries had agreed on the use of 625 lines, of which 576 were visible, so both systems followed this parameter. The two new alternatives were known as the Sequential Color with Memory (SECAM) color system and the Phase Alternating Line (PAL) color system. SECAM was designed by Henri de France, a French engineer who ran his own company, Compagnie Française de Télévision; and PAL was the work of a German inventor Walter Bruch, employed by Telefunken.[59] Both systems came into use around 1967, and the contest between them gave rise to yet another dispute, now a clash of national and corporate interests. Thus, even in the Global North, the ideologically hyped reality of television as a global medium was hardly at hand.[60]

The struggle over standards extended to other parts of the globe, as countries that were locked in the position of technology consumers were now compelled to select one of these three standards. In contrast with the image of spaceship Earth as seen from the moon, assumed to visually convey the ultimate irrelevance of political, social, and racial divisions, in the 1960s and 1970s, the world was being redivided not into kingdoms or empires but into huge techno-cultural, transcontinental, and transoceanic areas based on the adoption of these standards – a division that lasted until the arrival of digital television. The new global cartography had strong cultural, political, and economic implications since the standard chosen by each country determined its predominant exposure to content produced by the cultural industries of the countries that created the standards. Predictably, most of the Americas opted for NTSC, including Canada, Cuba, the Caribbean, Central America, and South America's Pacific Coast. Germany and most Western European countries, England, China, the Middle East, and several Commonwealth countries in Africa, Asia, and Oceania, went with PAL; SECAM was selected by France, the Soviet Union, and African countries that were former French or Belgian colonies. The resulting delimitations could be easily mapped onto the geographies of old and new colonization processes. And so it was that color, a perceptual category that is often and naively regarded as rooted in our shared perceptual apparatus, was effectively reinscribed into the emerging political framework of Cold War–era neoliberalism through its translation into electronic technologies.[61]

To some extent, this global state of affairs explains why, up to his death in 1965, González Camarena continued to believe that there could be a place for his invention in this shifting world. He concocted further elaborations of his design premise and obtained several new patents in Mexico. He patented a stereoscopic television system in collaboration with the American inventor James F. Butterfield, who filed for a similar US patent under his own name. This system was tested through Channel 5 broadcasts, as reported by *TV Guide* in an article titled "South of the Border: Fun with 3-D TV Down Mexico Way."[62] He also patented a design for a cathode-ray tube television set based on the aperture grille, a technique similar to the Trinitron system developed by Sony in the 1960s. More mysteriously, his children told me

70 *Backtracking*

that he had designed a Subjective Color Television System that sought to create the illusion of color in black-and-white monitors.[63]

The most important among these late works is a bi-color television system that was a direct evolution of the Chromoscopic Adapter.[64] This new system exploited the possibility of coordinating electromechanical and all-electronic functionalities: the camera was equipped with a color wheel using only two complementary colors (blue and orange), while the display was an all-electronic cathode-ray tube color television screen, also bi-color, where a group of horizontal phosphor lines would produce a primary color and a similar group, interspersed with the first, would produce the complementary. This made the system simpler and cheaper, although the scope of representable color was narrower than the trichromatic option. In spite of this, the bichromatic principle could easily match the quality of other commercial color television solutions available in those days. González Camarena was by now keenly aware of compatibility as a key criterion, and the fact that it paired an electromechanical camera with an all-electronic display meant that an image captured with this system could also be watched on an NTSC color television set. In general terms, it was a complete solution that enriched González Camarena's starting premise with innovations that were clearly responsive to the demands of the market. In that restricted sense, he can be said to have achieved his long-term goal of developing an affordable color television system made in and for Mexico. In his position as advisor for Telesistema Mexicano, he advocated for the adoption of this bi-color system as a national standard and made plans with Azcárraga to mass-produce bi-color television equipment under the brand name Majestic.

In 1964, Leslie Solomon introduced González Camarena's last design to the American public in the influential magazine *Electronics World*, describing it accurately as an alternative to existing standards based on the principles of simplicity and economy that prevailed, and continue to prevail, throughout the Global South: "This Mexican-developed color-TV system joins the NTSC, PAL, and SECAM. Although this Mexican system suffers from certain color deficiencies, it appears to use what are probably the simplest circuits of the four systems."[65] The article included a detailed explanation of the electronic transmission solution and emphasized the system's compatibility with the NTSC standard. That same year, the system was publicly demonstrated during the World Fair in Queens, New York, whose overall theme was "Man's Achievement on a Shrinking Globe in an Expanding Universe." The Mexican pavilion, designed by architect Pedro Ramírez Vázquez, was meant to showcase the results of a period of sustained economic improvement known as the Mexican Miracle.[66] Many reports of the time took note of the pavilion's audiovisual presentations screened on color television sets, but even though its brochure advertised "the development of an original color television process" as one of the country's achievements (alongside "the production of sponge iron by melting iron ore with natural gas" and "the manufacture of paper from sugar cane bagasse"),[67] no one seems to have made much of this exceptional fact: what was on display at the pavilion was, from a technical point of view, a true alternative to similar technological systems developed in the Global North. In that sense, and from the vantage point of his last efforts, we may surely frame González Camarena's projects as an example of the quest for technological autonomy in Latin America, as analyzed by Emmanuel Adler.[68] As I hope to have shown, however, González Camarena understood this autonomy as something to be achieved through a locally unique intercrossing of creative, social, economic, and political possibilities.

When a dramatic car accident interrupted his life, along with his ongoing projects in 1965, González Camarena was taking all the necessary steps to fill out his vision of an affordable color television system made in Mexico, covering all aspects of the industry, from technology design to programming. Nonetheless, soon after his death, Mexico adopted the NTSC standard, rushing to the decision under the pressure of the upcoming 1968 Olympic Games. As soon as González Camarena died, his company and projects came to an abrupt halt. The patents were known to the public, the electronic components were accessible, and several workers at the GonCam factory had the required experience to continue production, but clearly, the entire venture was too anchored to his individual drive. If we now ask ourselves again what could have driven the unfounded excitement about the reputed use of his system in the Apollo missions, we can read it now as the sign of a cultural mechanism that is often at work in the Global South: in places where the figure of the technical creator is not culturally coded, their work cannot be regarded as anything but an anomaly, even when the scale of their achievements is, as in this case, in plain view. This neglect is then overcompensated for by an uncritical retrospective celebration that, in fact, further entrenches their status as an anomaly. These cultural mechanisms are expressive of an uneasy relationship with technology, one that has taken on different forms throughout the Global South during the twentieth and twenty-first centuries. Although the effects can be partly remedied through careful archival and historical work, the sense of historical displacement that pervades many of these narratives, haunted as they are by the powerless specters of unrealized possibilities, can also be channeled into a contemporary practice that is based, as I have tried to show, on creative strategies of resignification and prospective archaeology. In that sense, the restitution of neglected achievements from the past is a function of our capacity to engage imaginatively with the media technologies of the present.

Notes

1 Dwight Steven-Boniecki, *Live TV From the Moon* (Ontario: Apogee Books, 2010), 91.
2 Bill Wood, "Apollo Television," 2005, www.hq.nasa.gov/alsj/ApolloTV-Acrobat5.pdf.

72   *Backtracking*

3 Paul Coan, *Apollo Experience Report: Television System* (NASA technical note, 1973), 10–15.

4 For a description of the system, see Larkin Niemyer, *Apollo Color Camera* (Baltimore: Westinghouse Defense and Space Center, 1969).

5 For a media-archaeological analysis of this device, see Friedrich Kittler, *Optical Media* (Cambridge: Polity, 2010), 211.

6 See Paul Sherman, *Colour Vision in the Nineteenth Century: The Young-Helmholtz-Maxwell Theory* (Bristol: Adam Hilger, 1981).

7 Susan Murray, *Bright Signals: A History of Color Television* (Durham: Duke University Press, 2018), 11–32. Mechanical television systems were demonstrated in 1926 in London and in 1927 in the United States (designed by Logie Baird and Herbert E. Ives, respectively); Baird's demonstration is regarded as the first television broadcast in the UK and possibly in the world. Also in 1927, both Philo Farnsworth and Vladimir Zworkin successfully tested all-electronic solutions, and in Europe, the Hungarian Kálmán Tihanyi developed a similar system in 1928. Hugo Gernsback and Charles Francis Jenkins started to work towards regularly scheduled television programming as early as 1928, as Ulises Armand Sanabria demonstrated yet another television system in Chicago. See Russell Burns, *John Logie Baird: Television Pioneer* (London: The Institution of Engineering and Technology, 2000), 19–41; Seth Shapiro, *Television: Innovation, Disruption, and the World's Most Powerful Medium* (New York: New Amsterdam Media, 2016), 1–44; Gary Edgerton, *The Columbia History of American Television* (New York: Columbia University Press, 2007), 3–59; and Kálmán Tihanyi, "Television Apparatus", US Patent 2158259, issued May 16, 1939.

8 Murray, *Bright Signals*, 60–156.

9 Kittler, *Optical Media*, 214.

10 Russell Burns, *The Struggle for Unity: Colour Television, The Formative Years* (London: The Institution of Engineering and Technology, 2008), 303.

11 The portrait was painted by artist Boris Artzybasheff and is held in the collection of the National Portrait Gallery. See "Frank Stanton," *National Portrait Gallery*, https://npg.si.edu/object/npg_NPG.83.TC1.

12 Steven-Boniecki, *Live TV*, 105.

13 Jeanette Becerra, "TV NASA, made in México. Las imágenes del alunizaje, tecnología de González Camarena," *Etius: Observatorio de comunicación y cultura*, July 27, 2009, https://qmedios.iteso.mx/2009/07/tv-nasa-made-in-mexico-las-imagenes-del-alunizaje-tecnologia-de-gonzalez-camarena.

14 González Camarena, Arturo and Guillermo Jr. Interview by author. Mexico City, 2010.

15 "Sistema mexicano de televisión en la NASA," YouTube video, 3:29, Arturo González Camarena, www.youtube.com/watch?v=Zb9hSMp1bRU.

16 See Phyllis L. Speser, *The Art and Science of Technology Transfer*. Hoboken, N.J, 2006.3–38

17 See, for example, the skillful historical reconstruction of such a process in mid-twentieth-century Colombia outlined by Gonzalo Sánchez and Donny Meertens in *Bandoleros, gamonales y campesinos: El caso de la violencia en Colombia* (Bogotá: El Áncora, 1983).

18 Coan, Paul. Interview by author. Santa Barbara – Austin, 2011.

19 Peter Goldmark, "Color Television," US Patent 2304081, issued September 7, 1940. As we now know, actually, three very similar electromechanical color television solutions were demonstrated and patented in parallel in three different countries, in the absence of any known direct connection between their creators. In addition to González Camarena's and Goldmark's, the third was the system designed by Logie Baird in England. See Murray, *Bright Signals*, 11–32.

The Color Wheel of Television History, Mexico, 1939   73

20 Peter Goldmark, *Maverick Inventor: My Turbulent Years at CBS* (New York: Saturday Review Press, 1973), 202–203.

21 James O'Neal, "Equipping Apollo for Color Television." *TV Technology*, July 2009, 19.

22 Renata Keller, *Mexico's Cold War: Cuba, the United States, and the Legacy of the Mexican Revolution* (Cambridge: Cambridge University Press, 2017), 13–48.

23 Ruben Gallo, *Mexican Modernity: The Avant-Garde and the Technological Revolution* (Cambridge: MIT Press, 2005), 1.

24 Ruben Gallo, "Wireless Modernity: Mexican Estridentistas and Russian Futurism," in *Latin American Modernisms and Technology*, edited by María Fernández (Trenton: Africa World Press, 2018), 59–92.

25 Manuel Maples Arce, "T.S.H.: El poema de la radiofonía," *El Universal Ilustrado* 308 (1927): 19.

26 See Lynda Klich, "Estridentismo, Mexican Modernity and the Popular," in *Latin American Modernisms*, 93–117; and María Fernández, *Cosmopolitanism in Mexican Visual Culture* (Austin: University of Texas Press, 2014), 194–219.

27 Patricia Jocirin, "La radio en la Ciudad de México, 1939–145" (Master's thesis, Universidad Autónoma Metropolitana Unidad Iztapalapa, 2007), 102.

28 "Historia de la televisión en México 1/4," YouTube video, 4:40, Arturo González Camarena, www.youtube.com/watch?v=hCRevouZGWE.

29 Celeste González de Bustamante, *Muy Buenas Noches: Mexico, Television, and the Cold War* (Lincoln: University of Nebraska Press, 1972), 1–46.

30 Meyer, Lorenzo. *Mexico and the United States in the Oil Controversy, 1917–1942*. Translated by Muriel Vasconcellos. Austin, 1977, 173–216.

31 Monica Rankin, "Mexico: Industrialization through Unity," in *Latin America During World War II*, edited by T. M. Leonard and J. F. Bratze (Plymouth: Rowman & Littlefield Publishers, 2006), 17–35.

32 See Antonio Luna, *Jorge González Camarena en la Plástica Mexicana* (Mexico City: UNAM, 1988); and Mónica Mateos-Vega, "Jorge González Camarena, el pintor de la historia de México," *La Jornada*, March 24, 2008, www.jornada.com.mx/2008/03/24/index.php?section=cultura&article=a10n1cul.

33 González Camarena, Arturo and Guillermo Jr. Interview by author. Mexico City, 2010.

34 Guillermo González Camarena, "Adaptador Cromoscópico para Aparatos de Televisión", Mexican Patent 40235, issued August 19, 1940.

35 Carlos Chimal, *Fábrica de colores. La vida del inventor Guillermo González Camarena* (Mexico City: Fondo de Cultura Económica, 2017); Jaime Muñoz Vargas, *Guillermo Gonzalez Camarena: Habitante del futuro* (Mexico City: Ediciones Sm, 2005).

36 "Victor Matrix MBS-092231. Río Colorado/Los Tres Diamantes," *Discography of American Historical Recordings*, https://adp.library.ucsb.edu/index.php/matrix/detail/200058136/MBS-092231-Ro_Colorado.

37 As philosopher Agnes Gayraud has argued, "pop music" can be both historically and ontologically determined as a form of music constitutively grounded on the recorded performance as a possibility. Gayraud further shows how recorded (and thus "deterritorialized") folk musics set the historical point of departure for this musical regime. See Agnes Gayraud, *Dialectics of Pop* (Falmouth: Urbanomic, 2019), 129–139.

38 "HNOS REYES Y TERESITA = RIO COLORADO," YouTube video, 3:06, Regallo Gallo, www.youtube.com/watch?v=YIe8yNJuxuE.

39 Hubert Luckett, "For $150 and a Bit of Work You Can Have Color Pictures on Your Present Television Set," *Popular Science*, October 1955, 136.

74 Backtracking

40 González Camarena, Arturo and Guillermo Jr. Interview by author. Mexico City, 2010.

41 See Roderic Camp, *Mexican Political Biographies, 1935–2009* (Austin: University of Texas Press, 2011), 33.

42 Horace Newcomb, editor, *Encyclopedia of Television* (New York: Routledge, 2004), 1483–1484. Columbia College awarded González Camarena an honorary doctoral degree in Sciences in 1954. See Chimal, *Fábrica de colores*, 80.

43 "Guillermo González Camarena, Logo Canal 5," YouTube video, 1:53, Revista Pantalla, www.youtube.com/watch?v=Q18MfcLQRTY.

44 The lexicon of contemporary Nahuatl uses the word *uekaixipkaxitl* to refer to television, but for the most part, its speakers simply use the Spanish word *televisión*.

45 Fernando González, *Apuntes para una historia de la televisión mexicana* (Mexico City: Fundación Manuel Buendía, 1999), 71–98.

46 Jennifer Jolly, "Technology and Revolution: David Alfaro Siqueiros and the Mexican Electricians' Syndicate Mural," in *Latin American Modernisms and Technology*, 119–144.

47 "Inauguración fachada de Televicentro," YouTube video, 32:10, Fundación Cultural Jorge González Camarena, www.youtube.com/watch?v=dAqaWNkTcdU. On the disappearance of the mural, see Verónica Díaz, "Historia de un mural perdido," *Milenio*, May 1, 2016, www.milenio.com/cultura/historia-de-un-mural-perdido.

48 O'Neal, "Equipping Apollo," 19.

49 Bradford Smith et al., "Voyager Imaging Experiment." *Planetary and Space Science* 21, no. 2 (1977): 103–127.

50 Smith et al., "Voyager Imaging," 108–125.

51 Bradford Smith. Interview by author. Santa Barbara – Santa Fe, 2012.

52 In a lecture at Universidad Nacional de Colombia, Hernán Thomas elaborated on his understanding of the resignification of technologies as follows:

> resignification of technologies: creative reuse of previously available technologies. The operations of resignification of technology are not mere "mechanical" alterations of a technology, but a reassignment of the meaning of that technology and its means of application. To re-signify technologies is to re-functionalize knowledge, artifacts and systems. The knowledge required is – in many cases – of the same nature as that required, for example, by the manufacture of the original machinery, and is similar in its conditions and characteristics to the basic design activity. Technological re-signification operations are located at the interface between social actions of technological development and the technological trajectories of specific social groups, in the "seamless fabric" of socio-technical dynamics. Thomas, "Tecnologías para la inclusión social y políticas públicas en América Latina"

53 Siegfried Zielinski, "Arqueología prospectiva." *H-ART. Revista de historia, teoría y crítica de arte* 8 (2021): 217–243.

54 The distinction between transmission and inscription technologies is developed in Douglas Kahn, *Earth Sound Earth Signal: Energies and Earth Magnitude in the Arts* (Berkeley: University of California Press, 2013), 17–24; and Jonathan Sterne, *MP3: The Meaning of a Format* (Durham: Duke University Press, 2012), 1–31. See also Ricardo Cedeño, *Portable Moving Images: A Media History of Storage Formats* (Berlin: Walter de Gruyter, 2017), 16–17.

55 "DLP Projector Technology," *Christie*, www.christiedigital.com/about/display-technology/dlp-projector.

56 "CUSF Landing Predictor 2.5," https://predict.habhub.org/.

The Color Wheel of Television History, Mexico, 1939   75

57 Bruno Latour and Dipesh Chakrabarty, "When the Global Reveals the Planetary," in *Critical Zones: The Science and Politics of Landing on Earth*, edited by Bruno Latour and Peter Weibel (Cambridge: MIT Press, 2020), 24–31.
58 See Tom Geismar, Sagi Haviv, and Ivan Chermayeff, *Identify: Basic Principles of Identity Design in the Iconic Trademarks of Chermayeff & Geismar* (Cincinnati: HOW Books, 2011), 20.
59 Murray, *Bright Signals*, 217–249.
60 Andreas Fickers, "The Techno-Politics of Colour: Britain and the European Struggle for a Colour Television Standard." *Journal of British Cinema and Television* 7 (2010): 95–114.
61 The arrival of color television strongly impacted the texture of everyday life. Among many other effects, advertisers and marketers refashioned the color of product packaging to resemble those seen on television screens, giving rise to the saturated and electronic colorscape of late capitalism. Peppino Ortoleva, *Un ventennio a colori: Televisione privata e società in Italia* (Florence: Giunti, 1995), 12–19.
62 "Fun With 3D-TV Down Mexico Way", *TV Guide*, October 30, 1954.
63 González Camarena, Arturo and Guillermo Jr. Interview by author. Mexico City, 2010.
64 Guillermo González Camarena, "Procedimiento Bicolor para Televisión," Mexican Patent 40235, issued October 16, 1962.
65 Leslie Solomon, "Simplified Mexican Color TV." *Electronics World*, July 1964, 48, 71.
66 William Beezley and Michael Meyer, editors, *The Oxford History of Mexico* (New York: Oxford University Press, 2010), 535–536.
67 *Mexico in the New York World's Fair 1964–1965*, brochure published by Secretaría de Industria y Comercio, Dirección General de Comercio.
68 Emmanuel Adler, *The Power of Ideology: The Quest for Technological Autonomy in Argentina and Brazil* (Berkeley: University of California Press, 2018).

Bibliography

Adler, Emanuel. *The Power of Ideology: The Quest for Technological Autonomy in Argentina and Brazil*. Berkeley: University of California Press, 2018.
Becerra, Jeanette. "TV NASA, made in México. Las imágenes del alunizaje, tecnología de González Camarena," *Etius: Observatorio de comunicación y cultura*, July 27, 2009, https://qmedios.iteso.mx/2009/07/tv-nasa-made-in-mexico-las-imagenes-del-alunizaje-tecnologia-de-gonzalez-camarena.
Beezly, William and Michael Meyer (eds.). *The Oxford History of Mexico*. New York: Oxford University Press, 2010.
Burns, Russell. *John Logie Baird: Television Pioneer*. London: The Institution of Engineering and Technology, 2000.
———. *The Struggle for Unity: Colour Television, the Formative Years*. London: The Institution of Engineering and Technology, 2008.
Camp, Roderic. *Mexican Political Biographies, 1935–2009*. Austin: University of Texas Press, 2011.
Cedeño, Ricardo. *Portable Moving Images: A Media History of Storage Formats*. Berlin: Walter de Gruyter, 2017.
Chimal, Carlos. *Fábrica de colores. La vida del inventor Guillermo González Camarena*. Mexico City: Fondo de Cultura Económica, 2017.

76 Backtracking

Coan, Paul. *Apollo Experience Report: Television System*, NASA technical note, 1973.

Edgerton, Gary. *The Columbia History of American Television*. New York: Columbia University Press, 2007.

Fernández, María. *Cosmopolitanism in Mexican Visual Culture*. Austin: University of Texas Press, 2014.

Fickers, Andreas. "The Techno-Politics of Colour: Britain and the European Struggle for a Colour Television Standard." *Journal of British Cinema and Television* 7 (2010): 95–114.

Gallo, Ruben. *Mexican Modernity: The Avant-Garde and the Technological Revolution*. Cambridge: MIT Press, 2005.

———. "Wireless Modernity: Mexican Estridentistas and Russian Futurism." In *Latin American Modernisms and Technology*, edited by María Fernández. Trenton: Africa World Press, 2018, 59–92.

Gayraud, Agnes. *Dialectics of Pop*. Falmouth: Urbanomic, 2019.

Geismar, Tom, Sagi Haviv, and Ivan Chermayeff. *Identify: Basic Principles of Identity Design in the Iconic Trademarks of Chermayeff & Geismar*. Cincinnati: HOW Books, 2011.

Goldmark, Peter. *Maverick Inventor: My Turbulent Years at CBS*. New York: Saturday Review Press, 1973.

González, Fernando. *Apuntes para una historia de la televisión mexicana*. Mexico City: Fundación Manuel Buendía, 1999.

González de Bustamante, Celeste. *Muy Buenas Noches: Mexico, Television, and the Cold War*. Lincoln: University of Nebraska Press, 1972.

Jocirin, Patricia. "La radio en la Ciudad de México, 1939–145." Master's thesis, Universidad Autónoma Metropolitana Unidad Iztapalapa, 2007.

Jolly, Jennifer. "Technology and Revolution: David Alfaro Siqueiros and the Mexican Electricians' Syndicate Mural." In *Latin American Modernisms and Technology*, edited by María Fernández. Trenton: Africa World Press, 2018, 119–144.

Kahn, Douglas. *Earth Sound Earth Signal: Energies and Earth Magnitude in the Arts*. Berkeley: University of California Press, 2013.

Keller, Renata. *Mexico's Cold War: Cuba, the United States, and the Legacy of the Mexican Revolution*. Cambridge: Cambridge University Press, 2017.

Kittler, Friedrich. *Optical Media*. Cambridge: Polity, 2010.

Klich, Lynda. "Estridentismo, Mexican Modernity and the Popular." In *Latin American Modernisms*, edited by María Fernández. Trenton: Africa World Press, 2018, 93–117.

Latour, Bruno and Dipesh Chakrabarty. "When the Global Reveals the Planetary." In *Critical Zones: The Science and Politics of Landing on Earth*, edited by Bruno Latour and Peter Weibel. Cambridge: MIT Press, 2020, 24–31.

Luckett, Hubert. "For $150 and a Bit of Work You Can Have Color Pictures on Your Present Television Set." *Popular Science*, October 1955.

Luna, Antonio. *Jorge González Camarena en la plástica mexicana*. Mexico City: UNAM, 1988.

Maples Arce, Manuel. "T.S.H.: El poema de la radiofonía," *El Universal Ilustrado* 308 (1927): 19.

Mateos-Vega, Mónica. "Jorge González Camarena, el pintor de la historia de México," *La Jornada*, March 24, 2008, www.jornada.com.mx/2008/03/24/index.php?section=cultura&article=a10n1cul.

The Color Wheel of Television History, Mexico, 1939 77

Meyer, Lorenzo. *Mexico and the United States in the Oil Controversy, 1917–1942*, translated by Muriel Vasconcellos. Austin: University of Texas Press, 1977.

Muñoz Vargas, Jaime. *Guillermo Gonzalez Camarena: Habitante del futuro*. Mexico City: Ediciones Sm, 2005.

Murray, Susan. *Bright Signals: A History of Color Television*. Durham: Duke University Press, 2018.

Newcomb, Horace (ed.). *Encyclopedia of Television*. New York: Routledge, 2004.

Niemyer, Larkin. *Apollo Color Camera*. Baltimore: Westinghouse Defense and Space Center, 1969.

O'Neal, James. "Equipping Apollo for Color Television." *TV Technology*, 21 July 2009.

Ortoleva, Peppino. *Un ventennio a colori: Televisione privata e società in Italia*. Florence: Giunti, 1995.

Rankin, Monica. "Mexico: Industrialization through Unity." In *Latin America During World War II*, edited by T. M. Leonard and J. F. Bratze. Plymouth: Rowman & Littlefield Publishers, 2006, 17–35.

Sánchez, Gonzalo and Donny Meertens. *Bandoleros, gamonales y campesinos: El caso de la violencia en Colombia*. Bogotá: El Áncora, 1983.

Shapiro, Seth. *Television: Innovation, Disruption, and the World's Most Powerful Medium*. New York: New Amsterdam Media, 2016.

Sherman, Paul. *Colour Vision in the Nineteenth Century: The Young-Helmholtz-Maxwell Theory*. Bristol: Adam Hilger, 1981.

Smith, Bradford et al. "Voyager Imaging Experiment." *Planetary and Space Science* 21, no. 2 (1977): 103–127.

Solomon, Leslie. "Simplified Mexican Color TV." *Electronics World*, July 1964.

Speser, Phyllis L. *The Art and Science of Technology Transfer*. Hoboken: Wiley, 2006.

Sterne, Jonathan. *MP3: The Meaning of a Format*. Durham: Duke University Press, 2012.

Steven-Boniecki, Dwight. *Live TV From the Moon*. Ontario: Apogee Books, 2010.

Thomas, Hernán. "Tecnologías para la inclusión social y políticas públicas en América Latina." Lecture presented at the Universidad Nacional de Colombia, Esocite, 2010.

TV Guide. "Fun with 3D-TV Down Mexico Way." *TV Guide*, October 30, 1954.

Wood, Bill. "Apollo Television," *NASA*, 2005, www.hq.nasa.gov/alsj/ApolloTV-Acrobat5.pdf.

Zielinski, Siegfried. "Arqueología prospectiva." *H-ART. Revista de historia, teoría y crítica de arte* 8 (2021): 217–243.

3 COMDASUAR: A Very Personal Computer, Chile, 1978

Introduction

In 1979, José Vicente Asuar, a composer and faculty member of the Music Department at the Universidad de Chile, self-published an LP titled *Así habló el computador* (Thus Spoke the Computer), described in the liner notes as intended to "illustrate the characteristics" of a "one-of-a-kind musical instrument."[1] The instrument is depicted in the cover (Figure 3.1) and, at first sight, appears to us now as a hybrid, featuring a typewriter-type keyboard and TV monitor appended to a vertical console with a few dozen controls, recalling the early integrated analog synthesizers that companies like Korg and Moog were producing at the time. Although the album's title, playing on that of Nietzsche's major work, might lead listeners to expect a historical breakthrough, what is actually on wax is, as Asuar acknowledged, more of a recorded demonstration. While Side A presents four compositions intended to highlight different features of the instrument (including a "parody of the musical academy" of which Asuar had been an active member for over two decades), Side B contains a side-long track titled "Illustration of how a computer composes and plays music," where Asuar offers a verbal account of his invention punctuated by examples. Asuar begins this recorded lecture by telling us in just what sense his device is a singular take on what a musical *instrument* should do, explaining that it can be used to play any score written using traditional notation but also to compose, thus taking on roles that are typically played by different individuals in traditional Western musical practice: that of the creator and that of the performer. Although the idea that a computer could perform a musical score would have merited enough attention at the time, the claim that it could also take on the role of the composer was meant to capture just how singular the device was. Accordingly, Asuar quickly turns to an account of how the computer can be used to compose by running through a series of ever more complex variations on a series of five tones. Each one of these variations, he explains, is obtained by allowing the computer to apply different probabilistic parameters to different aspects of their ordering, tonality, and rhythm. This, according to Asuar's liner notes, should allow his listeners to intuit that using the

DOI: 10.4324/9781003172789-5

computer as a tool for composition should not be regarded as a "something cold, impersonal, and excessively technical." Of course, there is a hidden and important shift in wording at this point of Asuar's account, for the computer is no longer described as composing music but described as a tool that can be used for composition. If we imagine a person listening to the recording at the time, we may ask ourselves: what did they imagine when they pictured themselves as possible users of Asuar's device? What kind of relationship to music-making was imaginatively afforded by a machine advertised as able to take over all the playing and even some of the composing?

It would be inaccurate to describe Asuar as advertising his instrument through the LP since there is no reason to assume that he regarded it as

Figure 3.1 Album *Así Habló el Computador* (LP) by José Vicente Asuar featuring the Computador Digital Análogo Asuar (COMDASUAR), Santiago de Chile, 1979.

Source: Courtesy of Claudio Asuar

80 *Backtracking*

a finished product. Only one of these instruments was ever made: it was designed and built single-handedly by Asuar, who named it the Asuar Digital Analog Computer, or COMDASUAR. Described in the LP liner notes as a "microcomputer adapted to receive musical data and transform them into sound," it had been the sole focus of Asuar's attention after 1975, when he had quit his position as director of the Laboratory of Musical Phonology at the Department of the Arts and Musical Sciences at Universidad de Chile and holed up in his lab in Santiago, "first at home and later on San Antonio street,"[2] to work on the project. The computer was assembled in 1978, and the music on the LP took three months to produce. By this time, Asuar had been working for more than two decades in the field of avant-garde music as a theorist, composer, teacher, popularizer, and technician. Around 1957, Asuar had designed and built the first studio for electronic music and sound processing in Chile, on which he wrote a thesis to obtain accreditation as a civil engineer. His 1958 composition *Variaciones espectrales* is likewise an early contribution to the field of electronic music, and one that, surprisingly, received a positive response from the audience when it was performed in Santiago. His 1959 essay "En el umbral de una nueva era musical [At the Threshold of a New Musical Era]" is one of the first Spanish-language contributions to the study of what were, at the time, the potentials to be glimpsed in new electronic technologies for musical creation and production.[3] Throughout these years, Asuar had developed a very high degree of technological resourcefulness and had brought it to bear on a corpus of compositions developed in conversation with technological experimentation (many of his most notable compositions were produced abroad, while traveling and working, allowing him access to equipment that was not available in Chile). The peak of his career as a composer at the international level took place in the 1970s, when he won two prestigious composition awards: the Dartmouth Arts Council Prize for his electro-acoustic composition *Divertimento* in 1970 (which he shared with Richard A. Robinson, who was at that time the director of the Atlanta Electronic Music Center) and the Bourges International Electroacoustic Music Festival award in 1975 for his work *Guaraira repano*, an award regarded as one of the most prestigious in the field of electro-acoustic music.[4] Later, he gained quite a bit of experience while assembling other sound studios in Germany and Venezuela, before conceiving and building the university lab that he directed until 1975.[5]

As a result of his frequent mobility and participation in academic environments both in Chile and in countries of the Global North over several years, Asuar had access to comprehensive information about the state of the art in music theory and technology, and he had from early on taken an interest in the possible relevance of computers to avant-garde music, at around the same time as leading international figures like Pierre Boulez and Iannis Xenakis. Indeed, when he decided to build a microcomputer in Chile, where there was no industrial framework to sustain his technical research, Asuar already had relatively long experience composing with computers and had even released a previous album of computer music in 1973, with the title *El computador virtuoso* (The Virtuoso Computer). As in the latter LP's title, here, Asuar seems willing to overstate the achievements of a music technology, even if, here, the description of a computer as a virtuoso clearly places the device on the side of the performer, rather than the composer. This simply signals a technological fact, for although Asuar was already interested in the computer's capacity to produce musical ideas, his emphasis around 1973 had been on getting a computer to control, or to play, an analog synthesizer. Indeed, this gap between the two parts of a system, one for composing and one for performing, was precisely what he wanted to breach when he took on the task of designing the COMDASUAR, with which he expected to integrate the control and production of sound into a single device. If Asuar emphasized, in naming the COMDASUAR, that it was a digital analog computer, he was pointing out the fact that his technological premise was that of a hybrid system, where sound would be digitally produced and analogically controlled and modeled. This slight adjustment could be said to have motivated a drastic shift, visible in Asuar's decision to relocate his work from the (comparatively bare bones) musical laboratory of the Universidad de Chile to his home. Indeed, the COMDASUAR was both built and meant to be used at home, and the efforts at integration were closely linked to a reconceptualization of what kind of device a music computer could be. This is a reconceptualization whose results we now find so familiar that we may fail to recognize the moment, or cluster of moments, of its emergence. Asuar's work can be described as at least one such point of emergence, for although he could hardly be said to have proceeded in isolation from a network of similarly oriented endeavors, his work on the COMDASUAR enacted a personal and institutional withdrawal from the space in which these kinds of projects had been unfolding until then. Accordingly, he produced a device that he conceived as capable of rendering the practice of musical composition and performance into a space for personal experience, emphasizing in the 1979 LP liner notes that "the instrument can be operated by a person who does not know how to play a musical instrument and who has only a basic knowledge of musical notation." The COMDASUAR, in other words, was conceived as a *personal* music computer, as a machine that could make the kind of exploration with sound that the musical avant-garde had been engaged in for the past decades into something that lay users could engage with.

Although Asuar deserves to be acknowledged as one of the few composers who was able to build – completely or partially – his own computer machine in order to produce his work, rather than using or adapting existing devices, the COMDASUAR also instantiated a personal position with respect to the technologies and institutions that had driven the practice of electro-acoustic music during the previous decades. This position can be said to determine what is remarkable about its design, which assembles a compendium of creative and inexpensive technical solutions in order to meet

82 Backtracking

demands arising from the vital intersection between the fields of technology and art. Arguably, it was only through a shift in design paradigm, driven by the tenet that complex possibilities in the production and organization of sounds could be reduced in size, from the lab room to the desktop, that these efforts at a technologically enabled reconfiguration of music could successfully converge. As Asuar understood it, the core of his innovation was linked to an understanding of the device as heuristic, and in that sense, what he was working towards was not simply a machine that, among other things, could produce compositional ideas at random, but rather a technologically enabled field of experience for new forms of musical thought and practice. What his technological paradigm condensed, then, was an approach to music-making that would feed from the past decades of radical experimentation to enable someone with no academic training to take on the position of the composer.

It was no incidental feature of this field that it should be able to fit inside the composer's home, away from the very different realm of radio or university studios. Such experience, which brings together advanced musical theory and technology with the idiosyncratic space of the personal vision, is quite common today, but it was hardly so at the time (one need only remember David Em, a pioneer of computer graphics and computer art, mentioning how important it was for him and others of his generation to be able to work at home in their own projects, without having to depend on the availability of time for using computers in a lab or an institution).[6] From that point of view, we can understand the COMDASUAR as a *very personal computer*, tailor-made for the creative needs of the composer who was able to make it and use it at home: the device was, in fact, doubly personal, being both non-institutional and custom-built in light of Asuar's own musical ideas, even though these ideas were channeled through the figure of a non-expert user. This, in turn, tells us something about the diversity of the processes that led to the rise of the personal computer as a device-type. The history of personal computers should not be told only from the point of view of a corporate brand that audaciously decided to introduce a computer into the domestic space under the paradigm of a portable office. Certainly, around 1981, the team working at IBM in the personal computer project had to put up quite a fight to position the idea that a computer could have a place out of government offices, universities, and big businesses.[7] The shift that ensued as societies around the globe embraced this newly available technology undoubtedly amounts to one of the most significant reconfigurations of the field of socio-technical possibilities in recent times. But we will not have a complete picture of this process unless we also consider cases where the home was experienced as a more radically personal space and where the computer enabled a reinterpretation of the value of isolation already built into spaces for creativity, like the studio. This is exactly what the COMDASUAR was designed for, although its history is such that we cannot quite tell whether its potentialities were ever actualized, leaving its identity as a functioning device in a somewhat indeterminate state.

An Instrument that Had No Users

Unfortunately, it is not possible to precisely determine to what extent Asuar was able to make the most out of his invention. The 1979 LP was conceived above all as something that could be useful for music teachers, allowing them to present general concepts and to introduce their pupils to electronic music. Indeed, although it sold fairly well, Asuar estimates that most purchases of *Así habló el computador* were made by educators. This lines up with the fact that, throughout his career, Asuar had maintained a productive parallelism between his roles as a teacher, popularizer, composer, and technician. This manner of acting at different levels of a field may have been structured in part by the conditions under which a practice like that of avant-garde music could be engaged with in a country like Chile, but it also seems to have been a reflection of Asuar's own mode of thinking (Figure 3.2).

To make matters a bit more perplexing, Asuar experienced a radical change in his professional life right before he jumped into his work on the COMDASUAR, cutting off ties with the Universidad de Chile's Music School, for whose journal he had written a series of articles that, as we will see, detail his path as a composer, theoretician, critic, technician, and

Figure 3.2 José Vicente Asuar working with the COMDASUAR in his studio, Santiago de Chile, 1979.

Source: Courtesy of Claudio Asuar

84 *Backtracking*

pedagogue. These factors make it hard to determine to what extent Asuar was unable to or uninterested in using the COMDASUAR to actually produce compositions in line with those for which he had been acclaimed by the avant-garde community. All that remains are the not properly preserved device, the design documentation, and an oddly quirky educational LP; as time went by, Asuar's album survived merely as an oddity and was soon forgotten so that by the late 1980s, students of music in Chile had no acquaintance at all with this or any of his previous experiments.[8]

To add to these uncertainties, Asuar's personal shifts took place in the context of a violent restructuring of Chilean society. Indeed, even though Asuar, in addition to publishing an album and an article on the COMDASUAR, also appeared on public television to present his work, his invention can probably be described as a casualty of the crisis that would hit all aspects of Chilean culture, and in particular those fields perceived as experimental, after the 1973 coup d'état led by General Augusto Pinochet. As Federico Schumacher has amply shown in his well-documented account of the development of electro-acoustic music in Chile since the 1950s, Asuar had the good fortune of developing his projects within a context that was, from a certain point of view, remarkably receptive.[9] Indeed, although he was unquestionably conversant with a wide range of projects in the Global North, local conditions also account for the fact that he would eventually take on the task of designing and assembling a personal computer for music composition. Science and Technology Studies scholar Eden Medina has undertaken an important historical account of the rich and long history of computation in Chile, beginning in the 1930s, when IBM opened an office in Santiago as part of its efforts to operate as a global company.[10] After that, Chile made continuous advances in the use of tabulators and was even involved in the industrial production of punched cards. In 1949, a Chilean scientist named Raimundo Toledo wrote a letter to the cybernetician Norbert Wiener describing his work on the development of an inexpensive advanced calculating machine based on a novel system for multiplication (Wiener's reply was dismissive, and he refused to comply with Toledo's request for a copy of *Cybernetics*, published only three months earlier). Later, during the early 1970s, an ambitious cybernetic management project named Cybersyn deployed a sophisticated strategy for the use of cybernetics in the context of economic policy.[11] As these examples suggest, there was an established commitment in Chile, at the levels of industry and politics, to explore the potentials of computer systems, which in turn sustained experimental endeavors at the academic level. In 1962, the Universidad de Chile's Department of Physical Sciences purchased a Standard Elektrik Lorenz ER-56, and that same year, the Universidad Católica acquired an IBM 1620; from that time on, it is possible to trace a sustained line of research on computation in Chilean universities.[12] This general atmosphere directly shaped Asuar's field of possibilities, and it accounts for his ability to gain access to specialized technical equipment for his first experiments with computer music in the early 1970s and for the existence of a network of educated and motivated students who would play important roles as collaborators and interlocutors. As Medina's research suggests, it was arguably the socialist government of Salvador Allende (1970–1973) that most strongly promoted an environment where these projects seemed to flourish.[13]

To some extent, the coup d'état that overturned the democratically elected socialist government of the Unidad Popular party on September 11, 1973, and the ensuing rule of the government junta led by Pinochet, crucially curtailed the tone and possibilities of these lines of inquiry, not only in the field of culture but also in academic work within strictly technical fields.[14] All levels of the Chilean government underwent dramatic shifts in administration with the arrival of the military regime, and university presidents were immediately replaced by individuals closer to the new ruling apparatus. As authors like Schumacher and Rolando Cori have argued, political changes in the 1970s had a strong and direct impact on Chile's cultural scene and particularly on the field of the avant-garde.[15] As a case in point, funding for all activities pertaining to electro-acoustic music at the Universidad de Chile's Music School, of which Asuar was a faculty member, abruptly ceased soon after the coup. Interest on the part of the general public for such innovative practices dwindled considerably under the effect of the conservative political atmosphere.[16] The process as a whole has been described as a "cultural blackout [*apagón cultural*]," setting the mood for what Schumacher describes as the "black years."[17] Asuar, who had been part of the Music School since the 1950s and a regular contributor to its journal, *Revista Musical Chilena*, gave up his position around 1980, when he was arguably at the peak of his career, and sought employment at the Engineering School in the same university, severing a valuable tie to a community that was perhaps the only context where his work on the COMDASUAR could have earned him some recognition. Although there are reasons to think that this change might have been directly related to the new political climate, Asuar himself claims that his move was due to his getting mixed up in serious personal problems ("palace intrigues") inside the department.[18]

And yet it would be short-sighted to attribute the COMDASUAR's fate to these surrounding personal and geopolitical circumstances, for there is something at the heart of the device itself that renders it resistant to the process of technological standardization. By virtue of being, as I have called it, "a very personal computer," the COMDASUAR had no actual users, even though it was conceived for a potential variety of users. We should not rush to see this as a paradox caused simply by circumstances, and the significance of such paradoxes to a media-archeological gaze can only be determined by taking a closer look.[19] Unquestionably, the COMDASUAR was an invention that could not properly come into being as a significant contribution to the field of musical practice, for as Bruno Latour explains, "the fate of a statement depends on others' behaviour. . ., if others do not take it up and use it as a matter of fact later on,"[20] it can have no meaning at all. Indeed, in

86 *Backtracking*

an elliptical statement about the fate of his machine, Asuar seems to argue that the fact that his achievement did not quite register as a historical event may have been part of the point:

> [There is] a book that I read when I was a teenager, . . . a book by Giovanni Papini called *Gog*. In that book there is a sculptor of smoke, a man who creates a campfire to get a column of smoke that grows in different colors of varying degrees with different reverberations, he may also have air currents that move the smoke from one side to the other with trowels. With a few movements, body figures were created, abstract images, clouds, and constellations, all of them coming out of the smoke. An ephemeral sculpture, but it can be very beautiful, it can be very beautiful. . . . [Computer music] would be a similar thing, in this case the smoke is what goes out from the computer and what the sculptor does with his tools is what a person can do with physical interfaces, it can be a handle, a mouse.[21]

Although in these lines Asuar envisages his device as something that could be used to give shape to ephemeral and cloud-like configurations of sounds, we can also read this image as a reflection of his attitude towards the ephemerality of his own technological invention. In this case, the interface itself is something for which appearance and disappearance were mutually implicit, and Asuar seems to be saying that it makes no sense to have regrets about this unique temporality. This attitude unveils, perhaps, the degree to which the dominant understanding of technologies is informed by ideologies of success, expansion, and perpetuation, and it gives us room for thinking, towards the future, about what can happen when technological developments are not subsumed by these paradigms, which tend to frame our understanding of technological development under conditions proper to capitalist enterprise. In that sense, Asuar's work, not in spite but rather because of its singular status as a market non-starter, might be an example to follow. In any case, there is no doubt that this odd fossil in the history of media technology has much to tell us and that its possibilities as an instrument are yet to be probed; in other words, we need not regard its fate as a statement as being conclusively sealed.

Composition and Computation

It may be inaccurate to describe Asuar as a pioneer in the field of computer music composition because the history of computation seems deeply connected, from early on, to radical shifts in the understanding and practice of music. In a sense, what we now know as computer music, as a space of cultural and artistic creative practice, has stood at the heart of a double process. This process can be regarded as a conversation between efforts to rework basic definitions of what constitutes musical sound and structure, often inspired by advances in physics and mathematics and technologically enabled practice. In that sense, even before there was such a thing as computer music, a field of converging concerns functioned as a testing site for the possibilities of mutual transformation between the technical and the aesthetic. These concerns can in turn be grouped around two lines of inquiry, one of which is based on the analogy between computing and composing, while the other seeks to expand the elements and structures of sound through technical production and reproduction. Inasmuch as Asuar sought to bring these two fields of possibilities into a single device, he can certainly be described as a pioneer.

Of course, these processes have led to what we now experience as a complete and perhaps already sclerotic restructuring of the music industry around digitality. As with many other spheres of cultural life, computation has impacted every single aspect of music in contemporary times, including sound production, recording, manipulation, distribution, and marketing. These areas did not change simultaneously, and the individual processes have been long and intricate, so it makes little sense to try to isolate a historical point that could be regarded as the founding moment of computer music. That being said, the first documents that attest to this entanglement between music-making and computation are arguably Ada Lovelace's influential notes and comments inspired by Charles Babbage's 1842 book on the Analytical Engine.[22] In these notes, where she perceptively alludes to the origins of the use of punched cards in the textile arts, Lovelace sketches a few important thoughts on the possibility of using the Analytical Engine for sound composition:

> The operating mechanism . . . might act upon other things besides number, were objects found whose mutual fundamental relations could be expressed by those of the abstract science of operations, and which should be also susceptible of adaptations to the action of the operating notation and mechanism of the engine. Supposing, for instance, that the fundamental relations of pitched sounds in the science of harmony and musical composition were susceptible of such expression and adaptations, the engine might compose elaborate and scientific pieces of music of any degree of complexity or extent.

Remarkably, what Lovelace immediately glimpsed as a possibility was a process that would articulate art and science, for she was not simply thinking about the possibility of reproducing established forms of music through a machine but rather about the redefinition of music as a field where scientifically informed technologies would determine new parameters for aesthetic practice and experience. Unfortunately, the Analytical Engine would never become fully operational, and a century would pass before the sagacity of Lovelace's anticipations could be assessed.

Nearly a century later, in 1941, the engineer Konrad Zuse created the first electro-mechanical binary computer, the Z3, and although it was a

88 *Backtracking*

machine designed solely to compute, it offers yet another, if unintended, illustration of the affinities between computational and musical operations. In 2001, Raul Rojas, professor of artificial intelligence at the Free University in Berlin, assembled a physical reconstruction of the Z3 and produced video documentation of the device at work, allowing us to get a sense of its experiential dimension, as the quick jumping motion of its many electromechanic relays created a complexly patterned sonic atmosphere, which has some similarities to avant-garde music of the same time period, for instance, the *music concrete*.[23] It doesn't seem far-fetched to imagine that something similar would have been the case with the Analytical Engine or the Difference Engine, although there is very little information about the sounds that these two machines might have produced. What is clear is that in these early devices, the work of computation was something that could be directly *heard*, and this was already more than an accidental overlap of two fields of human experience, one regarded as eminently intellectual and the other as sensory. Eventually, the analogy between a computer running a program and the action of performing a score would come to seem unavoidable, which in turn motivated an important conceptual shift in the notion of what the activity of composition might be like and on the role of subjectivity therein.

Following the research undertaken by composer Paul Doornbusch, we may date the intentional use of computers for sound generation and performance back to the work produced in Australia, around 1949, by the team of Trevor Pearcey, Maston Beard, and Geoff Hill, who built a digital computer (the CSIRAC) capable of generating sounds and playing music through software developed by Thomas Cherry.[24] Around 1951, in the United Kingdom, mathematician and computer scientist Christopher Strachey wrote an early piece of software designed to play sounds and musical sequences. Alan Turing gave Strachey instructions on how to use the Ferranti Mark I, one of the first commercially available computers, and there is even a recording of that machine playing the nursery rhyme "Baa Baa Black Sheep," made by the BBC during a visit to Manchester University for a children's show.[25] And at around the same time, the need to embrace a scientific approach to sound and to dismantle the culturally inherited understandings of basic notions like tone, melody, and harmony, embodied by traditional Western musical instruments, was being urgently felt by musicians who envisioned the possibility of technically decomposing sound into elements that could be independently manipulated. In this emergent field of conversation between artists and engineers, the roles of composer, designer, and performer were fruitfully destabilized.

The idea that mathematical procedures could be used to create musical ideas is already present in the *musikalische Würfelspiele* (musical dice games) popular in the eighteenth century, which were systems that randomly generated music out of previously composed musical segments.[26] Needless to say, once the possibility of computer composition became a field of inquiry for

Asuar and other professional musicians around the mid-twentieth century, the potential contribution of computers to the creative engagement with new musical forms was interpreted in very different ways. I will narrow my focus here by only mentioning the work of those researchers who Asuar himself acknowledged in his writings as influences: the chemists and composers Lejaren Hiller and Leonard Isaacson, the composer Iannis Xenakis, the electrical engineer Max Mathews, and participants on the research programs run by the University of Toronto and by Stanford University.

The first two cases exemplify efforts to apply the calculus of probability, with the help of computers, to determine the distribution and features of sound elements. In both cases, the computer was conceived as a device that could produce a score that would then be performed using traditional orchestral instruments. Hiller and Isaacson's *Illiac Suite* (1956), a piece developed at the University of Illinois Urbana-Champaign using one of the Illiac computers built on that campus, has often been described as the first computer-assisted composition. The work was conceived for performance by a string quartet and is divided into four segments titled "experiments," the last of which explores musical grammars through the use of probability and Markov chains.[27] Xenakis, one of the most influential composers in the musical avant-garde during the postwar period, not only promoted a sustained commitment to this approach to computer music but also cultivated a deep understanding of the relationship between mathematical models and musical innovation. This understanding was coded into his idea of a stochastic music that could reflect the dynamics of natural and social phenomena treading the line between order and disorder.[28] Importantly for Asuar, Xenakis did not leave computer-generated scores intact but modified them in order to obtain more interesting musical results, deploying an understanding of the computer as a heuristic device that composers could rely on to both challenge and enrich their subjective inclinations.[29]

The second two cases were models that would determine some of Asuar's technical decisions. While working at Bell Labs in 1958, Mathews was the first to implement a general method of Pulse-Code Modulation, which makes it possible to represent a continuous analog signal as a discrete series of binary samples. The signals can then be captured by an analog-to-digital converter (ADC) and transformed into sound files, which can then be played back through a digital-to-analog converter (DAC) that translates them back into analog signals (PCM is still today the standard technology for computer audio and other digital devices, from old CDs to contemporary smartphones).[30] The work done at the University of Toronto some time later, during the 1960s, would set the guidelines for experimentation with analog synthesizers controlled by computers. Asuar also points out that John Chowning, at Stanford University, developed a parallel method for creating digital sounds through FM synthesis and claims that this area of musical technology holds a great deal of promise in terms of the sounds that a computer could produce, although he made no attempt to implement

90 Backtracking

it in his own COMDASUAR.[31] As we will see, Asuar's writings show that he was remarkably in tune with other developments, both theoretical and technical, that were shaping global conversations on avant-garde music throughout the key decades of the 1950s, 1960s, and 1970s. Nonetheless, these few examples account for the range of issues that he would tackle in his own projects, all of which can be said to converge in the COMDASUAR. To summarize: Asuar was interested in the computer as a possible source of ideas determined by probability ranges, which composers could use to discover sounds and structures; he was also interested in the computer's capacity to control the production of electronic sounds at a great level of detail, thus coupling its capacity for calculation with the capacity to decompose and recompose sound elements demonstrated by electronic synthesizers. A device that could allow for a direct practical interaction between these two fields of play would be an instrument of computer music in a sense that both Asuar and his contemporaries were working towards, although Asuar may have been the first to schematize it as a personal computer.

Asuar's Writings: The Genesis of the COMDASUAR

When he quit the Universidad de Chile's Music School in 1980, Asuar lost the chance to publish his work in the *Revista Musical Chilena*, which had functioned as the key vehicle for his thought for over two decades. Like innovators Florence and González Camarena, Asuar devoted a good amount of time to writing about his work, and in fact, he was far better at it than the other two inventors, arguably in part because his experiments were taking place in an academic setting. Between 1958 and 1980, Asuar published about 20 papers in the journal, reporting on different aspects and phases of the contemporary musical context and innovations, and speculatively evaluating ongoing shifts in the elementary understanding of music and new trends in composition.[32] These essays tell the story of the path that led to the creation of the COMDASUAR in 1978 and offer a view into the problems that Asuar intended to address and the possibilities that he hoped to explore during each stage of his engagement with the creation of a system for computer music.

The earliest of his journal contributions show that Asuar was already critically aware of the mutual entailments between technical, theoretical, and aesthetic developments in music. His 1959 article, "En el umbral de una nueva era musical [At the Threshold of a New Musical Era]," even reads as a manifesto of sorts for a renewal, informed by the work that he had just completed assembling a laboratory studio in Santiago. Referring to recent developments in *musique concrète*, to which he had been introduced by his friend Fernando García, Asuar examines the technical and aesthetic capabilities of new musical instruments like the tape recorder, arguing for their use in composition and calling attention to potential difficulties, such as the lack of adequate notational conventions.[33] A paper published a few years later,

"Música electrónica: Poética musical de nuestros días [Electronic Music: Musical Poetics of Today]," was originally written as the text of a concert-lecture held at the Antonio Varas Theater.[34] After laying out a context for the emergence of electronic music within the Western musical tradition by pointing back to early definitions of music by Boethius and Hugh of Saint Victor, Asuar again celebrates the introduction of technical innovations as a factor motivating creativity and acknowledges the work of early twentieth century figures like Thaddeus Cahill, Léon Theremin, and Jörg Mager. Significantly, Asuar attributes to the artist and instrument maker Luigi Russolo, and especially to composer Edgard Varèse, a deeper understanding of the relationship between the creation of new instruments and what he describes as "an awareness on the part of a few visionaries of the crisis in harmonic thought and the need to seek for a new sound language" in the early twentieth century.[35] The concert-lecture also featured one of Asuar's own musical pieces, *Preludio: La noche*, which he had created in Karlsruhe while assembling a sound studio there in 1961. In order to make his audience aware of the possibilities of the studio as a technologically defined space for creative practice, Asuar explains that *La noche* was produced as a musical idea to be projected into space through a multispeaker system so that the monophonic version that they were about to hear could only be regarded as a sketch. He describes the work as structured by the choice of "an explosive electronic material, namely a large level of initial energy and a slow reverberated dissolution" so that the listener should experience it as the release of a quantum of sound energy reminiscent of the big bang.[36] Although his own work was produced exclusively through electronic means, Asuar goes on to argue that composers working within this new musical space should be creatively aware of the growing range of new means by which sound could be produced, including electrical generation, capture by microphone, processing by filters or magnetic tape manipulation, and mixing. Asuar argues that in this new kind of music there must be a "virtuous circle" between the choice of sound material and the realization of formal ideas, the latter determining the former but also the broader range of the former enabling the latter.[37] He then mentions a series of institutions where these new guidelines were being advanced, including radio studios and academic programs.[38] Interestingly, Asuar justifies the existence of such research organizations, and of studios in particular, by their ability to serve not only the creative needs of composers but also those of industries like cinema and television. We see then that by 1963, Asuar was firmly aware of the theoretical, aesthetic, technological, and institutional state of the art in avant-garde music composition and was clearly interested in outlining its potential and challenges for the local academic community and for a general audience.

A year later, in 1964, Asuar published "Mi fin es mi comienzo [My End is My Beginning]," a meditation on time grounded on notions drawn from the field of theoretical physics, with an emphasis on the roles of probability and statistics.[39] From this general conceptual landscape, Asuar zooms in on the

92 *Backtracking*

elementary constituents of musical sound (such as harmony, rhythm, tone, and color), to each of which he attributes a specific temporal modality, and whose relationships he illustrates through examples borrowed from classical and romantic music. Asuar then moves on to show that a new understanding of musical time, based on probability and statistics, is at work in pieces like Stockhausen's *Zeitmasse*, Messiaen's *Oiseaux exotiques*, and Amenabar's *Feedback*. Clearly staking out a position in a contemporary debate, a later text from 1969 titled "Fatalidades [Fatalities]" describes a "fatal" transition from a music characterized by *superstructure* (the standard example being serial music) to the proliferation of musical projects driven by an interest in randomness (exemplified by the experiments conducted by John Cage under the title of "music-happenings").[40] Tellingly, "Fatalidades" is also the first text where Asuar considers in writing the use of computers as a tool for composition, and his frame of thought on the subject was already quite nuanced. In line with Xenakis, Asuar thought that randomness could not be embraced by composers unless its laws were understood and modeled, a task for which computers were an obvious tool.[41] Although he stressed the fact that this technology could in that sense be the source of a new repertoire of possibilities, not only for composers but for popular music as well, Asuar clearly outlines the risk of creating a form of music-making that would be dominated by experts who had no interest in musical content, which he insists must be regarded as the living core of all technical innovation in music. Thus, it seems that Asuar was interested in the use of computers to create a space of interactions between the use of probability and other mathematical principles, and the subjectivity of musical creators and listeners. In that sense, he was wary of a path that would turn new music into a field removed from living culture and human experience, leading to an impasse analogous to that of serial music, which resulted in compositions that may have made sense on the page but whose significance could not be experienced by listening.

Three years later, in 1972, the use of computers as an aid to compositional practice had become a central concern for Asuar, and the paper "Música con computadores: ¿cómo hacerlo? [Computer Music: How to Make It?]" is entirely devoted to an assessment of the machine's possibilities. The text describes the computer as a pupil that can be fed with rules and instructions, and envisions the possibility of reaching a point at which the device would be able to compose music based on what it had learned. Using the metaphor of a spider's web, Asuar suggests an experimental system where pitch, intensity, velocity, density, and other sound parameters would be like threads constituting a structure that can be tested for variations by altering features of one thread while leaving the rest of the structure untouched. This, he suggests, would be analogous to a vector matrix that would make it possible to eventually fine-tune a computer's capacity to propose musical ideas coherent with a set of given musical tenets (a "style").[42] The guiding idea, then, is that a computer could learn how to create within a restricted style or idiom by being given a specific range of parameters within which it could meaningfully create random variations. Nonetheless, Asuar envisions this process as one by which the computer could function as an amplifier of the imagination and the process of composition as a collaboration between the composer and the machine. He then supplements these abstract and speculative ideas with an account of a project he launched in 1970 as part of the Universidad de Chile's Grupo de *Investigaciones en Tecnología del Sonido* (Research Group on Sound Technology) under the title "Probabilistic Forms Oriented to Music Creation." In this project, Asuar and his team set out to develop a system for computer-assisted music composition, with the particular aim of exploring the role of probability, distribution, and stochastic forms in musical creation. For these experiments, the team used an IBM 360 computer and software written in Fortran IV. Processing instructions provided by the team; the computer was able to produce 30 different musical sequences based on statistical models. The team selected the sound universe within which the computer should operate as that of serialism but used statistical tables, rather than series, to allow for a wider range of compositional options.[43] The computer produced results in the form of lists of values and graphs, and for the final composition, three of these sequences were selected, which Asuar then transcribed into musical notation himself. As he points out, the process of transcription entailed a final set of subjective decisions as to the order in which the sequences should be played, the instrumentation, and the *tempi*, allowing for a meaningful divergence between different transcriptions by different composers.[44] The first public performance of a piece of chamber music produced through this process took place in December 1971, conducted by Eduardo Moubarak with musicians from the Orquesta Sinfónica de Chile.

Although Asuar was consistently interested in exploring these spaces where human subjectivity could take over and elaborate ideas discovered by a computer, he was also clearly interested in developing his research program through the subsequent logical stages. He described it as going "from a creative program to synthesize a given musical style" to "an interpretative kind of program where an intermediate phase would translate musical structure and notation into the magnitudes of different sound parameters" (thus taking over part of the works of transcription and performance),[45] to be followed eventually by a final phase where an "instrumental program . . . would translate the creation into musical sounds."[46] In fact, Asuar was already at work in the second stage of this project, as can be seen in a paper published the following year, "Haciendo música con un computador [Making Music with a Computer]," a brief report describing the results of experiments conducted during the two previous years at the Universidad de Chile.[47] Looking to start a laboratory of Musical Phonology, the school had just acquired an ARP synthesizer equipped with modules to create sound and modify pitch (although it was designed to be controlled by a keyboard, this particular unit did not have one). This presented Asuar

94   *Backtracking*

with the opportunity to couple his interest in creative programs with an interpretive program that would allow a computer to control electronically produced sound: as he remarks, the absence of a keyboard meant that the university's ARP could only be used to produce "electronic music according to the traditional procedure," whereas controlling it through a computer would allow for the same range of performance as a keyboard and to "investigate new forms of performance that cannot be achieved by human performers."[48] In 1972, a group led by Asuar began to test possible ways of doing this by linking the ARP to a PDP-8 computer owned by the university's Physics Department. To determine the ways in which the computer could be used to explore modalities of sound production leading beyond those afforded by instrumental technique and traditional electronic music, Asuar singled out five fields in which the plasticity of the computer could be used to stake new ground: the subdivision of tone into scales and octaves could be further diversified to create precise microtonal scales and modules smaller than the octave; rhythm could be constructed out of units as small as a thousandth of a second, and all nuances that determine the expressiveness of a performance could be captured through precise rhythmic structuring; intensity could now be determined according to physical or psychoacoustic parameters, and an intensity score could be mapped onto a sequence of tones; transient variations (understood as values for attack and decay) could be assigned to all aspects of a sound, allowing for the creation of entirely new sounds; and sounds could now be articulated at speeds impossible to achieve manually, allowing for the construction of figures that would feature all manner of interval leaps, and for the possibility of "a succession of sounds to occur so rapidly that the ear would not be able to perceive the microsounds individually, but only fused into a single mass or sound continuum."[49] Although the paper does not offer much information about the technical configuration of the experiment, the results of Asuar's work with the PDP-8 were compiled in the 1973 LP *El computador virtuoso*, an album that seeks to show the degree of expression that can be achieved by using a computer to play a synthesizer. Indeed, the LP's subtitle describes the pieces as "music made by a computer and an electronic synthesizer," placing the computer in the position of performer capable of taking on the challenge of interpreting works by baroque and classical composers like Bach and Chopin. This album, which may be the first recording of computer music produced in Latin America, bears some resemblance to Wendy Carlos and Benjamin Folkman's well-known LP *Switched-On Bach* (released in 1968), performed by Carlos on a Moog synthesizer. The comparison is interesting, as it seems inevitable to experience the PDP-8's performance as rigid in light of Carlos's, even though Carlos's performance was considerably hindered by the fact that Carlos and Moog had to design a touch-sensitive keyboard and by the fact that each voice had to be recorded separately.[50]

As his writings clearly show, Asuar was constantly at work within several fields at once. He played the part of a popularizer, explaining new tendencies and theories in contemporary music, and reported on technical experiments that were both pedagogical and experimental, for engineers and musicians alike. It also seems clear enough that his contributions in all these spheres were in sync with cutting-edge developments in the Global North. Indeed, we may note that the IRCAM (Institut de Recherche et Coordination Acoustique/Musique), the Paris-based laboratory for electronic and computer music founded by Pierre Boulez, was established in 1977, the very year that Asuar started to work on the COMDASUAR (Figure 3.3). By then, he had already published two texts on computer music, released an album of computer music, and collaborated on two different projects of computer-based composition. In other words, Asuar had developed, through his practice as a composer, teacher, and researcher, a robust set of theoretical, aesthetic, and technical considerations by the time he set out to create his COMDASUAR, and he had already isolated and probed the different levels at which a computer could play a part in the process of conceiving, composing, and performing a musical work. Although he never achieved what he had established as the final stage of his research program, where all these layers would have been operated by an integrated digital

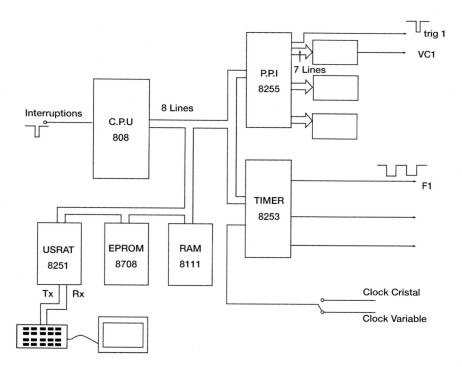

Figure 3.3 Technical drawings of COMDASUAR in "Un sistema para hacer música con un microcomputador," *Revista Musical Chilena* (1980).

Source: Courtesy of Revista Musical Chilena; vector-based image version by Pierre Puentes

96 *Backtracking*

system, it was clear that the COMDASUAR, as a digital-analog system, was intended to approximate this with means that could be available outside the context of a research institution. This, we may note, accounts for both a continuity and a discontinuity of his process once Asuar turned his attention to the COMDASUAR, exactly at the same time as he distanced himself from the institutional space where he had been able to access the limited technical resources that had allowed him to move forward. It may be said, indeed, that Asuar's interest in postserialist musical ideas was a key factor in his decision to develop his research in the direction of the *personal* computer, not in spite of but, because of the fact that he had also always been interested in a broader scope of interactions between technology and music, motivated by a critical distance with respect to the context of academic music. In that sense, his turn towards a different technological paradigm can also be read as a way of reworking his previous understanding of what the technology was for, a shift towards an understanding of music-making that Asuar never developed as such but with which we are now entirely familiar.

The COMDASUAR

The last paper published by Asuar in *Revista Musical Chilena*, in 1980, was an account of his work on the COMDASUAR, and someone who had read it at the time might have assumed that the system would continue to evolve during the next few years, following the guidelines outlined in the paper.[51] They may also have read the paper as an invitation to construct their own version of the system and to adapt it to their own needs through the schematics and detailed explanations provided by Asuar. The reasons why neither of these two possibilities materialized may be too complex to apprehend at a glance, although the personal and geographical landscape that I have drawn suggests that it was not due to issues with the system as such. This, however, simply confirms the claim that media technologies are never simply a system as such and that it is never easy, or accurate, to dissociate a technology from the conditions of its emergence.

His several years of experience had led Asuar to isolate a set of problems that he endeavored to tackle with his design. In spite of his skills, this was not a simple task, as there was no model known to him of a microcomputer capable of integrating all the solutions that he was trying to implement. For reasons that should now be clear, Asuar wanted to create a system that could respond to issues of musical performance and composition, and he had to design both software and hardware components that would allow for this flexibility and generality. The same machine, as he envisioned it, should be useful both as an instrument in the traditional sense, as a playback device capable of reading existing scores (which would also allow a composer to listen to a composition as he was working on it) and as a heuristic source of possibilities for computation-based composition in all manner of styles, from traditional to stochastic. As Asuar summarized them in the paper, the key features of his device were the following: It was inexpensive, with components costing less than 1,000 dollars, and could be used both "as a home piano" and for public musical performances, blurring the boundary between amateur and professional instruments. It could produce sound in real time, making it possible to listen as modifications were applied to the sounds. It was polyphonic, with six voices in the first version. It was equipped with a typewriter-type keyboard as input device and a television screen to be used as a display monitor for data input and memory content. It produced sound in the form of square waves that were then processed by analog units that could alter the color of the sound and equalize the six voices, allowing them to be directly recorded or broadcast. Finally, and most importantly, it could work heuristically, either playing with ideas that it was given or producing ideas on its own for a composer to develop.[52]

As Asuar remarks in the opening section of his paper, where he cites a list of antecedents to the project, Mathews and Chowning had set the template for his design architecture, but no attempt had been made to achieve these premises in a system based on a microcomputer. As I have suggested, there are many aspects of Asuar's career that account for the fact that he would have focused on this possibility, and they come into view in the virtues that he attributes to his device in the conclusion to the paper:

> It can be a means of leisure for amateurs who wish to create or recreate music, allowing them to obtain results in a brief amount of time. Also for music students and professionals, who may try out how certain complex scores sound, which it is sometimes difficult or impossible to reproduce on a piano. On the other hand, instruments like these may prevent many frustrations and materialize so many instrumental works that have never enjoyed the opportunity of being brought to the stage.[53]

This list of potential users and uses makes it clear that, for Asuar, it was not simply a matter of achieving a smaller version of systems that had already been achieved in university labs but that the reduction in size and cost entailed a virtual shift in the practice of music-making, potentially undermining the status of avant-garde music as tethered to scientific and mathematical thought that had originally inspired his approach to composition through probability. Although it would be easy to read this simply as a concession on his part to the idea that his system would have more of a future as a commodity if it could accommodate a wider range of users, Asuar's hybrid profile, and the circumstances within which he worked, suggest instead that the COMDASUAR embodied a new stance with respect to music, one which Asuar did not articulate as a theorist or composer but as a technician.

98 Backtracking

Asuar built the COMDASUAR from scratch, starting out with a board equipped with an 8-bit microcontroller. After considering the options available in those days within this emerging market, he finally opted for the Intel 8080 (once described as the "first truly usable microprocessor")[54] as the core of his system. This was a fairly logical choice since the commercialization of the 8080 in 1974 had brought on a significant change in the development of microcomputers and opened the doors to the production of personal computers and so-called single-board computers. In 1975, the company Micro Instrumentation and Telemetry Systems launched the Altair 8800, a microcomputer based on the 8080, lauded in *Popular Electronics* as the breakthrough of the year:

> The era of the computer in every home – a favorite topic among science-fiction writers – has arrived! It is made possible by the Popular Electronics/MITS Altair 8800, a full-blown computer that can hold its own against sophisticated minicomputers now on the market.[55]

The idea that computers were ready to become household items soon took hold. IMS Associates Inc. quickly developed a clone of the Altair 8800, the IMSAI 8080; and the Sol-20 computer, an Altair-compatible board, would become extremely successful, apparently being more reliable than the 8080 itself. A single-board computer based on the Intel C8080A, the Dyna-micro, also hit the market around that time, along with an operating system developed for the 8080 and conceived for a mass market, the Control Program/Monitor or CP/M.[56] About his decision to use the Intel 8080, Asuar said the following:

> On this CPU [Intel 8080]'s software one could work with the instructions that were given. There were 256 instructions of 8 bits each; numbering 256 in hexadecimal. . . . I was working without a compiler, directly into machine language, and that was due to several reasons: one of them was the limited memory. Anyway, at that time I had made great progress over the PDP-8, which only had 8000 bytes of memory; with the Intel 8080 I got 64000 bytes of memory, that is from 0000 to FFFF, those were the 64000 memory positions.[57]

As I have mentioned, in previous experiments Asuar had been able to get the PDP-8 computer to play its compositions through the ARP synthesizer, but now he wanted the computer to integrate the capacity for sound playback, so he had to design a solution for sound generation. To this end, Asuar worked out a hack on another Intel product, the 8253 chip, a Programmable Interval Timer, which he was able to modify for use as a sound generator.[58] The 8253 was designed to be used as an 8080 microprocessor peripheral and endowed with three counters that could be programmed independently. Each of these counters had an input from the clock, a gate, and an output. Asuar used the 8253 by getting a high frequency in the input from the clock (2048 kHz) and then dividing that frequency by the number in the gate, thus obtaining an audible output frequency. He programmed that process three times, one for each counter. Asuar also altered the timer's quartz clock in order to control its speed through a potentiometer, to which he added a multiplexer and a Programmable Peripheral Interface chip, the Intel 8255. Thus, by using two 8253s, Asuar was able to get six audible frequencies out of the timers, allowing the device to determine six independent frequencies. At the end of each of the six outputs, he then installed a digital analog converter, a decision that, as I have already remarked, merits some attention. As I have noted, there are many examples in the history of computer music of devices that were able to create tunes, play basic sounds, and perform musical pieces, but the shift by which the field came properly into its own is arguably linked to the appearance of the Pulse-Code Modulation (PCM) solution, in combination with the digital-to-analog converter envisioned and developed by Mathews in 1957.[59] In line with this structural guideline, the COMDASUAR also generated tones digitally, but Asuar settled on a special use of digital analog converters to render the frequencies audible (Figure 3.4). Because he was certainly aware of the possibility of

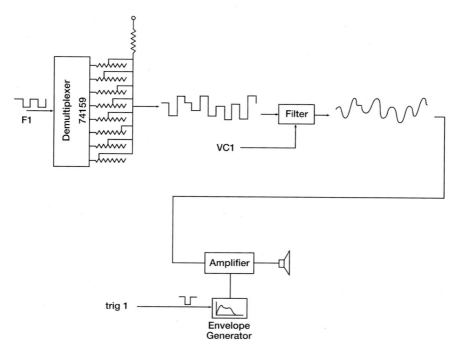

Figure 3.4 COMDASUAR's sound generation system in "Un sistema para hacer música con un microcomputador," *Revista Musical Chilena* (1980).

Source: Courtesy of Revista Musical Chilena; vector-based image version by Pierre Puentes

100 Backtracking

using the PCM, it is not quite clear why Asuar decided to create his own system to generate the sounds, rather than adapting earlier solutions put forward by Mathews and Chowning. The most likely reason is that Asuar's hardware had some limitations, especially its CPU and available memory. His decision to work with timers as the source of divided frequencies in order to obtain specific notes was functional, but it strongly limited the range of sounds that could be obtained, and it consequently limited the kind of compositions that could be produced with it, something that Asuar later lamented:

> The pitches were not obtained in an analogue way; the pitches and different heights were obtained in a digital way, but with the limitation that the wave obtained in the output of the timers was a square wave, that is a very pure sound, similar to or even the same as pitches that come from a cell phone and many other electronic systems that need an acoustic communication with the user. I used this kind of square wave pitch that is easy to produce, so the problem that I faced was that of making the sounds more attractive. . . . The Intel [8253] timers had frequency dividers. It was a circuit board where one can introduce a fixed frequency, one high frequency tone, it had a clock, a very stable quartz clock. . . . It was a programmable frequency divider; the frequency that went out could have a proportional value to the number in the divisor, therefore it changed when the input was a different number; subsequently there is another frequency, and one can obtain the output of the frequency divider, so it was possible to obtain different frequencies, I mean, different musical pitches; with the duration of every pitch it was possible to have a melody, a sequence of pitches. Every timer had three independent frequency dividers; I used two timers, so you have the six frequencies. There was one limitation: all of [the sounds coming from the timers] were harmonic, or all these colors were harmonic, all produced with the natural scale of harmonics.[60]

The fact that the COMDASUAR was not an entirely digital solution clearly shows that Asuar was forced to solve, in the analog domain, problems for which he could not find a solution in the digital domain, such as that of creating a nuanced range of sounds on the basis of the original square waves produced by the six timers. To do this, Asuar equipped each of the timer outputs with a set of analog controls: a filter with voltage control (using a digital analog converter for each output), an envelope generator, and an amplifier with voltage control. In spite of this, he was not able to obtain the kind of sound universe that he would have been interested in exploring as a composer:

> So, to have different sounds, I passed them over to the transient generator and the amplifier and it sounded different. . . . After passing through

COMDASUAR   101

the filter, it passed the band's Q variable, in that way I could get many sounds, but with the limitation, which of course I dislike a lot, . . . that they were all harmonics. The instrument was good for making a kind of harmonic music, or to type out melody lines, or lines whose heights could be distinguished aurally and as chords, meaning that the combinations could also be distinguished.[61]

It is significant that Asuar was willing to strike a compromise between the range of possibilities that the computer could explore and the range of sounds that his digital-analog solution could produce, knowing that he had already coupled the PDP-8 to the ARP and was clearly aware of the limitations to composition that his new system entailed. We may read this as a provisional concession to the COMDASUAR's design premise, which clearly could not have been fulfilled by resorting to an analog synthesizer. Under this premise, the computer should eventually be able to control every aspect of the sound, including generation and modelling, allowing users to explore unheard musical universes, but Asuar was willing to limit the range of sounds to the harmonic in order for his system to be a music computer, rather than a computer coupled with a synthesizer. Similarly, Asuar's programming also grew out of an inventive confrontation with the available hardware, as he struggled to make room in the limited memory space for what he took to be a sufficient range of tools, which forced him to write a new operating system:

> [T]he kit that I bought came with a pre-installed operating system, it was 2 kilobytes, . . . [it was the] incorporated operating system [that] initializes all the counters, puts everything on the screen to be seen, is all set to make the thing start to operate. I wrote the operating system again and the same operating system was reduced by half in terms of memory capacity, so that means that the new operating system was only 1 kilobyte.[62]

Asuar's decision to work directly in machine language allowed him to save space for instructions, although it had a negative consequence: the software thus produced was not portable at all. In other words, Asuar's software was hardware-specific, making it almost impossible for other composers or musicians to use it or to adapt it for use on a different device.[63]

Clearly, the reason for this additional compromise was that Asuar needed space for the two sets of operations that were at the heart of his system: the musical codes, which allowed for all aspects of a traditional score to be transcribed into a very economic code, and the heuristic programs, which contained the commands that would allow users to engage with the computer as a creative partner.[64] In his paper, Asuar describes six of these heuristic programs, some of which would generate musical figures on the basis of set parameters, while others would produce variations on the basis of a given figure (Figure 3.5). The latter comprised four of the six programs,

102   Backtracking

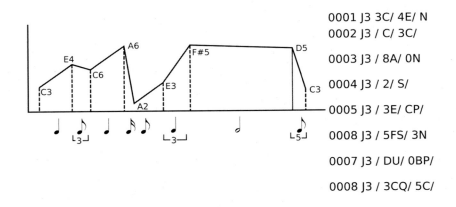

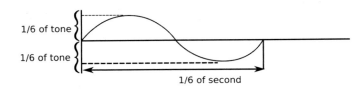

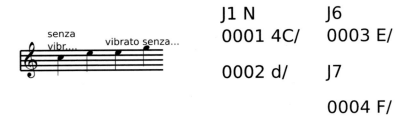

Figure 3.5 COMDASUAR's compositional system and methodology in "Un sistema para hacer música con un microcomputador," *Revista Musical Chilena* (1980).

Source: Courtesy of Revista Musical Chilena; vector-based image version by Pierre Puentes

and they allowed the computer to create counterpoint figures like canon, retrograde, and transpositions of tone and duration between two voices. The fifth probability program would allow the computer to use a probability table to create sets of tones according to all the variables that the computer could control, namely, register, pitch, duration, harmony, and texture. As an example, Asuar explained that the computer could produce a sequence of 100 tones to each of which a different octave could be assigned probabilistically. The sixth program was conceived as a way of mitigating the monotone and inarticulate nature of such sequences of tones by distributing duration and pauses, also probabilistically. These two programs seem to come closest to the idea of a computer as an amplifier of the imagination that had inspired Asuar's previous efforts at assisted composition, although they might not seem as exciting in their actual realization as they are described on paper. More tantalizingly, but in less detail, Asuar goes on to describe a seventh group of heuristic programs that he had used, some of which had allowed to him to produce "in two or three hours" compositions that "an unadvised listener would have confused with works by one of the composers of [the serialist school]."[65] Although Asuar was interested in the system's capacity to be used to produce music in all manner of styles, including "classical, popular, and experimental,"[66] it is worth recalling that, as his background clearly suggests, he would have desired a system capable of going far beyond serial music, which had been the point of departure, rather than arrival, of his own work as a composer. Thus, both in hardware and software, the system would have been extremely limited for him in the role of a serious composer, although we should not read this as a sign that Asuar acknowledged any such a hierarchy between the roles of technician, pedagogue, and composer: instead, it seems fair to say that the COMDASUAR was a successful technical articulation of these three roles to the extent that it created a space where a plurality of musical roles could interact and hybridize.

Conclusion

This portrait of the COMDASUAR as a music computer, coupled with the LP that Asuar produced to promote it, might lead us to think that it was, even for its designer, a very provisional step in a process that was unfortunately interrupted, hindered by limitations acknowledged by Asuar and which he could have overcome had he been working in a different location and with a different budget. And yet we could hardly be said to *know* what this instrument was capable of unless we actually played it – after all, it was conceived as a music-making device. Since the heart of the COMDASUAR was a set of programs to be used creatively, we can hardly say that we have a solid sense of what it is if we reduce it to an existence on paper alone, where it risks becoming a mere abstraction, requiring us to engage in a dubious imaginative exercise by which we could hardly be able to experience its

104 *Backtracking*

logic *at work*. It seems clear that, in the case of a media technology, and more so of a device conceived as an active participant in a process of musical creation, the potentialities that are concretely embedded in the design can only unfold if the device is made and put to work. For this reason, and in collaboration with Professor Andrés Cabrera from the Media Arts and Technology graduate program at the University of California, Santa Barbara (UCSB), I attempted to build a functional prototype of the COMDASUAR using currently available technologies (we named this prototype COMDAS-UAR MK II). The prototype was conceived as an open and accessible model that others could replicate and interact with, including a GitHub repository with the code. Cabrera, who was one of the developers of the landmark Csound programming language and compiler, which has been extensively used for sound generation and music composition since 1986, has a deep knowledge of the relationship between sound, composition, and programming, and he shared my interest in exploring the COMDASUAR's heuristic programs.[67] For this reason, we chose to focus on reconstructing the COMDASUAR's software component, although we did design a tailored hardware configuration that complied in structure with Asuar's published descriptions. That being said, we were not interested in getting the system to generate the sounds in the same manner as the original computer but rather in modeling the COMDASUAR's composition methods with the use of current sound processing software. Thus, our project was meant to show that by using only the elements and structures described in Asuar's paper, it was indeed possible to engage in a computer-assisted process of musical composition, which we regarded as the key to the design's personality as a creative tool.

The reconstruction was done using a Raspberry Pi board (Figure 3.6) and software developed with Csound.[68] We also used a Wiring board for controlling the potentiometers, a small Korg MIDI keyboard to record the compositions note by note, and an external black-and-white video monitor.[69] We installed the Csound software on the Raspberry Pi to model Asuar's heuristic software. Being very versatile and precise, Csound allowed us to model some of the musical operations that Asuar himself had programmed so that the resulting model was sufficient to prove the technical consistency of the device as described in Asuar's papers – with an unexpected and revealing twist. Once we engaged with the software at the practical level, it became clear that it could be extremely helpful in developing repetitive forms of composition based on progressive variations. The COMDASUAR's code can easily generate iterative sequences that can be continuously adjusted by adding simple variations. Thus, the instrument was particularly suited for the creation of fluid alterations that stand out aurally against the backdrop of repetitive sonic sequences, a kind of musical structure characteristic of techno music and which would probably not have fallen within the aesthetic parameters that Asuar was hoping to explore with the help of his device. This discovery can be thought of as one productive point of departure for

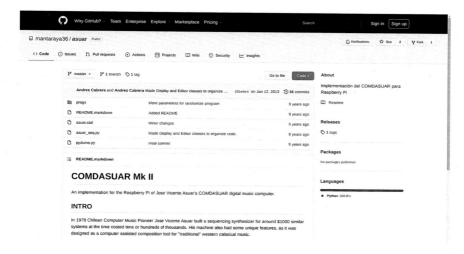

Figure 3.6 "COMDASUAR MK II" code repository; it runs on a Raspberry Pi board.
Source: Andrés Cabrera and Andrés Burbano, 2012

the practical resignification of the COMDASUAR, and through the prototype, it is possible to pinpoint several others.

Another feature of the COMDASUAR calling for further exploration is the module that, in its original desktop configuration, would have allowed users to manipulate the sound analogically. This module, which bears roughly two dozen physical interfaces, like potentiometers, all of which can be manipulated in real time, adds a virtual layer of performative ways of interacting with the machine, to which Asuar paid no particular attention in his own accounts of the device. By exploring these and other features, we may yet gain a better sense of the COMDASUAR as a sonic technology, something that is only possible as this technology finds what did not have at the time of its emergence: users. Although the COMDASUAR may seem limited in light of ongoing experiments with machine learning, where all possible variations in harmony or melody can be produced at great speed on the basis of any musical idea, the COMDASUAR MK II open prototype may prove more attractive to composers whose creativity is energized by the challenge of achieving musical expressivity through fewer possibilities. It is also worth noting that the development of popular electronic music after the 1970s, in places as remote as Dusseldorf and Detroit, is arguably the result of a conversation between musical styles, leading to a fusion of the idioms of experimental electronic music and African American music that enabled the emergence of what we now know as techno music. In that sense, by virtue of being a design directed at an indeterminate range of users,

106 *Backtracking*

the COMDASUAR may be said to anticipate what we would now define as a music production station, a device-type that allows the figure of the producer to take on the flexible and hybrid role of technician, composer, and performer that Asuar embraced in his own practice.

An effort at resignification enabled by the COMDASUAR MK II could also allow us to elaborate creatively on the COMDASUAR's structure as a digital-analog solution, digitally generating sound that would then be processed analogically through the use of filters. In our postdigital times, sound has come to stand out as one of the cultural fields where the difference in quality between analog and digital media has been queried and reinterpreted, yielding what can now be described as a new space of signification. This is visible in the fact that LPs now sell in larger numbers than CDs or in the emergent market of analog tube-based amplifiers, many of which combine analog and digital solutions to sound generation and processing. Here, too, Asuar's hybrid approach to design proves to be relevant in a contemporary setting. Now that we have an open-source version of the COMDASUAR, the virtual plurality of users that Asuar envisioned may become concrete, which will sharpen our understanding of the fact that not all sound software processes and conceives sound in the same way. Thus, as individual users test and engage with the approach to sound that is coded into Asuar's design, we will see just how much it has to offer. The fact that these and other possibilities for resignification were not anticipated by Asuar should not lead us to conceptualize them as incidental, for it is exactly through them that a media technology can have a history, something that Asuar's device has not been able to have until now. Thus, we may see this approach to resignification as a radical historical operation, if we understand these experiments as retroactive manifestos for past avant-gardes. This mode of thinking through practice invites us to grasp the need to diversify and delinearize our technological present by exploring forms of audiovisual and computational technology that point beyond those that surround us, showing us that sometimes going back is a way of going beyond.

In light of Asuar's example, the history of computer music can be understood as informed by the intertwinement of local technological realities with singular geographical and historical networks, often intercultural but never entirely global in a neoliberal sense. If we consider the early experiments with computer music conducted in Australia in 1949, we have reason to envision a new understanding of music technology as a constellation of diverse processes, each of them configured by specific forms of interaction between the local and the international at the levels of the technical, the theoretical, and the aesthetic. Asuar's story is a small piece in a large puzzle, and assembled with other hidden stories from other geographical locations, his case is likely to lead us to a new understanding of the intellectual and physical geography of computer music, a task for which we have yet to develop an adequate set of fine-tuned conceptual and historical tools.

Notes

1 Translations of this and other texts by Asuar are my own.
2 Federico Schumacher, "José Vicente Asuar: El compositor virtuoso," *Revista Musical Chilena* 71, no. 227 (2017): n.p., http://dx.doi.org/10.4067/s0716-27902017000100265.
3 J. V. Asuar, "En el umbral de una nueva era musical," *Revista Musical Chilena* 13, no. 64 (1959): 11–32.
4 F. Schumacher, "50 años de música electroacústica en Chile," *Revista Musical Chilena* 61, no. 208 (2007): 66–81.
5 He retained his faculty position at the Department of the Arts and Musical Sciences, which he had joined in 1962, until 1980. In 1969, he had founded the Sound Technology program, for which the lab had been designed and built. See J. V. Asuar, "Recuerdos," Revista Musical Chilena 29, no. 132 (1975): 5–22.
6 David Em, "Twenty-two Paradigm Shifts," in *Media Arts and Technology Seminar Series* (Santa Barbara: University of California, 2010), www.mat.ucsb.edu/595M/?p=310.
7 See A. Pollack, "Big I.B.M.'S Little Computer." *The New York Times,* August 13, 1981. Retrieved March 1, 2021.
8 R. Cori, "Remembranzas de Juan Amenábar," *Revista Musical Chilena* 62, no. 209 (2008): 62.
9 F. Schumacher, "50 años," 66–68.
10 E. Medina, "Big Blue in the Bottomless Pit: The Early Years of IBM Chile," in *IEEE Annals of the History of Computing* (October–November 2008): 26–41.
11 E. Medina, *Cybernetic Revolutionaries. Technology and Politics in Allende's Chile* (Cambridge, MA: MIT Press, 2011), 9–10, 245–6.
12 J. Alvares and C. Gutierrez, "El primer computador universitario en Chile: El hogar desde donde salió y se repartió la luz," *Bits de ciencia,* no. 3 (2012): 2–13.
13 Medina, *Cybernetic Revolutionaries*, 15–41.
14 P. Guillaudat and P. Mouterde, *Los movimientos sociales en Chile, 1973–1993* (Santiago de Chile: LOM, 1998), 103.
15 Cori, "Remembranzas," 61–65.
16 A. Dorfman, P. Aguilera, et al., *Chile: The Other September 11: An Anthology of Reflections on the 1973 Coup* (Melbourne: Ocean Press, 2006), 1–6. It is worth noting that neighboring Argentina also experienced a military coup d'etat in that decade and that Brazil had experienced one a decade before, which meant that these three countries faced the transition from the 1970s to the 1980s under the yoke of military rule. Those were years of tempestuous transitions filled with stories of desperation, exile, and death. The consequences of those years are highly controversial, and still today, the responsibility for many of the government's actions is heavily disputed. The impact of these political events shaped the transformation of South American societies in radical ways, not in the least by implementing particular technological policies. See E. Adler, *The Power of Ideology* (Berkeley: University of California Press, 1987), 223–226.
17 F. Schumacher, "50 años," 68–69.
18 Cori, "Remembranzas," 61–65. Although Asuar is fairly vague on the details, it seems clear that he had conflicts with his former collaborator, Juan Amenábar, who had been elected as chair of the school.
19 A similar case in the American context can be found in the work of composer David Cope, who developed his Experiments in Musical Intelligence (EMI) at UCSC. Like Asuar, Cope was interested in the relationship between human-computer interaction and musical creativity, and his technical experiments in that direction likewise failed to achieve the impact and recognition that they deserve.

108 *Backtracking*

See David Cope, "Experiments in Musical Intelligence." Accessed March 1, 2020. http://artsites.ucsc.

20 B. Latour, *Science in Action* (Cambridge, MA: Harvard University Press, 1987), 104.

21 A. Burbano and I. Nieto, "Interview with José Vicente Asuar," unpublished Ms., Santa Barbara – Santiago de Chile (2008).

22 L. Menabrea and A. Lovelace, "Sketch of the Analytical Engine Invented by Charles Babbage," *Scientific Memoirs*, no. 82 (October 1842): 118.

23 R. Rojas, "The Architecture of Konrad Zuse's Early Computing Machines," in *The First Computers – History and Architecture*, edited by R. Rojas and H. Hashagen (Cambridge, MA: MIT Press, 2002), 237–261. R. Rojas, *Der Nachbau der Rechenmaschine Z3* (video, 2001), www.zib.de/zuse/Inhalt/Rep/Z3/Z3Rep/Videos/z3-2.mpg.

24 P. Doornbusch, *The Music of CSIRAC, Australia's First Computer Music* (Melbourne: Common Ground Publishing, 1995), 13. This means that it is quite plausible to argue that computer music is an art form that originated outside of the Global North, which confirms how important it is to explore alternative genealogies of the interaction between computers and sound.

25 J. Fildes, "*'Oldest' Computer Music Unveiled*" (London: BBC Science and Technology, 2008), http://news.bbc.co.uk/2/hi/7458479.stm.

26 Probably the most famous of these games has been attributed to Mozart, although there is an open debate regarding its authorship. Unsurprisingly, this musical game was one of the first to be translated to a computer program around 1956, and it was later programmed again by John Cage. See L. Hiller and L. Isaacson, *Experimental Music. Composition with an Electronic Computer* (New York: McGraw-Hill, 1959), 54.

27 Hiller and Isaacson, *Experimental Music*, 141–150.

28 I. Xenakis, *Formalized Music: Thought and Mathematics in Composition* (Stuyvesant: Pendragon Press, 1992), 1–176.

29 Asuar, "Un sistema," 6.

30 C. Roads, "Interview with Max Mathews," in *The Music Machine: Selected Readings from Computer Music Journal*, edited by C. Roads (Cambridge, MA: MIT Press, 1989), 5–12. Mathews's contributions do not stop at his having solved that huge problem, for he was also the main developer of the influential MUSIC N software series. However, Asuar argues that Mathews's PCM methodology consumes too many computational sources, making it difficult to obtain sounds in real time.

31 Asuar, "Un sistema," 7. J. Chowning and D. Bristow, *FM Theory and Applications: By Musicians for Musicians* (Tokyo: Yamaha Music Foundation, 1986). Asuar was unaware of other, less-known composers and engineers who, like him, were doing independent work and whose findings were accordingly not well documented or published. Among these composers and engineers who were also producing computer music using personal or microcomputers at around the same time as Asuar was building his own, we may mention Martin Bartlett, Maurice Rozenberg, Marc LeBrun, David Oppenheim, Jean-Francois Allouis, John Bischoff, and Curtis Roads. See M. LeBrun, "Notes on Microcomputer Music," *Computer Music Journal* 1, no. 2 (1977): 30–35.

32 All the volumes of *Revista Musical Chilena* from 1942 to 2012 are available online at the following link: www.revistamusicalchilena.uchile.cl/index.php/RMCH/issue/archive.

33 J. V. Asuar, "En el umbral de una nueva era musical," *Revista Musical Chilena* 13, no. 64 (1959): 11–32.

34 J. V. Asuar, "Música electrónica: poética musical de nuestros días," *Revista Musical Chilena* 17, no. 86 (1963): 12–20. The concert featured works by Bruno Maderna, Francois Bernard Mache, Henri Pousseur, and Mario Davidovsky,

among others. The article also discusses the important role played in the new musical scene by composers from Latin America, especially Argentineans like Mauricio Kagel and Edgardo Canton.

35 Asuar, "Música Electrónica," 19.

36 Asuar, "Música electrónica," 17.

37 Asuar, "Música electrónica," 16–17.

38 Asuar mentions Radio Studio in Cologne, the RTF in Paris, the RAI in Milan, the Radio Tokyo studio, Radio Warsaw, and Radio Stockholm, along with the Technical University of Berlin, Columbia University, the University of Toronto, and the University of Buenos Aires.

39 J. V. Asuar, "Mi fin es mi comienzo," *Revista Musical Chilena* 18, no. 89 (1964): 43–78.

40 J. V. Asuar, "Fatalidades," *Revista Musical Chilena* 23, no 107 (1969): 33–45.

41 As Xenakis put it, it was not a matter of simply "playing heads or tails to decide on this or that matter of detail" but of a "philosophical and aesthetic concept ruled by the laws of the theory of probabilities and by the mathematical functions that formulate them, of a coherent concept within a new domain of coherence." I. Xenakis, *Musiques formelles* (Paris: Stock, 1981 [originally published in 1963]), 37.

42 J.V. Asuar, "Música con computadores: ¿cómo hacerlo?", *Revista Musical Chilena* 26, no. 118 (1972): 39–40.

43 Asuar, "Música con computadores," 51. Interestingly, Asuar remarks that the group chose serialism as the style, rather than classical or traditional music, because their concerns were creative, rather than musicological. It follows that he thought that this system could also be used as an aid in musicological analyses of, say, canonical or folklore music.

44 Asuar, "Música con computadores," 66.

45 It should be noted that in Spanish, a person who performs a musical instrument is typically referred to as *intérprete*, and a performance of a musical score as an "interpretation."

46 Asuar, "Música con computadores," 43.

47 J. V. Asuar, "Haciendo música con un computador," *Revista Musical Chilena* 27, no. 123–1 (1973): 81–83.

48 Asuar, "Haciendo," 81–82.

49 Asuar, "Haciendo," 82.

50 Carol Wright, "Wendy Carlos. Something Old, Something New: The Definitive *Switched-On*", www.wendycarlos.com/wright.html.

51 J.V. Asuar, "Un sistema para hacer música con computador," *Revista Musical Chilena* 34, no. 151 (1980): 5–28.

52 J.V. Asuar, "Un sistema," 8.

53 Asuar, "Un sistema," 26.

54 P. Rony, *The 8080A Bugbook, Microcomputer Interfacing and Programming* (Indianapolis: Howard W Sams & Co., Inc., 1977), 11.

55 H. E. Roberts and W. Yates, "ALTAIR 8080," *Popular Electronics* (January 1975): 33–38.

56 Rony, *The 8080A Bugbook*, 39.

57 Burbano and Nieto, "Interview with J.V. Asuar."

58 K. Kant, "Programmable Interval Timers INTEL 8253 and INTEL 8254," in *Microprocessors and Microcontrolers, Architecture, Programing and Design* (New Delhi: PHI, 2006), 313–331.

59 See Roads, "Interview with Max Mathews," 5–12.

60 Burbano and Nieto, "Interview with J.V. Asuar."

61 Burbano and Nieto, "Interview with J.V. Asuar."

62 Burbano and Nieto, "Interview with J.V. Asuar."

110 Backtracking

63 It is worth noting that other composers pursuing similar concerns also turned to machine language and programming in languages like FORTRAN and COBOL. See, for example, Roads, "Interview with Max Matthews," 7.

64 The COMDASUAR was equipped with a total of 26 programs, one for each letter of the alphabet to be found in the keyboard that would be used as an interface. These were divided into five groups: (1) operating instructions that determined the handling and display of data; (2) the musical codes, which allowed users to program tones and sequences of tones by determining pitch, duration, and textures, like glissando and vibrato, using redundancy to minimize the amount of space to be occupied by the coding of figures like tremolos and trills; (3) the heuristic programs, defined as those "where the computer has creative intervention (originating a score in the memory) or recreative (manipulating a score recorded on the memory)"; and (4)–(5) sound conversion and peripheral control (reading from and copying to magnetic tape). Asuar, "Un sistema," 9–19.

65 Asuar, "Un sistema," 18–19.

66 Asuar, "Un sistema," 28.

67 Csound is a programming language for sound processing and a compiler; it is written in C and was initially designed as a portable version of MUSIC 11 (in other words, it is a direct descendant of the MUSIC N software series initiated by Max Mathews). R. Boulanger, *The Csound Book: Perspectives in Software Synthesis, Sound Design, Signal Processing and Programming* (Cambridge, MA: MIT Press, 2000), 5–63.

68 We chose the Raspberry Pi board over other options on the market because it already integrates several important technical solutions. The Raspberry Pi is a small computer developed by the Raspberry Pi Foundation in the United Kingdom, running on an ARM11 processor and equipped with video and audio outputs, and Ethernet and USB ports. Raspberry Pi runs on Debian GNU/Linux as operating system, so it is affordable, open-source, versatile, and fast. In that sense, we found the Raspberry Pi to be a tool that reflects the spirit of Asuar's endeavor in a contemporary mode. See G. Halfacree and E. Upton, *Raspberry Pi User Guide* (London: Wiley, 2012), 1–10.

69 For our filter console prototype, we used the Wiring board, which receives the data from potentiometers to control the sound filter parameters. As will be shown in Chapter 5, Wiring is the board that functioned as the point of departure for the Arduino board, and it is likewise an open hardware initiative running the *Wiring* language, a Processing-like programming language. Our console was equipped with an array of potentiometers that allowed for real-time manipulation of sound parameters like filters and envelopes. C. Reas and B. Fry, *Processing Processing: A Programming Handbook for Visual Designers and Artists* (Cambridge, MA: MIT Press, 2008), 1–16.

Bibliography

Adler, Emanuel. *The Power of Ideology: The Quest for Technological Autonomy in Argentina and Brazil.* Berkeley: University of California Press, 1987.

Álvarez, Juan and Claudio Gutiérrez. "El primer computador universitario en Chile: El hogar desde donde salió y se repartió la luz." *Bits de ciencia*, no. 3 (2012): 2–13.

Asuar, José Vicente. "En el umbral de una nueva era musical." *Revista musical chilena* 13, no. 64 (1959): 11–32.

———. "Música electrónica: poética musical de nuestros días." *Revista musical chilena* 17, no. 86 (1963): 12–20.

COMDASUAR 111

———. "Mi fin es mi comienzo." *Revista musical chilena* 18, no. 89 (1964): 43–78.

———. "Fatalidades." *Revista musical chilena* 23, no. 107 (1969): 33–45.

———. "Música con computadores: ¿cómo hacerlo?" *Revista musical chilena* 26, no. 118 (1972): 36–66.

———. "Haciendo música con un computador." *Revista musical chilena* 27, no. 123–1 (1973): 81–82.

———. "Recuerdos." *Revista musical chilena* 29, no. 132 (1975): 5–22.

———. "Un sistema para hacer música con computador." *Revista musical chilena* 34, no. 151 (1980): 5–28.

Boulanger, Richard. *The Csound Book: Perspectives in Software Synthesis, Sound Design, Signal Processing and Programming.* Cambridge: MIT Press, 2000.

Chowning, John and David Bristow. *FM Theory and Applications: By Musicians for Musicians.* Tokyo: Yamaha Music Foundation, 1986.

Cori, Rolando. "Remembranzas de Juan Amenábar." *Revista musical chilena* 62, no. 209 (2008): 61–65.

Doornbusch, Paul. *The Music of CSIRAC, Australia's First Computer Music.* Melbourne: Common Ground Publishing, 1995.

Dorfman, Ariel et al. *Chile: The Other September 11: An Anthology of Reflections on the 1973 Coup.* Melbourne: Ocean Press, 2006.

Em, David. "Twenty-two Paradigm Shifts." In *Media Arts and Technology Seminar Series.* Santa Barbara: University of California, 2010.

Fildes, Jonathan. " 'Oldest' Computer Music Unveiled." *BBC News,* June 17, 2008, http://news.bbc.co.uk/2/hi/7458479.stm.

Guillaudat, Patrick and Pierre Mouterde. *Los movimientos sociales en Chile, 1973–1993.* Santiago de Chile: LOM, 1998.

Halfacree, Gareth and Eben Upton. *Raspberry Pi User Guide.* London: Wiley, 2012.

Hiller, Lejaren and Leonard Isaacson. *Experimental Music: Composition with an Electronic Computer.* New York: McGraw-Hill, 1959.

Kant, Krishna. *Microprocessors and Microcontrolers, Architecture, Programing and Design.* New Delhi: PHI, 2006.

Latour, Bruno. *Science in Action.* Cambridge: Harvard University Press, 1987.

LeBrun, Marc. "Notes on Microcomputer Music." *Computer Music Journal* 1, no. 2 (1977): 30–35.

Medina, Eden. "Big Blue in the Bottomless Pit: The Early Years of IBM Chile." *IEEE Annals of the History of Computing* 4, no. 30 (2008): 26–41.

———. *Cybernetic Revolutionaries. Technology and Politics in Allende's Chile.* Cambridge: MIT Press, 2011.

Menabrea, Luigi and Ada Lovelace. "Sketch of the Analytical Engine Invented by Charles Babbage." *Scientific Memoirs,* no. 82 (October 1842): 691–731.

Pollack, Andrew. "Big I.B.M.'s Little Computer." *The New York Times,* August 13, 1981.

Reas, Casey and Ben Fry. *Processing: A Programming Handbook for Visual Designers and Artists.* Cambridge: MIT Press, 2008.

Roads, Curtis. "Interview with Max Mathews." In *The Music Machine: Selected Readings from Computer Music Journal,* edited by Curtis Roads. Cambridge: MIT Press, 1989, 5–12.

Roberts, Edward and William Yates. "ALTAIR 8080." *Popular Electronics,* January 1975.

112 Backtracking

Rojas, Raul. "The Architecture of Konrad Zuse's Early Computing Machines." In *The First Computers: History and Architecture*, edited by Raul Rojas and Ulf Hashagen. Cambridge: MIT Press, 2002, 237–261.

Rony, Peter. *The 8080A Bugbook, Microcomputer Interfacing and Programming*. Indianapolis: Howard W Sams & Co., Inc., 1977.

Schumacher, Federico. "50 años de música electroacústica en Chile." *Revista Musical Chilena* 61, no. 208 (2007): 66–81.

———. "José Vicente Asuar: El compositor virtuoso." *Revista Musical Chilena* 71, no. 227 (2017): n.p.

Wright, Carol. "Wendy Carlos. Something Old, Something New: The Definitive Switched-On." *Wendy Carlos*, www.wendycarlos.com/wright.html.

Xenakis, Iannis. *Musiques formelles*. Paris: Stock, 1981.

———. *Formalized Music: Thought and Mathematics in Composition*. Stuyvesant: Pendragon Press, 1992.

Part II
Sidetracking

4 Lua: The Scripting Side of the Moon, Brazil, 1993

Introduction

In this chapter, I will investigate a unique kind of artifact: a programming language. The first thing to say about programming languages in the present context is that they are quite difficult to describe and conceptualize in terms that go beyond the theoretical and practical framework of the computer sciences. Although within that framework, programming languages are characterized by a relatively small set of profound concepts (compositional semantics, binding structure, domains, transition systems, and inference rules),[1] this is a conceptual field that does not seem to connect directly with the questions that drive my research, which hinges on the cultural, creative, social, and historical implications of the conception, design, and implementation of media technologies. Of course, programming languages can be understood as media technologies as such, but they are, above all, used to write media technologies. Nonetheless, if we focus on the fact that programming languages are forms of *writing*, it may be less difficult for us to perceive them as the kind of socio-technical artifacts whose deep history I have been attempting to expose in previous chapters.

It might be good to take a moment to wonder to what extent programming languages are indeed *languages* or whether this is a label that is used simply as a matter of convenience or out of habit. Like so-called natural languages, programming languages are said to have a syntax, a grammar, a semantics, and a performative dimension, although in the latter case, the performers are machines that do (or fail to do) as they are instructed. Also, like natural languages, programming languages are created and shared by a community whose use of the language causes it to evolve; but this all happens under very different conditions and in a very different sense in each of the two cases. To some extent, programming languages are the heirs of efforts by twentieth-century logicians like Gottlob Frege to develop an artificial language capable of capturing the putatively true ideal structures of rational thought, which these logicians assumed were in fact obscured by natural language.[2] The sense that there is an inferential form underlying all correct thought regardless of its content captures a dimension of the kind

DOI: 10.4324/9781003172789-7

116 *Sidetracking*

of abstraction that a programming language should be capable of – but that is, at most, half of the story. Computer code is written in order to be interpreted or executed by a machine, and it always comes down to bits and bytes that translate into hardware instructions. This means that programming languages have to negotiate between criteria of clarity, order, and efficacy that can apply to human thought and expression, and analogous criteria whose ultimate substrate are physical processes mediated by technical systems. So a programming language is part of a hybrid construction that emerges out of intersecting layers of abstraction, and for that reason, it can be assessed under very different parameters: in light of its formal qualities, of its functionality as an engineering component, or of its capacity to get things done.

The Lua programming language was created in Brazil in the early 1990s and is now used in a vast and growing range of industries (most prominently in video game development), a range that may by now be difficult to gauge as Lua has found a place in the sprawl of the Internet of Things.[3] Lua is the work of a small team of academics based in Rio de Janeiro who have carefully managed its evolution since 1993 through a considered approach to the open-source philosophy. The team's three core members are Roberto Ierusalimschy and Waldemar Celes, both professors of computer science at Rio's Pontifical Catholic University (PUC-Rio), and Luiz Henrique de Figueiredo, a mathematician who works for the National Institute for Pure and Applied Mathematics (IMPA). In the early 1990s, Ierusalimschy, Celes, and Figueiredo were all working for a research lab Tecgraf, based in PUC-Rio and served the needs of various industrial partners. One of these partners was Petrobras, Brazil's state-owned oil company, and Lua was originally designed as a language that could be used to program tools to be used by the company's engineers and scientists.[4] Although it was created to address fairly local and specific technical needs, Lua has gained an incredibly numerous and assorted global community of users, most of whom are quite likely unaware of its origins (Figure 4.1). This raises the question: does it – or should it – matter where a programming language is from? This question points to a well-known set of quandaries about the valorization of the local in the framework of a so-called global economy and specifically about the meaning of concepts like "local" and "origin" within the current market-dominated technological regime.

Lua is the only one of my case studies that can be described without qualifications as a global success story, although as with other software creations, this success is not to be measured in terms of financial returns. The sense in which Lua is a successful language is nonetheless straightforward: it has been widely adopted (in May of 2022, it ranked 22 in the worldwide PYPL index, which tracks Google searches for language tutorials), and the reasons for its surprising spread are, to some extent, fairly easy to determine.[5] As Figueiredo puts it, Lua's key virtue in comparison to other languages is "the existence of a single data structure: the table," although he acknowledges

Figure 4.1 Lua programming language logo, 1998.
Source: Created by Alexandre Nakonechnyj; courtesy of Lua team

that it "can take a while for a programmer to get used to the total freedom this gives."[6] This structural feature exemplifies the Lua team's overarching design premise, which assembles simplicity, flexibility, and an extremely judicious use of memory and computing resources (Lua needs less than 200 kilobytes to run in a machine with 1 megabyte of memory). The language has by now been evolving for over three decades, and this typically leads to heavier versions as developers try to respond to the concerns and suggestions of new users, but the Lua team has held fast to their original design premises and carefully managed its growth in conversation with a thriving community of users and enthusiasts. For that reason, Lua is a language that can run pretty much everywhere, from a mainframe to a smartwatch, and it is actually used in just about every kind of existing platform.

118   *Sidetracking*

Although the language is extensively used by the Petrobras technicians for whom it was created and was later implemented in Ginga, the middleware for Brazil's digital television system, in the past, the Lua team have acknowledged that it had "always bothered" them that the language had remained relatively unknown in Brazil for many years.[7] This apparent paradox is, to some extent, a commonplace narrative among professionals working in the Global South whose criteria and parameters for thought and action are determined elsewhere, whether by academic institutions or market trends in the Global North. It is not hard to imagine, for instance, Latin American scholars who return to their countries of origin after getting a Ph.D. in Latin American Studies at a US university and whose scholarly output will be produced for and evaluated by an academic community that, in a strong sense, speaks and thinks in American English, even if many of its members come from the Global South (the book you are now reading is a case in point). Lua's story, however, is far from commonplace, and its international propagation has played out through a sequence of fortuitous linkages that vividly illustrate the origins of our current socio-technical landscape.

Can Software Be from Somewhere?

I have asked whether it makes any sense to refer to the place of origin of a programming language as a significant fact, and in the case of Lua, this question has actually been answered. Between 2005 and 2008, computer scientist and STS scholar Yury Takhteyev did fieldwork in Rio de Janeiro for an ethnographic study of the city's programmer cultures, and one of his research questions was whether it was possible to claim that knowledge work was truly emerging as a place-independent professional field that would allow inhabitants of peripheral regions to participate as equals in a globalized economy. Takhtevey interviewed Lua's creators, along with workers and executives from other local software companies, to assess their perceptions of their own position within the world of commercial software products and services; his conclusion was that, strictly speaking, Lua could not be described as a Brazilian programming language – or more generally, that "one cannot talk about 'Brazilian software' in the same way one talks about 'Brazilian music.'"[8] Like the Lua team, Takhteyev was struck by the fact that even local programmers who were acquainted with Lua and its virtues were more often than not compelled to use products by international well-known companies for their local customers, for various reasons: these client companies may already have service contracts with foreign software providers, or they may have doubts about the future implications of using a local software not associated with a major company, or they may have an outright prejudice against local products. Beyond Lua's limited relevance to the local software market at a time when it was already being widely used abroad, Takhteyev also argued that even though it had been developed in order to meet a very specific range of demands for a local client, the language had been written by professionals who, like my imaginary Latin American Studies scholar, spoke in the lingua franca of their field: English. The takeaway, as he sees it, is that the globalization of an industry like software does not enable the emergence of local ways of writing software but rather creates a set of dynamics that cannot be said to undermine the overarching dominance of academic, commercial, and industrial institutions from the Global North.[9]

In his study, Takhteyev pays particular attention to the way in which Rio's software developers deal with those parts of the code where natural languages are used, like the reserved words and the comments. Reserved words are so-called because their meaning is fixed in the language and cannot be defined by a programmer; most widely used programming languages draw their reserved words from English to define basic elements of the syntax: "if" and "else" (conditionals); "int," "float," and "long" (data types); "and," "or" (logical operations); and others. In his fieldwork, Takhteyev found that even local Rio programmers who are not necessarily proficient in English are quite familiar with English reserved words like "if," "break," or "loop." Along with other items of programming, business, and cultural lingo, these foreign linguistic units simply impose themselves as the right ones to use, and to a point, the Rio programmers do not really regard them as being part of the English language, nor do they perceive their use as a concession to a foreign culture. Comments, however, are written statements that are not part of the code and that may contain explanations or clarifications directed at a user who may not be a programmer. Comments, Takhteyev notes, are sometimes written in Portuguese, as when the staff of the company for whom the software has been designed cannot be assumed to be able to read them in English, but in the case of Lua, *both* reserved words *and* comments were written in English from the inception of the project, along with most contributions to its mailing list and its first book-form manual, written by Ierusalimschy. This means that, although they in no way expected or anticipated the language to be used by the English-using global software community, Lua's designers did write it under the criteria that prevail in that community, led by a kind of internalized globalization. In Takhteyev's terms, the Lua team "preemptively disembed[ded] Lua from the local language, avoiding a tie that would have forever limited its use to Portuguese-speaking places," a process that he thinks is often driven by what he calls a "subvocal imagination," a disposition to project "imagined futures that are treated as too unlikely to be publicly presented as a rationale for action, but that nonetheless can affect action profoundly."[10]

Although Takhteyev's explanatory framework veers at times a bit too close to the psychological, it is clear that he has honed in on a very significant puzzle. There are, of course, counterexamples: Potigol, a programming language also developed in Brazil, does take its reserved words from the Portuguese language, and Qriollo, from Argentina, goes further and uses *Porteño*, the unique strain of Spanish spoken in Buenos Aires.[11] But

120 *Sidetracking*

these are both pedagogical projects intended to introduce young people with no access to the English language to the principles of programming (in the case of Potigol) or to allow advanced users to understand how a programming language is made (in the case of Qriollo). It seems fair to assume that pupils who are introduced to the field of programming by way of these two experimental languages and who then wish to continue on this path will soon find themselves in the same hybrid linguistic space as Takhteyev's Rio programmers since they will eventually have to begin using programming languages with English reserved words. As natural as it seems to wish for developments in technology that are responsive to cultural specificity and the needs of those who are left behind by the mindsets of neoliberalism and globalization, these efforts to align programming languages with natural languages may be begging the question: just what is it that we would like a local software to be? At each degree of locality, questions will inevitably arise about the reasons why a language like Portuguese or *Porteño* can play the part of the local language and legitimize themselves as the proper means of access to the culture of a particular enclave and its own most concerns.

It is certainly a mistake to regard software as a "*naturally* placeless" product,[12] but the sense in which a programming language can be said to have a place of origin is far from evident if we attempt to go beyond the anecdotal. The use of English alone does not warrant the assumption that there is a global culture whose values and ways of doing things are thoroughly or predominantly mediated by the most powerful players, and the very idea of a natural or local language is a simplification of a tiered and ongoing process of historical layering. Lua is written using the Latin script, its name means "moon" in Portuguese, and it takes its reserved words from English: these are so many imprints of past and ongoing processes of local, global, and imperial power formations referring back to Latin's tenure as the language of the learned and of the Catholic church, of Portuguese as the language of colonization and the postcolonial state, and of English as the language of Cold War geopolitics and globalization. To this we must add differences in class and education among developers and users in the local context and, just as importantly, the availability of different kinds of hardware and of technicians who are able to operate and maintain it. Although a programming language is just written code, it is palpably traversed by an incredible array of fluctuating and evolving factors. We see then that the description of Lua as an "internationally successful programming language from Brazil," as simple as it sounds, places us in yet another complex nexus where cultural, socio-technical, and historical strands are woven in a unique way: a singularity that, nonetheless, is from Rio in a sense that is far from incidental.

The Languages of Computational Media

The emergence of programming languages drastically redefined communication practices at different levels: with other humans through technology, with machines through programs, and with nature through machines. Although they are a recent arrival, there is certainly a depth to their historicity. Through their links to natural languages, they are obviously intertwined with cultural networks, and they are inextricable from historical configurations of cultural and economic power. To this we must add their kinship with formal languages, mathematics, and the formalisms of modern physics and engineering, each of which has a complex history of its own. As Warren Sack has shown, these different layers have been coevolving since the proto-historical strata of computational cultures, which he traces back to a series of profound transformations in the structure of classical Western educational systems. According to Sack, what we now call software has its roots in a historical conjunction that took place in the context of the French Encyclopedia, whose epistemic structure attempted to integrate the skillsets of the mechanical arts (such as the creation of types) and of the liberal arts (such as the development of clear and convincing arguments).[13] Sacks's suggestive archaeological framework resonates with my own efforts to explore the hybridity of media technologies, something that may seem hard to visualize in the abstract realm of programming languages but that is nonetheless actually there, as a kind of *formal hybridity*. His argument suggests that a formal construct can assemble components extracted from a diverse range of human practices, from the rhythms of manual labor and the classification of artisanal materials to the systematization of knowledge, the pragmatics of public discourse, and the mathematical study of nature. The historicity of such formal constructs calls for an awareness of the geohistorical dynamics of emergence, displacement, relocation, and others.

The contemporary conception of a functional programming language dates back to the mid-1940s, when the German engineer Konrad Zuse created the Plankalkül, described by some as the first high-level programming language. Zuse's language was designed but not implemented, and due to its historical and geographical coordinates, it did not have an immediate impact on the field. The four pillars in the history of programming languages would only appear about a decade later, all of them known by their acronyms: Fortran (Formula Translation, 1957), Lisp (List Processing, 1958), Algol (Algorithmic Language, 1958), and Cobol (Common Business-Oriented Language, 1959). Three of these languages were created in the United States, and the fourth, Algol, was developed in Switzerland by an international team that also included American scientists – one of them was a woman, Jean E. Sammet, who would later make important contributions to the study of the history of programming languages. The group also included the Swiss mathematician Heinz Rutishauser, who had already created Superplan, a language that built on some of Zuse's ideas, and who is responsible for the creation of the reserved word "for" (derived from the German word *für*) to refer to repetitions.[14] Out of this foundational group, Algol stands out for being the first to clearly embrace an international approach: the documentation for Algol 68 was published in numerous languages, including

122 *Sidetracking*

German, French, Russian, Japanese, and Braille, and in the Soviet Union, its standard became the Gost 10859 standard, which included non-ASCII and non-Unicode characters.[15]

It is customary to visually represent the evolution of programming languages through a tree diagram, which depicts new languages as stemming from earlier ones, but the logic of ramification, common root, and hierarchy sheds little light on the historicity of a language like Lua. Most languages take and adapt components from other languages, both previous and contemporary, and in that regard, Lua could be inscribed in the lineage of one of the four inaugural languages, Lisp.[16] Nonetheless, it also shares features with more recent languages like Scheme and Awk, and it is clearly part of a generation that includes JavaScript, Icon, Python, and Tcl, all of which came into existence during the first half of the 1990s.

The sense in which a language is new is not strictly chronological or technical, as each new language is responsive to specific issues that its creators need or wish to address. At the same time, the creation of a programming language requires a deep knowledge of the fundamentals of computing and a thorough understanding of existing languages, which undoubtedly is only possible through acquaintance with the English language and its attendant cultural and institutional opportunities and constraints. This may be unproblematic for those who think that, if the English language is the vehicle of globalization, its origins as a neocolonial language pale against its capacity to enable communication between the most diverse and distant communities. This line of thought is even more compelling when we are concerned with technologies, their development and use, since technology is likewise regarded as an operator of deterritorialization understood as a positive process by which the local power dynamics and traditions of inequality of so-called developing countries can be upended. Nonetheless, lack of access to the English language and to academic or corporate settings in the Global North remains one of the most direct and naturalized forms of exclusion from this and other neoliberal utopias. The Lua team certainly did have access to some of these advantages, but the case remains that their approach to creating the language was undoubtedly informed by the fact that they were working from the periphery. What we need, in a sense, is a keener sense of what these peripheries are actually like or better: of how they are constituted by overlapping layers of territorialized, deterritorialized, and reterritorialized assemblages.

Sunset to Moonrise

Creating a programming language is an extremely demanding task – and yet new languages turn up at a fairly quick rate. The list of those created around 2010 alone includes Google's Go (2009), Mozilla Research's Rust (2010), Apple's Swift (2014), and Facebook's Hack (2014), along with a few more developed by Microsoft. All these examples have the backing of strong companies that provide these languages with support and a solid ground to grow on, offering users an incentive to try it out and contribute to its evolution. In the absence of a strong institution that legitimates them in the eyes of programmers, other languages from the same generation, like Julia (2012), have had a harder time finding a community of users. This may well have been Lua's fate if a series of contingencies had not lined up to make its virtues visible to users who could have easily missed them. Lua is the product of a singular set of circumstances, and its institutional setting is already somewhat unique: although its three main creators came from an academic environment, and Ierusalimschy in particular was engaged in theoretical research on programming languages, the language itself was not an academic exercise. The specific context for Lua's emergence may be described as one of collaboration between academic research and an industrial sector historically inflected by state intervention.

The state company Petrobras was created in 1953 with the mission of securing oil self-sufficiency at a time when Brazil did not have any oil resources to speak of. This meant that, unlike most national oil companies, which are created to extract oil that has already been found, Petrobras was forced to behave like international oil companies and engage in a long-term effort to find oil deposits through scientific analysis and technological innovation. Well into the 1970s, Brazil struggled with oil dependency, but the company was eventually able to use cutting-edge seismic stratigraphy to determine the existence of deep-water deposits and became a leader in the use of new off-shore drilling technologies to extract it.[17] In the process, the Brazilian state became a major consumer of scientific and technological expertise, and this is the background for the creation of Tecgraf, the lab where Lua was conceived.[18] In the early 1990s, Tecgraf was a small lab staffed by PUC-Rio professors and students, and its job was to create interactive graphical programs for several client organizations, including Petrobras. At the time, Ierusalimschy was a consultant at Tecgraf, and Figueiredo was a full-time postdoctoral fellow; Lua is the off-shoot of work that they were doing separately for Petrobras.

Figueiredo's point of departure was DEL, a language that he created in 1992 to fill a very precise gap. Petrobras produced oil extraction simulations using what Figueiredo describes as "huge programs that were very old and refined, and they didn't want to give them up."[19] The simulators were "legacy code that needed strictly formatted input files – typically bare columns of numbers, with no indication of what each number meant."[20] These old programs, however, did not have effective graphic interfaces that would allow users to easily enter the data to be applied in the simulation. Figueiredo created DEL (for Data Entry Language) as a tool for writing data-configuration interfaces, or front ends, that could receive and validate the data and create outputs that could be processed by the various simulation programs. On their end, Ierusalimschy and Celes, who was his Ph.D. student at the time, had created another language for Petrobras, called SOL

124   *Sidetracking*

(for Simple Object Language). SOL was designed to write a different kind of program, "a configurable report generator for lithology profiles"[21] that should have allowed users, mostly geologists, to configure information in different ways using a column-based graph. They equipped SOL with an interpreter, a program that, roughly speaking, translates instructions in a higher-level language into commands that a machine can execute, which in this case was implemented as a C library linked to the main program. They also included an API (application programming interface) through which the main program could access configuration information.[22] In programmer lingo, both DEL and SOL were little languages, one tailored to data configuration and the other to data description. For different reasons, at around the same time, both of these little languages proved insufficient, and Figueiredo, Ierusalimschy, and Celes decided to create a full-blown language to solve their problems. They chose the name LUA, whose initials stand for Language for Application Users in Portuguese but which also means "moon," to signal its connection to SOL, which means "sun."

Lua soon proved to be a highly efficient tool in both Tecgraf and Petrobras, which is exactly what it had been intended to be – and for the team, that may have been enough. From the start, however, the language was certainly conceived with criteria that exceeded those of the context in which it was "embedded," to use Takhteyev's terminology. However, rather than saying that it was "preemptively disembedded," we can see the language as an expression of converging local conditions, some of them coming from Tecgraf and its clients, and others from the team's aims as designers. Undoubtedly, the language was informed by Ierusalimschy's academic and theoretical approach, which drove the team to embrace very exacting criteria of simplicity based on an awareness of how the language could function and grow by being put to work within different systems. These criteria took on a singular shape through the contingent fact that, inspired by SOL, the team built the language around the key idea of using it as an auxiliary tool to be used alongside applications written in more complex languages like C. Figueiredo told me this:

> The main process (at the intellectual level) is to control the conflict between expressiveness and simplicity. This conflict results in the elegance of the language of programming. It is crucial that all major structures of programming and data abstraction can be used in the language, but that does not mean that they have to be directly included in the language design. For example, Lua has only one data structure: the table. With it, we can elegantly implement all other data structures. This requires that tables are implemented very well, but at the same time, it allows the implementation effort to focus on the performance of tables.[23]

This approach was informed by the team's concern for portability, which was in turn directly motivated by the variegated population of their surrounding hardware landscape. As Ierusalimschy told Takhteyev, "In the beginning our goal of portability was Tecgraf's set of computers. . . . So it must run on DEC, on VAX, on *ta ta ta*."[24] The team's design premise was thus to simplify the code by giving the language a modular structure, making it easy to connect with other pieces of code written in other languages according to the needs of individual programmers.

The team also built on SOL's use of an interpreter structured as a library with a C API, and this meant that the language was well-suited to function as a scripting language, which in the context of Tecgraf's interface-oriented projects was an obvious virtue.[25] In the global context, however, the need for this type of functionality was making itself felt, and this accounts for Lua's generational affinities with other scripting languages like Python and JavaScript, created around the same time. Indeed, the Lua team considered using an existing scripting language, but the only one available at the time, Tcl, "had unfamiliar syntax, did not offer good support for data description, and ran only on Unix platforms."[26] They wanted their language to have a simple syntax that would make it accessible to non-professional programmers, data description was one of their key target fields of use, and they needed their language to be multiplatform: in their particular situation, this meant that they should create their own new language, and it so happened that they were in a position to do exactly that.

Lua's success in Tecgraf and Petrobras did not lead it to be used by Brazil's local industry, something that according to Takhteyev may have counted in its favor since "stronger contacts with the [local] industry would have likely entangled the language in local relationships so closely as to make its later international success quite difficult."[27] Presumably, these entanglements would have emerged once Lua had been culturally and legally inscribed, in one way or another, as a commercial product with local commitments. Arguably, however, the conditions under which it was created meant that the Lua team felt no pressure to seek commercial avenues for it at home or abroad – instead, the fact that they were working within Brazil's academic system pushed them to present their work in international academic events within the discursive framework of computer science as a discipline. One might say that this gave the Lua team *time* to track and tackle the evolution of their language at a certain pace, and one could go further and argue that it is access to this kind of pace or *temporality* that is a distinctive function of Lua's embeddedness within a local form of life.

During Lua's first years of existence, the team in Rio continued working on it without being fully aware of its path to global recognition. As Ierusalimschy puts it, they would now and again receive smoke signals as to what was going on, and by the mid-1990s, the project began to consolidate gradually as the team came to realize just how powerful the language could be. In December 1996, the team published an article in an issue of the now-mythical *Dr. Dobb's Journal* devoted to scripting languages. *Dr. Dobb's* was

126 *Sidetracking*

a kind of *Popular Mechanics* for coders, and it typically featured articles that focused on applied digital culture. Bret Mogilefsky, a chief software developer at LucasArts, read that article, and in 1997, he contacted the Lua team with some inquiries about the language. In keeping with the secretive nature of the video game industry, he was far from straightforward about the reasons for his inquiries, but he did let on that he may be using Lua for a project; sure enough, a year later, LucasArts released the AAA computer game *Grim Fandango*, which embedded Lua. As the team later discovered, Mogilefsky went on to become Lua's superspreader in Silicon Valley. In 1999, at the Game Developers Conference in San Jose, California, there was a panel on the topic of scripting languages. The panelists were presenting work samples and discussing the limitations and disappointments that they had encountered in working with various scripting languages, which prompted Mogilefsky, who was in the audience, to share his recent positive experience with Lua. When the Lua team held their first Lua workshop at Adobe in San Jose, in 2005, several of the attendees mentioned that panel as their very first encounter with the language.

To some extent, the particular way in which the language spread after this breakthrough is linked to another crucial factor in this context: licensing. A licensing framework provides clear legal foundations to which developers can refer if they want to use a programming language in their own projects. A sign of its original embeddedness is that Lua's licensing took about a decade to stabilize. Lua 1.1 was released in 1994 under a restrictive license that made it available for academic purposes free of charge but which required commercial uses to be negotiated. This kind of license can easily scare off even those academic projects that may potentially move on to become market-oriented endeavors at a later stage. Growing interest from abroad, and the difficulties involved in any attempt to structure it as a commercial product under Brazilian law, led the team to gain further acquaintance with open-source culture, and they eventually decided to place later versions under an open license. Their first attempt at it was not entirely successful: the Lua team wrote the document themselves and created a kind of collage based on the text of other licenses; the resulting document left many users confused as to the scope of the license, its degree of openness, and its compatibility with the General Public License (GPL), under which users both modify and share modified versions of the software (such licenses are known as a reciprocal licenses). They eventually settled on the MIT license, which is permissive rather than reciprocal.[28] A permissive license allows users to distribute their modified version of a software under a different license, including proprietary licenses; this decision cleared the path for Lua's growth since it allowed proprietary software companies to use it in their commercial products without any further licensing conditions. And so it was that a major media corporation like LucasArts could commercially profit from an indirect product of the Brazilian state's efforts towards resource autonomy.

Learning from Brazil's Computer History

When we dig a little further into the local background for the creation of Lua, we come across a unique and complex deep history. Following the media-archaeological premises of this book, I would now like to activate a retrospective perspective to expose a set of historical conditions that allow us to draw in broad strokes the landscape of computational history in Brazil and to expose the deep roots of computer science and engineering in that South American country. This will allow us to see the contingencies that determined the development of Brazil's technological policies and to high-light the crucial role of underlying historical tensions between autonomy and dependency and between national interests and international techno-logical trajectories.

We have already come across the figure of Konrad Zuse, who created the foundational Plankalkül programming language. Zuse also designed the first Turing-complete computer in 1942 (the Z3), and a few years earlier, in 1936, a mechanical computer (the Z1).[29] A German inventor named Helmut Schreyer (1912–1984) assisted Zuse in developing the design and implemen-tation of the Z1 and Z2 computers, we will see how this branch of develop-ment of computers connects with the developments in Brazil. In late 1939, Zuse was drafted for military duties, and Schreyer requested the German government that he be exempted on account of the potential relevance of their work to the war effort; he submitted a plan to build a large electronic computer, but it was rejected on the basis of what the German military regarded as an extremely long timeline (they apparently did not anticipate the war lasting more than a couple of years). Zuse was eventually excused from duties and went on to work on the Z3, while Schreyer developed his own model. According to Mexican scholar Raúl Rojas, Schreyer himself may have been excused from military service because he had been a member of the National Socialist Party since 1933; in any case, he certainly seems to have enthusiastically devoted his engineering talents to the war effort and spent a great deal of time on a design for an accelerometer for the V2.[30] Schreyer's own model was destroyed as he was trying to bring it to safety on a train to Vienna during the last days of the war. After losing it, he man-aged to reach Vienna and contacted an officer at the Brazilian Embassy who issued him a Brazilian passport that allowed him safe travel to the country, where he was offered work at the Army's Technical School (the ETE).

In 1950, Schreyer published with the ETE a book in Portuguese on the subject of electronic digital computers that featured circuit designs, and in 1960, while teaching at the PUC-Rio's school of engineering, he and other faculty members led a group of students in an end-of-term electronics pro-ject that consisted in designing and assembling a computer. The result, nick-named "Lourinha" ("blondie"), is the first computer to be designed and assembled in Brazil, although it should be noted that Lourinha's design was not directly influenced by Schreyer's earlier projects.[31] There is still much

128 *Sidetracking*

research to be done in this area, but Schreyer's activities in Brazil clearly exemplify the kind of accidental and truncated routes by which information and know-how about new technologies found its way to the subcontinent through most of the twentieth century, the importance of the PUC-Rio.

During his term as president of Brazil (1956–1961), Juscelino Kubitscheck pushed for a plan of accelerated industrial development, and in 1958, under encouragement from Gerardo Maia, a naval officer who had recently completed graduate studies in electrical engineering in the United States, the government created a working group whose task was "to analyze the use of electronic computers in budget calculations."[32] A year later, the government created the Executive Group for the Application of Electronic Computers, which negotiated the purchase of the first two computers to reach the country: a UNIVAC 1105 for the Brazilian Institute of Geography and Statistics (IBGE) and a Burroughs B-305 for PUC-Rio's recently created Center for Data Processing.[33] Apparently, the Kubitscheck administration pushed the IBGE to use the UNIVAC computer to process the results of the 1960 census, which led to all manner of difficulties; the computer's thousands of vacuum tubes consumed great amounts of energy and air conditioning, and there were not enough trained technicians to keep it working. These difficulties pushed the Brazilian government to initiate collaborative programs with local universities, and in particular with PUC-Rio, hoping to create a workforce capable of supporting its efforts to computerize governance within a short timeframe.[34]

The history of computing in Brazil took a drastic turn during the late 1970s and early 1980s. Since 1964, the country had been under a military regime that gave Kubitscheck's development agenda a spin of its own, engaging in a very unique process of nation-building that has been carefully reconstructed by Uruguayan scholar Emanuel Adler.[35] In 1972, the government created CAPRE, an agency whose task was to ensure that the government's computer purchases were adequately evaluated; although this seems like a fairly circumscribed assignment, the agency would play an incredibly important role in Brazil's digital future. CAPRE pushed for the creation of a local computer industry, and a hike in oil prices made the government sympathetic to the policy since it seemed like a plausible way of holding on to some of the foreign currency that they would otherwise have to hand over to multinational corporations like IBM.[36] The policy was also favored by a technological shift: the introduction of the microprocessor by Intel in 1971 meant that the Brazilian market for the upcoming generation of minicomputers was not yet controlled by IBM and the like.[37] Unlike mainframes, minicomputers could be assembled in Brazil from parts obtained from different suppliers in response to local needs, so the idea of kick-starting a local minicomputer industry that could service the needs of local government and industry was able to gain a hold.[38]

In 1974, a computer production company called Cobra was created as a joint venture between the Brazilian state, a local private company, and the

British company Ferranti. Cobra was originally created in response to the Brazilian Navy's purchase of a Ferranti computer system for its vessels, and its mandate was to produce a local computer that could interact with the Ferrantis. Ferranti held a 3% share in the company and agreed to a process of full technology transfer. The company produced the first minicomputers assembled in Brazil, the 700 Series, and after closing a similar technology transfer deal with a small American company, Sycor, went on to produce a second model, the 400 Series, conceived to be sold to local businesses and industry.[39] Cobra also produced Brazil's first domestically designed minicomputer, the G-10, which started out as an academic project, with hardware designed at the University of São Paulo and software from PUC-Rio. The G-10 became the Cobra 500, which was made using mostly locally produced components, but Cobra never managed to carve out a local market beyond its initial client base of government institutions and the armed forces. When IBM announced its intent to bring their own minicomputer to the market (the System 32), Cobra's fate seemed to be doomed, but 11 local banks joined to acquire 39% of its shares and keep it afloat.[40] This crisis precipitated the creation of what came to be known as Brazil's market reserve policy.

Under the new policy, the Brazilian government effectively pushed its academic and industrial sectors to develop a strong infrastructure capable of sustaining research and development in the field of computer science (known in Brazil as "informatics"). Although it is succinctly described as a protectionist program, Adler has argued that Brazil's efforts to create a national computer industry exemplify a "pragmatic" understanding of economic and technological dependency, which he contrasts with the "structuralist view that the world capitalist system necessarily leads to stagnation and to eternal dependence."[41] As Adler puts it, the economists who developed this approach, led by José Pelúcio, argued that "Brazil would acquire autonomy not by rejecting foreign technology but by attaining the ability to make technological decisions."[42] An agency called FINEP, led by Pelúcio and attached to the National Development Bank (BNDE), was assigned the task of steering local industry towards the nation's technological needs and the National Research Council–funded fellowships and research programs in local research and academic centers.[43] The government eventually formulated the market reserve policy, whose guiding assumptions have been described by Ivan da Costa Marques as follows:

> The Brazilian state could not possibly increase funds for research (financial applications without direct return) in the proportion needed to keep the pace of growth of the teams of professionals if a program for local development of technology was not taken seriously. Financial resources for product conception and design would have to come directly from the market, and business firms were the consecrated form of organization for this kind of job. Finally, if on the one hand foreign capital was

130 *Sidetracking*

> not interested in investing in the development of minicomputer systems in Brazil, and on the other hand Brazilian private capital was not interested in investing in minicomputer manufacturing in Brazil, it was a priori understood that, under a regime of "free competition," the game was lost to foreign technology.[44]

The market reserve, implemented in 1977 through CAPRE, sought first and foremost to use import controls to favor minicomputer production companies that conducted research and development locally, and to thus create a context in which the entire life cycle of minicomputer technologies could be handled locally.[45] As Da Costa explains, the assumption was that a market for locally produced hardware could not be expected to emerge otherwise and that once it did, Brazilian companies would tend to prefer computers designed specifically to meet their needs.

As I have noted, throughout this process, Brazil was ruled by a military dictatorship, and Adler somewhat paradoxically attributes the relative success of the market reserve policy to what he describes as a "subversive elite" made up of technocrats who were able to promote an antidependency ideology within an unlikely political setting.[46] Takhteyev, for his part, reads the market reserve as "an alliance in pursuit of globalisation"[47] between engineers educated abroad, who wanted to create local versions of the institutions where they had learned their profession, and a government that was looking to modernize its practices in an effort to be perceived as a player in the global community of nations. In any case, by the mid-1980s, the policy, which was defined in terms of the minicomputer as a paradigm, was put to the test by the PC revolution. Initially, the Brazilian government regarded the new microcomputers as a mere extension of the minicomputer and placed them under the same restrictions, but at this point, the local market basically overgrew the policy as Brazilians were able to buy smuggled IBM PCs at a third of the price of the locally produced minis.

A 1984 law attempted to adapt the market reserve policy to the new situation, but it was clearly destined to disintegrate eventually. Nonetheless, and although the country's shift to democracy in 1989 brought a swift end to its protectionist inclinations, the Brazilian state has maintained an active approach to policy with respect to computer technologies. The next law on the subject, brought to Congress in 1991 by Fernando Collor, Brazil's first democratically elected president after the dictatorship, was swiftly approved and instated an abrupt opening to the global market, following the neoliberal tenet that open competition with foreign companies would strengthen the local sector. The law also purported to incentivize the continuance of local research and development and collaboration with local academic institutions through tax exemptions, and its two following revisions in 2001 and 2004 attempted to ensure a greater degree of control over these tax-exempt research activities.[48] As one of Takhteyev's interviewees argues, the context in which Lua was created was directly impacted by these circumstances: the sudden downsizing of Brazil's homegrown hardware industry left behind many unemployed electrical engineers who switched to software development as a tenable professional alternative.[49] At that point, moreover, academic institutions, chief among them PUC-Rio's Department of Computer Sciences or Informatics, were already well established as advanced research centers with links to local industry. As the Lua team put it in their own historical account, the market reserve also informed the practices of companies like Petrobras, which "could not afford, either politically or financially, to buy customized software from abroad" since "they would have to go through a complicated bureaucratic process to prove that their needs could not be met by Brazilian companies,"[50] which is why Petrobras relied on Tecgraf to fulfill its programming needs. Just as importantly, under the market reserve, Petrobras "had a limited choice of what computers it used, depending on who had been allowed to bring computers into Brazil in a particular year,"[51] which created the hybrid assortment of hardware that motivated the Lua team to design a highly portable language.

The Visibility of Code

After a brief and necessarily incomplete expedition through the deep historical context of computer history in Brazil, in which PUC-Rio has played a major role since the 1960s, it may also be useful to revisit a sequence of events that will allow us to gain a broader perception of the socio-cultural ambiance within which Lua was created. As Adler's book *The Power of Ideology* clearly demonstrates, Brazil's historical efforts towards technological autonomy played an extremely important role in configuring local attitudes and practices.[52] But it can be argued that Brazilian culture also established a very unique dialogue with technology through a long-standing engagement with techno-aesthetics through the practice of the media arts. From quite early on, Brazilian artists explored and adapted protocomputational and early computational technologies with creative purposes, and their artistic experiments clearly elaborate on some of the key topics discussed in this chapter: writing, computational language, programming, and image codification in a variety of meaningful ways.

The emergence of computing as a media technology in fact predates the arrival of actual computers in Brazil. Geraldo de Barros was a paramount visual artist who made remarkable contributions to Brazilian concretism, establishing meaningful international connections with many artists, including the founders of the Ulm School of Design. The broad spectrum of his production, which spans experimental photography, abstract painting, furniture design, and other creative media, attests to his creative versatility. Around 1949, De Barros was working as a part-time employee at Banco do Brasil, where he came into contact with a group of colleagues who were working with tabulators, pre-computer algorithmic devices that used punched cards to store information (Brazil's census results had actually been processed with tabulators since the 1920s). De Barros was intrigued by the matrix-like cards peppered with rectangular holes and brought a few of them to his darkroom to use in some photographic experiments. He replaced the negative with the punched cards and came up with a set of experimental photographic works bearing distinctive geometric patterns that even today we could easily identify as instances of digitally coded information (Figure 4.2). De Barros produced seven pieces using the cards and included them in a large series of constructed photographs that he called *Fotoformas*, where he suggested a kind of visual architecture by juxtaposing different idioms of visual abstraction.[53] These seven images are one of the earliest attempts to transform units of coded binary information – the bits represented by filled or empty rectangles in a card – into a constructive visual element analogous to the pixel, all of it by photochemical means. With them, De Barros posed questions that we are still grappling with, about the blurring of the boundaries between the readable and the visible, and the mutation of these notions when they are removed from the naturalized substrate of the human agent.[54] The *Fotoformas* series is regarded today as one of the landmarks of artistic photography made in Brazil, and the Instituto Moreira Salles holds the archive in Rio de Janeiro. Recently, the seven

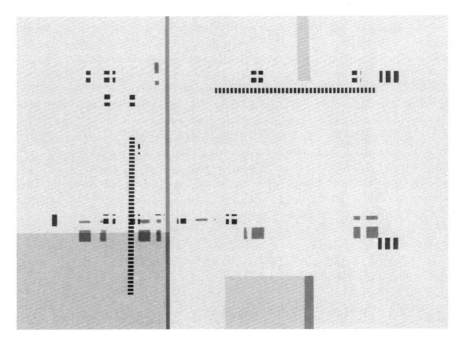

Figure 4.2 Fotoforma by Geraldo de Barros; single copy composed in the dark room with tabulator's punched cards, 1949–1952.

Source: Courtesy of Fabiana de Barros and Musée de l'Elysée, Lausanne

Fotoformas made with punched cards have been gaining the attention and recognition that they deserve as contributions to the history of the interaction between the arts and technology, and one of them has been acquired by New York's Museum of Modern Art.

In 1952, De Barros was one of the founding members of Grupo Ruptura, an avant-garde collective that developed various aesthetic strategies grounded on a unique local take on concretism. Brazilian concretism in the visual arts was closely connected to the Argentine movement of the same name and to the ideas of the Swiss artist and designer Max Bill; they were also closely related to a group of poets who were interested in the use-value of the materiality of language as exemplified by new experiments in graphic design and advertising.[55] Another member of Ruptura was Waldemar Cordeiro, a Brazilian artist of Italian origins who in the 1960s set out on a fruitful collaboration with Giorgio Moscati, a professor in the Institute of Physics at the University of São Paulo. In 1968, Cordeiro and Moscati began to work on a series of experiments regarded today as the earliest examples of computer art in Brazil.[56] Their first project in this direction was a program aptly called *BEABÁ* (ABCs), which generated new six-letter words by alternating consonants and vowels.[57] They continued to work in the same direction and eventually assembled the results of their aesthetic explorations with computer-generated linguistic artifacts under the title "Informative Content of Three Consonants and Three Vowels Treated by Computer." Cordeiro and Moscati then switched their interest from language as a result to language as a material for producing and reproducing visual information through algorithmic formalization (Figure 4.3).

They began to work with typographic characters and symbols to explore the codification of figurative images, and to do so, they wrote a program in Fortran that could be used to produce printed images through an IBM 360 Model 44 that received data input via punched cards. Their concern was now to use the computer to apply mathematical transformations to images appropriated from the popular media and to translate them into a configuration of letters and characters that could be used to create a basic grayscale palette.[58] In 1969, they exhibited a triptych titled *Derivadas de uma imagem* (Derivatives of an image) produced by translating a photo from an illustrated "Dia dos Namorados"[59] (The day of the lovers) advertisement using a proto ASCII system. The two derivatives of the original image were created by applying two mathematical principles, transposition and unfolding (Figure 4.4). As Moscati explained, the piece was an effort to make mathematically modelled physical principles visible through computerized procedures:

> [Cordeiro] gave me a numerical matrix, which represented the varying intensity of darkness. . . . [Y]ou can see the zero-order image, the original. I would say – and I believe Cordeiro would agree with me on that – that this zero-order image is nothing; it isn't art, it's just a transcription without any meaning. What is meaningful though is the transformation

134 Sidetracking

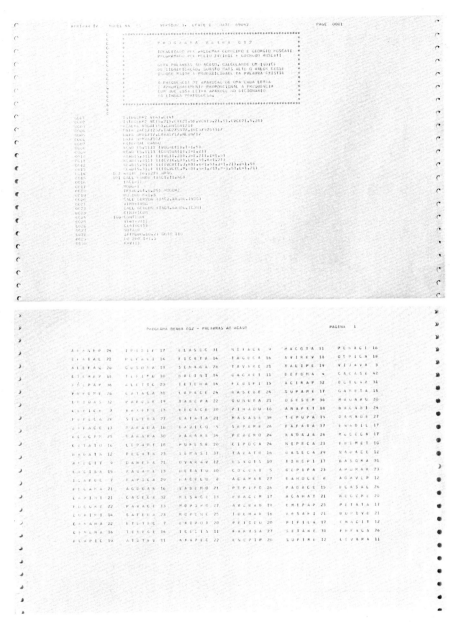

Figure 4.3 BEABÁ computational experimental poetry by Waldemar Cordeiro and Giorgio Moscati, 1968.

Source: Courtesy of Analivia Cordeiro and ZKM | Zentrum für Kunst und Medien, Karlsruhe

Figure 4.4 Derivadas de una Imagen, the first computer visual art project made in Brazil by Waldemar Cordeiro and Giorgio Moscati, 1969.
Source: Courtesy of Analivia Cordeiro and ZKM | Zentrum für Kunst und Medien, Karlsruhe

136 *Sidetracking*

process: the zero-order image and then the derivative, the comparison between both of them; but each one is meaningless in isolation; that's how I see it.[60]

The *Derivadas* have been described as a search for a universal language by American scholar Adrian Anagnost,[61] and they can be said to presciently outline a field of interaction between natural language, code, and visual media that continues to inform the work of many contemporary media artists. As Moscati insists, their intended achievement was not the image that resulted from applying the derivative to its own previous degree but the program that allowed them to produce both the zero-degree image and its derivatives. This, he claims, connects to "an open question about biological, anthropological, [and] perceptual evolution,"[62] yet another accurate (if ambitious) intuition as to the potential repercussions of the new kind of formal exercise in which they were engaging. These artists experienced code as a portal that could be used to travel between the realms of nature, culture, and technology, and for that reason, they were able to see beyond its boundedness to expensive machines and industrial pragmatics.

Like De Barros, Cordeiro and Moscati were interested in denaturalizing the phenomenological immediacy of the photographic image and in destabilizing the sense that our visual world is made out of mid-sized objects perceived against a background. They sought to do this by factoring in the code-like constituents of perception and culture, although they could be said to have been working in reverse directions: De Barros used the photographic process to produce images that were of more than one kind simultaneously – a representation of an object, the trace of a chemical process, and a morsel of coded data. Cordeiro and Moscati, in turn, translated figurative imagery bearing a coded commercial message into a visible structure of characters and symbols, allowing many layers of meaning to permeate, reinforce, and undermine each other. De Barros brought digital information into the realm of visual objects, while Cordeiro and Moscati dissolved visual objects into the infinite malleable realm of code. In both cases, however, it was the capacity to transform one kind of image into the other that led the artists to take an interest in tabulators, computers, and code as tools for atomizing and recomposing cultural givens. Although limited, these are two very telling examples of how a local cultural setting can receive or engender media technologies and inscribe them within a continuum of cultural practices that is not predetermined by the concerns of foreign designers or manufacturers.

The aforementioned creative uses of computational technologies in the 1950s and 1960s highlight the role of Brazilian artists who were the first to tap into the creative interactions between code-writing and image-making. In the altogether different cultural domain of the computer sciences, this was exactly what the Lua team were concerned with when they created the language. In the algorithmic artworks programmed in Fortran by Cordeiro and Moscati, the images are made out of constitutive elements drawn from the atoms of written language: letters and typographic characters – they certainly did not create anything as complex and abstract as a programming language, but they were keenly aware of the fluid and porous relationship between the linguistic and the computational.[63] Somewhat provocatively, Lua, too, can be read as part of this lineage, not only because it originated as a data visualization program but also through its evolution as a scripting language that would go on to have a significant impact on a contemporary form of industrialized artmaking: video game development.

Conclusion

When I asked Ierusalimschy about the reasons why Lua was so quickly embraced by the video game industry, he claimed that it was "with a bit of luck,"[64] and his appreciation seems correct. Although the language was conceived under entirely unrelated circumstances, it was fortuitously designed in a way that made it extremely suitable for use as a scripting language in game development. As I have mentioned, Lua's suitability stems first and foremost from its ability to work in tandem with heavy and complex languages like C and C++. A game's engine, for example, is a vast and intricate program that developers cannot afford to make significant changes to, and Lua's functionality as a code for embeddable programs allows them to use it as a module that handles graphics and other computationally costly real-time processes in conversation with the engine. Lua's portability also made it particularly suitable for video game developers because games need to run on different devices, including proprietary CPUs, specific consoles, and iOS and Android smartphones. In response to the needs of these users, the Lua team worked to further "[reduce] the dependency of Lua's core on the standard C library" and make the language optimally operational in platforms that do not support the "full standard C library."[65]

As the community of users has grown, the Lua team has carefully crafted new versions in response to concerns like these, but they have done it without sacrificing any of their original design premises. An American game developer interviewed by Takhteyev claims that this is one of the reasons why the language has a distinctively elegant structure. He explains this remark by comparing Lua's evolution to that of a likely contender, JavaScript. In his view, JavaScript suffered from a "premature stabilization" precipitated by its massive and rapid embrace by web developers just when that field was exploding. Because it had standardized so quickly in response to the needs of an instantly large and varied community, the language was cluttered and complicated, while Lua had developed much more gradually for a few years within a small community, which allowed its developers to fix bugs and introduce innovations without sacrificing the consistency and simplicity of the language.[66] These appreciations by an industry user reflect the Lua team's own programmatic commitments.

138 Sidetracking

In the 2007 edition of the ACM History of Programming Languages Conference (HOPL), an event that happens only every 15 years, the team was invited to talk about Lua's history (Figure 4.5). HOPL is organized by the Association for Computing Machinery's Special Interest Group on Programming Languages, and it typically features presentations by their authors on the history of languages like C, Algol, Lisp, and Haskell (the fact that back in 2005 Lua was already regarded as a member of this group is outstanding). In the conclusions to their presentation, the team describes the rationale behind Lua's unique evolution as follows:

> With hindsight, we consider that being raised by a small committee has been very positive for the evolution of Lua. Languages designed by large committees tend to be too complicated and never quite fulfill the expectations of their sponsors. Most successful languages are raised rather than designed. They follow a slow bottom-up process, starting as a small language with modest goals. The language evolves as a consequence of actual feedback from real users, from which design flaws surface and new features that are actually useful are identified. This

Figure 4.5 Luiz Henrique de Figueiredo (left) and Roberto Ierusalimschy (right), photo taken at the third *ACM Conference on History of Programming Languages, HOPL*, June 9, 2007, San Diego, California, USA.

Source: Courtesy of Lua team

describes the evolution of Lua quite well. We listen to users and their suggestions, but we include a new feature in Lua only when all three of us agree; otherwise, it is left for the future. It is much easier to add features later than to remove them. This development process has been essential to keep the language simple, and simplicity is our most important asset. Most other qualities of Lua – speed, small size, and portability – derive from its simplicity.[67]

As the team elaborates, "Lua is best described as a closed-development, open-source project," which means that "even though the source code is freely available for scrutiny and adaptation, Lua is not developed in a collaborative way."[68] This modus operandi signals a unique way of embracing the open-source philosophy, by which Lua remains rooted in its point of origin and the community that raised it. Of course, the Lua community has developed many strategies to mobilize the collective intelligence of Lua programmers around the world, but the fact that all crucial decisions are reviewed by a small and efficient team has proven to be extremely wise. In that sense, and although Takhteyev is right in suggesting that it makes no sense to speak of Brazilian software as one would of Brazilian music, one is nonetheless tempted to say that Lua remains *located* in Brazil, to the extent that this location is a condition of its controlled evolution.

This exercise of control over the evolution of the language, however, must be balanced against the fact that, due to its license, Lua has by now taken on a dizzying array of guises and mutations. Take as an example the massively popular multiplayer online role-playing game *World of Warcraft* (WoW), released in 2004. Since then, a large community has been constantly at work expanding the game, and several books have been published with the programming environment. The language used to write expansions of the game is known within this community as the World of Warcraft programming language, but it is in fact Lua. WoW programmers have created a massive collection of libraries that are disconnected from Lua's main development track, and they have thus collectively generated an entirely separate world. A similar and more recent example is Roblox, an extremely successful online game platform. Roblox is very popular among teenagers worldwide because it also allows users to create simple games on their own (Figure 4.6). The language to code in Roblox is also Lua, and this has led many teenagers to take their first steps in programming with Lua – indeed, one of the most widely used programming manuals for Lua in Roblox was actually written by a thirteen-year-old gamer and developer, Brandon LaRouche, which goes to show just how simple and elegant the language is.[69]

Lua's spread among these gaming communities determines its remarkable – if somewhat invisible – role as a media technology with an impact on global culture. As these few examples show, this impact must be characterized as multiple and dispersed through the variety of communities that have

140 *Sidetracking*

Figure 4.6 Boy visits Roblox-Lua booth. Roblox is an online entertainment platform that encourages users to program games and play games made by other users; the language to program the games is Lua. Booth during CEE 2019, the largest electronics trade show in Ukraine.

Source: Photo by panama7; courtesy of Depositphotos

come to embrace the language. In his insightful book *Cultural Code*, Phillip Penix-Tadsen has studied the way in which video games are used and experienced in Latin American societies. In his account, games uniquely exemplify the capacity of media technologies to introduce positive feedback loops that open up new spaces for social creativity: as he puts it, games use culture and culture uses games, which entails that the distinction between the producers and the consumers of a media technology is never clear-cut.[70] This line of analysis can be rephrased in terms of a broader question that has surfaced in different ways throughout this book: as we have seen, while technological development is often a driver for cultural change, it is itself inflected by the cultural settings where they emerge or into which they are brought. In the present context, we might say that through its specific role in video game development, Lua is a technology from Latin America that is now an agent of change within an extensive and globally distributed variety of positive feedback loops between technology and culture.

Lua is also an established presence in more secluded settings of the digital world: it is widely used by hackers and network security analysts in applications like Nmap, which can be deployed to verify open ports and determine which programs are running in each machine within a system. Again, these users know the language that they are using as the scripting programming language of Nmap, with no awareness of its source or of the many other settings in which the same language is used. The recently growing use of Lua in object-embedded applications makes this situation even more extreme: in 2020, Celes was hanging out with a friend who had recently acquired a new Volvo car and, as he flipped through the manual, came across Lua's name in the licenses section (Lua is embedded in the vehicle's control panel). As I later discovered, Mercedes Benz also uses Lua in 3 of 11 components that feature embedded computational tools in its C-Class 205 model (the head unit, the taximeter, and the emergency system). The Lua team does not keep track of who is using the language, but Lua licenses appear in the manuals of products from a growing range of major companies, including Logitech, Huawei, Olivetti, Technicolor, Samsung, Verizon, and Cisco. As the industrial version of the Internet of Things expands, embedded systems are developed in response to very particular conditions, and as a result, they yield a very fragmented landscape; by being inscribed within these myriad systems, Lua is becoming dispersed into a fluid multiplicity of disconnected worlds. The resulting paradox might even lead us to question the identity criteria for an artifact like Lua: is Lua the located language carefully raised like a plant by Ierusalimschy, Figueiredo, and Celes, and rooted in their lifeworld, or is its identity dissolved in the dispersed and multitudinous adaptations and transformations of its code in the fathomless world of applications? The resulting double image of what Lua is could be said to count as an appropriately intractable representation of the kind of network that constitutes the contemporary global socio-technical landscape.

With this in mind, we can now return to our starting question about the relationship between a programming language and its place of origin. Takhteyev describes Lua as a "an attempt to bring into alignment a wide range of resources, both local and global, in the production of a global project aligned with local needs."[71] As I have suggested, one of these local resources is time or, rather, a temporality that is not directly hooked to that of the global hardware and media industries. Our present time, drunk on the idea of acceleration, has embraced a simplistic view of Moore's law of semiconductor industry evolution that postulates an exponentially faster expansion of the capabilities of hardware. As a result, many software tools, including programming languages, are developed under the assumption that hardware will eventually have the power to run all manner of programs with no limitations. The risk seems obvious: a haphazard and ad hoc approach to programming that banks on a speculatively bloated and commercially driven hardware industry whose environmental repercussions are already making themselves felt. Disengaged from these accelerated timeframes, the Lua team works under a different interpretation of Moore's law: in their view, the acceleration of hardware performativity simply entails that there will be a wider variety of hardware made up of accumulated historical layers, which means that a programming language should be able to

142 *Sidetracking*

function in computational machines both old and new. As we have seen, this approach is a direct consequence of the particular circumstances in which Lua was created, but it is also an indirect reflection of the pathways that configure the global technoscape as a heterogeneous and historically layered space. The hardware environment within which Lua was created, populated by the assorted uncoordinated systems that for one reason or another were in use at Tecgraf and Petrobras, is in fact a metonymy for the true global technoscape as it looks from the Global South, where the present is not exhausted by market novelty but is rather composed of a cluttered and noisy texture of times, locations, and languages.

Notes

1 John C. Reynolds, *Theories of Programming Languages* (Cambridge: Cambridge University Press, 1998), ix–xii.
2 In his classic 1919 essay on "Thought," Frege defined language as a sensible vehicle for expressing thought, which he understood as non-sensible. Any attempt to speak about thought, he then argued, would inevitably lead to a "struggle with language" since "the sensible imposes itself repeatedly and results in an image-like expression that is therefore inauthentic." Gottlob Frege, "Der Gedanke", in *Logische Untersuchungen* (Göttingen: Vandenhoek & Ruprecht, 2003), 46. The task of a formal logic understood as an artificial language inspired by mathematical formalism would be to prevent these struggles.
3 Rajive Joshi, "Working with Strongly Typed Data Models in Lua for Building Industrial Internet of Things (IIoT) Applications," paper presented at the Lua Workshop 2016, San Francisco, October 13–14, 2016.
4 Federico Biancuzzi and Shane Warden, *Masterminds of Programming: Conversations with the Creators of Major Programming Languages* (Sebastopol: O'Reilly Media, 2009), 165.
5 Lua's first and most impactful user base outside its place of origin has been among computer game developers. Successful games such as *Escape from Monkey Island, World of Warcraft, Angry Birds,* and more recently, Roblox all use Lua extensively. An inventory in Wikipedia lists literally hundreds of games that use it. Lua is also available in MediaWiki, which means that Wikipedia itself uses it as its template scripting language. Lua is used in embedded systems for keyboards, routers, and automobiles; it has been used in interface development, most notably in Adobe's Photoshop Lightroom. The influential GitHub online code platform uses Lua in its Pages hosting service.
6 Luiz Henrique de Figueiredo, interview with author, May 11, 2021.
7 Roberto Ierusalimschy, Luiz Henrique de Figueiredo, and Waldemar Celes, "The Evolution of Lua," paper presented at the Third ACM SIGPLAN History of Programming Languages Conference (HOPL-III), San Diego, June 9–10, 2007, 9.
8 Yury Takhteyev, *Coding Places: Software Practice in a South American City* (Cambridge: MIT Press, 2012), 99.
9 Takhteyev, *Coding Places*, 93–114.
10 Takhteyev, *Coding Places*, 55.
11 See: GitHub, "Potigol," accessed August 1, 2021, https://github.com/potigol; GitHub, "Qriollo," accessed August 1, 2021, https://qriollo.github.io/.
12 Takhteyev, *Coding Places*, 94.
13 Warren Sack, *The Software Arts* (Cambridge: MIT Press, 2019), 57–78.

14 Heinz Rutishauser, "Über Automatische Rechenplanfertigung bei programmgesteuerten Rechenmaschinen." *Zeitschrift für angewandte Mathematik und Mechanik* 31, no. 8–9 (1951): 255.

15 Peter Naur, "The European Side of the Last Phase of the Development of ALGOL 60." *History of Programming Languages* (1978): 92–139.

16 Ierusalimschy, Figueiredo, and Celes, "The Evolution of Lua," 4.

17 Tyler Priest, "Petrobras in the History of Offshore Oil," in *New Order and Progress: Development and Democracy in Brazil*, edited by Ben Ross Schneider (Oxford: Oxford University Press, 2016), 64–65.

18 Takhteyev, *Coding Places*, 143.

19 Takhteyev, *Coding Places*, 143.

20 Ierusalimschy, Figueiredo, and Celes, "The Evolution of Lua," 3.

21 Ierusalimschy, Figueiredo, and Celes, "The Evolution of Lua," 3.

22 Ierusalimschy, Figueiredo, and Celes, "The Evolution of Lua," 3.

23 Figueiredo, interview.

24 Takhteyev, *Coding Places*, 151.

25 Ierusalimschy, Figueiredo, and Celes, "The Evolution of Lua," 4.

26 Ierusalimschy, Figueiredo, and Celes, "The Evolution of Lua," 4.

27 Takhteyev, *Coding Places*, 157.

28 On the history of the MIT license see Jerome H. Salzer, "The Origin of the 'MIT License.'" *IEEE Annals of the History of Computing* 42, no. 4 (2020): 94–98.

29 Andrés Burbano, "Between Punched Film Stock and the First Computers: The Work of Konrad Zuse." *Relive: Media Art Histories* 1 (2013): 135–148.

30 Raúl Rojas, "Helmut Schreyer: Eine deutsche Karriere," *Telepolis*, January 24, 2010, www.heise.de/tp/features/Helmut-Schreyer-eine-Deutsche-Karriere-3384053.html.

31 Marilza de Lourdes Cardi and Jorge Muniz Barreto, "Primórdios da computação no Brasil." Paper presented at the II Simpósio de História da Informática na América Latina e Caribe, Medellín, October 1–5, 2012, 2, 4. Co-author Muniz Barreto was in fact part of the group of students who assembled Lourinha.

32 Lourdes Cardi and Muniz Barreto, "Primórdios," 3.

33 Lourdes Cardi and Muniz Barreto, "Primórdios," 3.

34 Takhteyev, *Coding Places*, 104–105.

35 Emanuel Adler, *The Power of Ideology: The Quest for Technological Autonomy in Argentina and Brazil* (Berkeley: University of California Press, 1987), 151–198

36 Takhteyev, *Coding Places*, 108.

37 Emanuel Adler, "Ideological 'Guerrillas' and the Quest for Technological Autonomy: Brazil's Domestic Computer Industry." *International Organization* 40, no. 3 (1986): 684.

38 Takhteyev, *Coding Places*, 108.

39 Adler, "Ideological 'Guerrillas,'" 689.

40 Adler, "Ideological 'Guerrillas,'" 690.

41 Adler, "Ideological 'Guerrillas,'" 686.

42 Adler, "Ideological 'Guerrillas,'" 686.

43 Adler, "Ideological 'Guerrillas,'" 688.

44 Ivan da Costa Marques, "Brazil's Computer Market Reserve: Democracy, Authoritarianism, and Ruptures." *IEEE Annals of the History of Computing* 37 (2015): 4.

45 Da Costa Marques, "Brazil's Computer Market Reserve," 6.

46 Adler, "Ideological 'Guerrillas,'" 705.

47 Takhteyev, *Coding Places*, 110.

144 *Sidetracking*

48 Henrique Luiz Cukierman, "Computer Technology in Brazil: From Protectionism and National Sovereignty to Globalization and Market Competitiveness." *Information & Culture* 48, no. 4 (2013): 482–502.
49 Takhteyev, *Coding Places*, 111.
50 Ierusalimschy, Figueiredo, and Celes, "The Evolution of Lua," 3.
51 Takhteyev, *Coding Places*, 152.
52 Adler, *The Power of Ideology*.
53 See: Danielle Stewart, "Geraldo de Barros: Photography as Construction." *H-ART: Revista de historia, teoría y crítica de arte* 2 (2018): 76–77.
54 Andrés Burbano, "Photo(Info)Graphy: Gerardo de Barros and the New Media," in *Gerarde de Barros*, edited by Fabiana de Barros (São Paulo: Sesc, 2013), 325–329.
55 For a brief outline, see art historian Irene Small's introductory remarks to her curatorial project *Verbicovisual: Brazilian Concrete Poetry*, www.lehman.cuny.edu/ciberletras/v17/introjacksonsmall.htm.
56 Rachel Price and Giampaolo Bianconi, "Rachel Price on Waldemar Cordeiro's Computer Art"." *Post: Notes on Art in a Global Context*, May 23, 2018, https://post.moma.org/rachel-price-on-waldemar-cordeiros-computer-art/.
57 Priscila Arantes, "Waldemar Cordeiro e a Arteônica." *Modos: Revista de história da arte* 5, no. 2 (2021): 87–98.
58 Moscati and Cordeiro divided the image into a matrix with a total of 10.976 points, with a grayscale of 7 points. Cordeiro manually made the grid and then manually assigned a number from 0 to 6, depending on the black level of the point.
59 Celebrated on June 12, somehow similar to Saint Valentine's Day but with important cultural differences.
60 Giorgio Moscati, "Art and Computing," *Ekac.org*, n.d., www.ekac.org/moscati.html.
61 Adrian Anagnost, "Internationalism, Brasilidade, and Politics: Waldemar Cordeiro and the Search for a Universal Language." *Hemisphere: Visual Cultures of the Americas* 3, no. 1 (2010): 23.
62 Moscati, "Art and Computing."
63 In 1972, Cordeiro established the Center of Image Processing at the University of Campinas Art and designed a project for the Instituto de Artes (the implementation came to a halt because of his sudden death). In 1973, he died of a heart attack when he was 48, in São Paulo.
64 Roberto Ierusalimschy, interview with author, February 15, 2021.
65 Ierusalimschy, Figueiredo, and Celes, "The Evolution of Lua," 23.
66 Takhteyev, *Coding Places*, 142.
67 Ierusalimschy, Figueiredo, and Celes, "The Evolution of Lua," 23.
68 Ierusalimschy, Figueiredo, and Celes, "The Evolution of Lua," 23.
69 Brandon LaRouche, *Basic ROBLOX Lua Programming* (n.p.: CreateSpace Independent Publishing Platform, 2012).
70 Phillip Penix-Tadsen, *Cultural Code: Video Games and Latin America* (Cambridge: MIT Press, 2016), 18–29.
71 Takhteyev, *Coding Places*, 117.

Bibliography

Adler, Emanuel. "Ideological 'Guerrillas' and the Quest for Technological Autonomy: Brazil's Domestic Computer Industry." *International Organization* 40, no. 3 (1986): 673–705.

Lua   145

————. *The Power of Ideology: The Quest for Technological Autonomy in Argentina and Brazil*. Berkeley: University of California Press, 1987.

Anagnost, Adrian. "Internationalism, Brasilidade, and Politics: Waldemar Cordeiro and the Search for a Universal Language." *Hemisphere: Visual Cultures of the Americas* 3, no. 1 (2010): 23–41.

Arantes, Priscila. "Waldemar Cordeiro e a Arteônica." *Modos: Revista de história da arte* 5, no. 2 (2021): 87–98.

Biancuzzi, Federico and Shane Warden. *Masterminds of Programming: Conversations with the Creators of Major Programming Languages*. Sebastopol: O'Reilly Media, 2009.

Burbano, Andrés. "Between Punched Film Stock and the First Computers: The Work of Konrad Zuse." *Relive: Media Art Histories* 1 (2013): 135–148.

————. "Photo(Info)Graphy: Gerardo de Barros and the New Media." In *Gerardo de Barros*, edited by Fabiana de Barros. São Paulo: Sesc, 2013, 325–329.

Cukierman, Henrique Luiz. "Computer Technology in Brazil: From Protectionism and National Sovereignty to Globalization and Market Competitiveness." *Information & Culture* 48, no. 4 (2013): 482–502.

Da Costa Marques, Ivan. "Brazil's Computer Market Reserve: Democracy, Authoritarianism, and Ruptures." *IEEE Annals of the History of Computing* 37 (2015): 2–13.

De Lourdes Cardi, Marilza and Jorge Muniz Barreto. "Primórdios da computação no Brasil." Paper presented at the II Simpósio de História da Informática na América Latina e Caribe, Medellín, October 1–5, 2012.

Frege, Gottlob. "Der Gedanke." In *Logische Untersuchungen*. Göttingen: Vandenhoek & Ruprecht, 2003, 35–62.

Ierusalimschy, Roberto, Luiz Henrique de Figueiredo, and Waldemar Celes, "The Evolution of Lua." Paper presented at the Third ACM SIGPLAN History of Programming Languages Conference (HOPL-III), San Diego, June 9–10, 2007.

Joshi, Rajive. "Working with Strongly Typed Data Models in Lua for Building Industrial Internet of Things (IIoT) Applications." Paper presented at the Lua Workshop 2016, San Francisco, October 13–14, 2016.

LaRouche, Brandon. *Basic ROBLOX Lua Programming*. N.p.: CreateSpace Independent Publishing Platform, 2012.

Moscati, Giorgio. "Art and Computing," *Ekac.org*, n.d., www.ekac.org/moscati. html.

Naur, Peter. "The European Side of the Last Phase of the Development of ALGOL 60." *History of Programming Languages* 13, no. 8 (1978): 92–139.

Penix-Tadsen, Phillip. *Cultural Code: Video Games and Latin America*. Cambridge: MIT Press, 2016.

Price, Rachel and Giampaolo Bianconi. "Rachel Price on Waldemar Cordeiro's Computer Art." *Post: Notes on Art in a Global Context*, May 23, 2018, https://post.moma.org/rachel-price-on-waldemar-cordeiros-computer-art/.

Priest, Tyler. "Petrobras in the History of Offshore Oil." In *New Order and Progress: Development and Democracy in Brazil*, edited by Ben Ross Schneider. Oxford: Oxford University Press, 2016, 53–77.

Reynolds, John C. *Theories of Programming Languages*. Cambridge: Cambridge University Press, 1998.

146 *Sidetracking*

Rojas, Raúl. "Helmut Schreyer: Eine deutsche Karriere," *Telepolis*, January 24, 2010, www.heise.de/tp/features/Helmut-Schreyer-eine-Deutsche-Karriere-3384053. html.

Rutishauser, Heinz. "Über Automatische Rechenplanfertigung bei programmgesteuerten Rechenmaschinen." *Zeitschrift für angewandte Mathematik und Mechanik* 31, no. 8–9 (1951): 255.

Sack, Warren. *The Software Arts.* Cambridge: MIT Press, 2019.

Salzer, Jerome H. "The Origin of the 'MIT License.'" *IEEE Annals of the History of Computing* 42, no. 4 (2020): 94–98.

Stewart, Danielle. "Geraldo de Barros: Photography as Construction." *H-ART: Revista de historia, teoría y crítica de arte* 2 (2018): 73–92.

Takhteyev, Yury. *Coding Places: Software Practice in a South American City.* Cambridge: MIT Press, 2012.

5 Wiring: Tangible Interaction, Intangible History, Italy, Colombia, 2003

Objects Subjects

To dive into the topic of this chapter, I would like to refer to Friedrich Kittler's *Aufschreibesysteme 1800/1900* – or rather, to its cover.[1] Both the original German edition and the English translation of Kittler's book are embellished with a reproduction of a poster designed by Teodoro Wolf Ferrari to advertise a product launched by Camilo Olivetti at the dawn of the twentieth century. In the image, we see a portrait of Dante Alighieri pointing his finger at a new kind of object: a typewriter. The sober gesture draws a circle that connects the origins of literature in the modern sense and the advent of writing as an industrialized practice; two cultures of writing, more than 600 years apart, are brought into direct contact, as though to validate the inevitable transition from the author to the artifact and from the subjectivity of the early humanists to the subjectivity of machines. At the bottom of the ad, we find a bit of commercial copy: "*Prima Fabbrica Italiana. Macchine per Scrivere. Ing. C. Olivetti e Co. Ivrea* [First Italian Factory. Typewriter by Eng. C. Olivetti and Co. Ivrea]." The image is a perfectly suggestive gateway into Kittler's profound analysis of the cultural and creative transformations brought on by the arrival of writing technologies in the nineteenth and twentieth centuries. Interestingly, the technological artifact that will occupy us in this chapter came into being in the very same location where Camilo Olivetti established the factory that produced his M1 typewriter in 1912: the small city of Ivrea in Northern Italy.

Nowadays, some readers may even recognize Ivrea as the birthplace of Arduino, an astonishingly successful product that may be said to have spearheaded physical computing as a popular field of exploration. Arduino is undoubtedly an uncommon sort of device: a board with a microchip that can be programmed using a relatively simple language to be used in an incredible variety of ways. The board is equipped with a set of inputs and outputs that allow it to read sensors and control actuators; it is an ergonomic and compact solution that makes it easy for non-engineers and non-experts to work with electronics. Arduino is a *programmable thing* whose identity is determined by those who program it, and thanks to its open-source

DOI: 10.4324/9781003172789-8

148 *Sidetracking*

philosophy and dynamic community, it has contributed substantially to the consolidation of a global culture of makers. During the Covid-19 pandemic, for example, this community banded to create and distribute prototypes of DIY devices, such as electronic thermometers, ventilators, and other artifacts assembled using Arduino.[2]

Arduino was created by a team of five people linked to Ivrea's Interactive Design Institute (known as the IDII). The team was led by a member of the IDII faculty, Massimo Banzi, who at some point indicated that the board had been originally conceived as a tool for teaching interactive design.[3] The IDII was an apposite birthplace for a project like Arduino: the school was explicitly conceived in the spirit of adventurous design schools like the Bauhaus, Vkhutemas, and Ulm, and like these predecessors, it was a short-lived affair, lasting only from 2000 to 2005.[4] The IDII envisioned design education as a means for confronting new social realities through a creative approach to technology and commercial endeavors. Undoubtedly, this vision was informed by the recent emergence of a reconfigured Europe that promised to coalesce into a new economic force driven by a model for political openness and collaboration. The 2005 exhibition *Making Things Public*, curated by Bruno Latour and Peter Weibel at the ZKM, captured the spirit of the age through the image of a parliament of parliaments, a political space where a long history of disparities could be redirected through a commitment to continentality as a framework for dialogic democracy.[5]

The choice of Ivrea as a location for the school was far from incidental. For almost a century, the city's fate had been tied to that of the company Olivetti, well-known as a manufacturer of typewriters, calculators, and computers. Adriano Olivetti, who in the 1930s took over the firm founded by his father, refashioned the industrial city as an experimental and radically progressive social space, and for decades, commissioned modern architects to bring his ideas into concrete structures.[6] The resulting architectural complex was acknowledged as a World Heritage site by UNESCO in 2019, and it can be described as one of the most sustained and cohesive efforts to deploy design as a discipline that can create and mediate positive feedback loops between technological artifacts and cultural and social life. The IDII, which was sponsored by Olivetti and Telecom Italia, specifically framed interaction as the field to which a new design culture could most effectively contribute:

> When machines were mechanical, there was a direct, physical way to interact with them. You wound up your watch and turned a wheel to set its time; clicked a dial to make a kitchen mixer go slower or faster; flipped a switch to sew in reverse, and could see the mechanism which allowed this. But a machine controlled by a computer chip is different. It may require us to master menus and modes, and it responds to us, and often to stimuli independent of us, in more complex, less transparent, and sometimes downright mysterious ways. We rely increasingly on such devices, yet our interaction with them is too often awkward, baffling and lacking in grace and pleasure.

For the few students who were fortunate enough to experience it, the IDII study program was intense and immersive. It was described as a "convent with an airport": a place that required dedication and concentration through a strenuous academic curriculum and constant visits by a wide variety of scholars, creators, and professionals.[7] It was in this space of international exchange, discussion, and practical experimentation that the Arduino board was born. The Arduino team developed, produced, and tested the board at Ivrea, and the project was even named after a local pub. When the school closed, the project successfully morphed into a company that continued to sell "Made in Italy" boards to a steadily growing community of users.

In 2014, the fate of the company was shaken by a trademark dispute. Arduino LLC was the company founded by the team that had developed the board in Italy around 2005, comprising Massimo Banzi, David Cuartielles, David Mellis, Tom Igoe, and Gianluca Martino, who had joined the team at a later stage as the designer and manufacturer of the board itself. A company called Smart Objects, founded and run by Martino, had been functioning as the manufacturing branch of the project, producing and selling the boards. As *Wired.it* reported in 2015, Martino disagreed with his peer's efforts to internationalize production of the boards through alliances with foreign companies.[8] Martino wanted the name Arduino to be bound to the boards being produced by his factory in Italy, and for this reason, in 2014, Smart Objects changed its name to Arduino SRL and, under the leadership of Federico Musto, who had not been part of the initial team, initiated a dispute that was eventually resolved in 2017 with the merger of the two companies.[9] The legal struggle nonetheless brought on a wave of scrutiny into the origins of the project, which revealed the existence of what seemed like an unacknowledged predecessor: a very similar device known as the Wiring board, designed by a young Colombian engineer and designer, Hernando Barragán.

The Wiring board had been Barragán's thesis project at IDII, and Banzi had been one of his advisors, but for many years, the Arduino team seems to have downplayed or even denied the relationship between the two projects. Although Barragán himself was not particularly vocal or critical of this attitude, in 2016, he decided to write his version of the story in order to clear the air. As he saw it, there were no substantial differences between Wiring and the first version of Arduino: the code that he had written for Wiring had been forked for Arduino, and the sole crucial change in the board's design had been the use of a cheaper microcontroller, a possibility that he himself had considered from the start. He also claimed that he had never been asked to join the Arduino team and that some effort had been made by them to misrepresent his role, at times hinting that Banzi's position as his thesis supervisor entitled him to authorship of the project, at others suggesting that Barragán had not agreed to explore the alternatives that would lead to Arduino, suggesting that he wanted the project to be closed source and more expensive than it needed to be.[10] Although in the meantime these concerns about acknowledgment have been remedied to some extent, the significance

150 *Sidetracking*

of the fact that this new paradigmatic example of a globally explosive innovation had its roots in the interstice between the Global North and Global South deserves some attention.

The Interface as Solution, the Interface as Problem

As the M1 typewriter contributed to activating a massive transformation in what Kittler calls "discourse networks" or writing systems, the input-output board introduced a radical shift in our way of interacting with electronics and facilitated the rise of an international scene of designers, artists, engineers, and makers who have advanced a different understanding of the potential role of electronics in the world of objects. Going further, we might even say that the input-output board signaled the arrival of a new regime of objects, a lineage of computing objects that no longer rely on an operational structure based on separating the computer on the one side and the embodied user on the other, with forms of mediation characterized by that unique mixture of the abstract and the concrete: the interface.

As the discipline of material culture has taught us, new kinds of objects do not emerge in a void. The program of material culture as a field of study is to decipher the spectrum of properties that permeate material objects when they inform and are informed by specific cultural contexts. Its diverse repertoire of methods and techniques range from the analysis and description of materials and their key features to the on-site study of manufacturing processes. Gradually, this research program has taught us to treat objects as subjects, that is, as entities whose roles in our social dynamics far surpass the modes of subservient usefulness typically attributed to tools and instruments. Artifacts may once have been experienced as inanimate solid constructions that were there to facilitate daily life activities, like holding a liquid for washing or drinking, or else invested with sophisticated cultural values embodying immaterial properties, as with symbolic objects used in political or religious ceremonies.[11] With the arrival of mass-produced objects and heavy machinery, both public and domestic landscapes were invaded by new forms of interplay between objects and actions; not only production and transportation became different but also cooking, teaching, and playing. Our lifeworld became a landscape of artifacts that both responded to and refashioned old and new ways of doing things, and the sense that manufactured objects were subservient to their makers soon gave way to a feeling of dread inspired by the overwhelming presence of mechanized systems.[12]

This process came to a turning point when these new families of objects were endowed with an electronic soul. The first electronic devices were not necessarily capable of performing new feats, and many of the effects that we associate with their arrival were previously achieved by mechanical systems. The Z1 computer, produced in Germany by Konrad Zuse in the 1930s, was arguably the first operational computer of the twentieth century, and it was entirely mechanical.[13] At first, electronics transformed existing devices previously powered by mechanical energy captured through the use of a crank, like the gramophone and the film camera. The new electron-driven incarnations of these devices took advantage of the theoretical and experimental achievements of pioneers like Faraday and Maxwell, who had probed the interactions between electricity, light, and magnetism in the nineteenth century.[14] Soon enough, a culture of electronic media emerged, set on exploiting the potential of circuits boosted by newly invented components like Flemming's vacuum tubes and thermionic valves. Existing objects were reconfigured, and new objects arrived: the radio, the telegraph, the telephone, television, radar, and early computers like the Atanasoff Berry and the Colossus.

Undoubtedly, a crucial moment in the development of our contemporary technoscape was the arrival of the integrated circuit known as the MOS (metal-oxide-semiconductor) or MOSFET (metal-oxide-silicon field-effect transistor), designed in the late 1950s by two immigrants to the United States (from Egypt and Korea).[15] The integrated circuit enabled the miniaturization of objects like the radio and the computer and, thus, kicked off a process that continues to unfold, bringing technology to unexpected places, closer to the skin and out into the farthest reaches of space. Through this shift in scale, integrated circuits and microprocessors have rendered material culture into a new kind of realm. Our material culture has been reconfigured by the emergence of a teeming and growing diversity of electronic artifacts that continue to challenge our sense of how humans and objects can interact,[16] and the concept of non-human agency has moved on from being an abstract construct to becoming a component of our everyday life.[17] The temporality of these shifts is arguably unique and certainly disconcerting, and an archaeological radiography of our culture will undoubtedly display many crossroads where objects of all sorts, the products of more than one industrial revolution, still await for deeper understanding. The rates at which hardware has come to be produced and implemented have radically tested our ability to engage reflexively with objects that have, in fact, altered how we go about reflecting. In this slippery time warp, institutions like the contemporary academy often seem condemned to belatedly come to terms with (and occasionally overinterpret) an already outdated set of conditions. Although no one doubts that computing, broadly understood, is the area from which most of these lines of flight emanate, it seems fair to say that the objecthood of computing has been understudied from a critical perspective. Nevertheless, there are exceptions, notably the remarkable work of Paul Dourish and Jean-François Blanchette.

Although we may perceive material objects that are able to perform calculations and computations through automated processes as relative newcomers, recent research confirms that their presence in material cultures dates quite a while back. The discovery of the Antikythera mechanism has shown that operational calculations were already being explored in Ancient Greek civilization,[18] and the study of the automaton created in the context of the Arab Renaissance, like the astounding hydraulic musical devices designed by the Banū Mūsā in the ninth century, likewise suggests that robotics has

152 Sidetracking

more than a thousand years of documented history.[19] Closer to computation as we know it, researchers who have tracked attempts to build the Analytical Engine during the first industrial revolution in England have shown that the computer as a technology predates both electricity and the binary principle.[20] These archaeological layers are a reminder that computers are objects and that the fact that we don't quite perceive them as such is an effect achieved by equally objective means: it is by their *interfaces* that computing artifacts present us with specific possibilities for action, including intellectual and creative activities, and it has been a guiding premise of interface design to allow us, or compel us, to relate with computers as if they somehow more than the thing at hand.

The personal computer paired the reduction in size enabled by microcontrollers with one crucial innovation: the operating system paired with a graphical interface. The possibility for technically unskilled users to engage with complex computing devices created a wider dimension of usability. The Macintosh introduced a standardized set of input and output interfaces (the keyboard, the mouse, and the monitor), and product design philosophy and practice mutated to probe the computer's capacity to emulate the use values of other machines.[21] This was first and foremost framed as a problem in software design and development: computer programs were expected to reproduce and enhance the properties of other technical objects, and interfaces were tasked with replicating established modes of use in order to allow users access to compute by disguising often-unfamiliar processes as good old friends, predominantly modeled on the experiences of urban office workers. Even today, a visually and culturally narrow world of desktops, folders, and trash cans is the naturalized environment for the vastly diverse kinds of things that people can do with computers.

As we have seen, before the personal computer had consolidated as an object type, technically minded creators like the Chilean composer José Vicente Asuar had used some of the first commercially available microcontrollers to design their own devices and probe the specific ways in which computing could enhance their field of practice.[22] To use a personal computer as a musical instrument was to place computation in conversation with a source of input that called for an interface with a certain range of sensitivity: the human body and its musical skills, capable of producing a large amount of nuanced values. The problems that came into view at that point are still with us, as interface and interaction designers attempt to make computational capabilities available through objects that a growing variety of users can engage with in tactile interactions. Computers, of course, are no longer personal and domestic: they are portable, and the idea of an interface that can be handled or manipulated is no longer bound to hand-based anthropometric parameters. Portability has brought computers into closer conversation with the highly individual cognitive processes of different kinds of users and challenged the way in which top-down technological development makes decisions on their behalf. A DIY culture of global proportions has arisen, which by embedding circuitry into physical elements and pluralizing the field of interaction between inputs and outputs to microcontrollers – and thereby linking computation to both human and non-human forms of agency – is redefining the objecthood of objects. Computing objects need not be consumer products embodying a monolithic point of view; they can be activators of a multiplicity of meanings to be drawn from the possibilities of circuit design and programming by individual and creative users engaged in productive, scientific, critical, or artistic activities.

The field of physical computing has channeled many of these efforts around a set of principles that envision technological creativity as a function of community building that resembles early computer hacking and hobbyist subcultures that thrived before the increased standardization and commodification of computing devices.[23] These new communities have put forward the open-source philosophy as a condition for a new way of designing software, hardware, and interfaces, forging along the way new kinds of linkages between the Global North and the Global South; they have also managed to impact technological developments at a global scale, signaling a new path in the potential unfolding of technological innovation. The case of the Wiring input-output board is an exemplary instance of the kind of process that brought this reconfigured landscape into being (Figure 5.1).

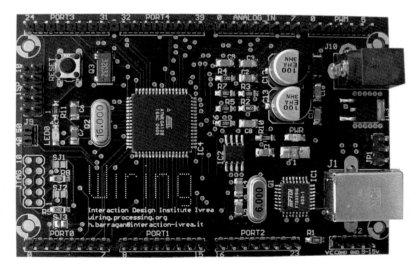

Figure 5.1 A Wiring board with the silkscreen visible, including information about IDII and the wiring font designed for the project; the URL is subdomain at Processing: wiring.processing.org, 2003.

Source: Courtesy of Hernando Barragán

154 *Sidetracking*

Code Matters

In the early 1990s, Hernando Barragán was an undergraduate student in computer engineering at one of Colombia's most prestigious private universities, the Universidad de los Andes in Bogotá. At the time, Colombian society was experiencing a wave of dramatic changes. In 1991, an elected assembly representing diverse and even conflicting political views drafted a new political constitution for the country, which many saw as an opportunity for a new start under the premise of a plural civil society. President César Gaviria promoted what he described as an "opening" of the country's economy. Gaviria presented his embrace of neoliberal policies as an effort to draw the country into the networks of the globalized economy and as consistent with the structural and cultural changes expressed in the new constitution. Colombia's deep-rooted and enduring social conflicts hardly vanished: instead, they mutated and became even harder to map out, as the illegal drug trade created an economy in which players from all political corners and social layers were involved.[24] The "opening" of Colombia certainly allowed a new generation of young urban dwellers to feel like they could participate in, rather than simply witness, the development of new possibilities. As elsewhere, the arrival of the Internet was interpreted as a crucial vehicle for social, economic, and political deprovincialization, and the Universidad de los Andes played an important role in the process (by managing the. co domain, among other things).[25] In this context, then, it was exceptional but plausible that a young undergraduate like Barragán could envision a career as a computer engineer capable of taking on a creative role in technological development.

As Barragán has stated, the reasoning behind Wiring, which was absorbed wholesale by Arduino, was grounded on the premise of creating a tool for interaction design that could allow non-engineers to approach electronics-based design in an open and creative way. Barragán's own sense of creativity was shaped by his involvement, during his student days, in a wave of enthusiastic experimentation by Colombian artists with newly available digital devices. The university was perhaps the only possible location for this kind of encounter at the time, and Barragán's curiosity was piqued by some of the classes being taught at the Arts Department. At the time, this was an unusual combination of interests, and he was lucky to find a degree of coursework flexibility at Los Andes that was unusual in Colombia's universities. The Catalan media artist Xavier Hurtado, a former student of the Interactive Telecommunications Program at New York University, was a visiting professor at the Arts Department, where he taught students how to apply the Basic Stamp microcontroller as a tool to develop sculptural interactive art projects. Recently introduced to the market by Parallax, the Basic Stamp was a microcontroller and board that ran a simplified version of the Basic programming language called PBasic. By the mid-1990s, the Basic Stamp was being used in some media art programs around the world, and Hurtado's students at Los Andes came up with extremely interesting proposals like *Peligro biológico*, a trash can robot designed by Martha Patricia Niño. This was Barragán's first experience with the capabilities and limitations of microcontrollers and a clear precedent to his later approach to Wiring.

After graduating, Barragán relocated to New York City, where he found work as an IT developer for Utensil, a studio that specialized in developing computational media for artistic projects. For a while, he turned his attention to the WWW and focused on mastering the recently introduced Java programming language, created by James Gosling, Mike Sheridan, and Patrick Naughton just before the World Wide Web revolution took off.[26] In 1999, Barragán returned to Colombia and was appointed as director of the Advanced Computer Center MOX at Los Andes. The lab's job was to provide a high-level computational infrastructure to the university's scientific community, and it was equipped with several exceptional hardware devices and high-performance platforms, including a Cray supercomputer (for a while, MOX was among the most advanced labs of its kind in Latin America). There, Barragán often worked with new and old Silicon Graphics machines running Unix, which allowed him to hone his skills in the use of different operating systems. All the while, he continued to explore the relation between computing and artmaking in conversation with a growing community of like-minded scholars and artists. By then, Los Andes had introduced several new courses that urged students and faculty to explore the creative possibilities of digital media and artistic uses of the Internet, and an entire generation of Colombian artists and designers who now had some degree of access to current developments in media and digital arts embraced the role of disseminators, initiating a vital South-North dialogue around the potential uses of media technologies.

Back then, I myself was a faculty member at Los Andes, and in 2001, soon after meeting Barragán, I asked him to be part of a project that counts as a good example of the atmosphere that prevailed in the local scene that brought together people interested in art, science, and technology. The project, *Hipercubo/ok/*, was an experimental publication that included a book, a CD-ROM, and a website. The publication as a whole was conceived as a platform for the work of Latin American creators interested in media technologies. Barragán contributed an essay to the book, which also included compiled texts exploring the emerging scene of art, sciences, and technology in Latin America, with contributions by Francisco Varela, Eduardo Kac, Rafael Lozano Hemmer, Alejandro Duque, Tania Ruiz, and others. Barragán's essay, titled "Software: ¿arte?" (Software: Art?), may well be the first attempt to critically examine the relationship between code and art in Colombia. Barragán begins by reminding his readers that the framing of digital arts as media arts had forced them into the lineage of video art and reinforced a tendency to regard code itself as merely a means to produce visual or sound effects, rather than as a creative medium in its own right:

> [I]n this way, the medium that makes change possible lacks a form of its own and is thus pure operation. . . . In that sense, digital means are

156 *Sidetracking*

perceived as immaterial, seeming to be pure function and untouchable by form. Code is then a language with aesthetic and formal possibilities, a coding that has a transformative power that brings about transformations in the digital medium, which itself might also generate new forms.[27]

As Barragán notes, in 2001, the Transmediale festival had introduced software art as a prize category, indicating that code as such could be regarded as a creative medium. To make this into a tangible proposition, Barragán outlined two ways in which coding could come to the fore as a creative medium: as a "universal transformer of information" that can take, say, an auditory input and render it as a visual output; and through interactivity, which he describes as a region where "the artistic process lies in the very act of writing the code."

Barragán was not content with arguing for this possibility: he also exemplified it by writing three code experiments, or software art pieces, which were included in the small CD-ROM that accompanied the book. The first of these was *Hiperlook*, an experimental browser that could read HTML and CSS languages from online websites and interpret and display them in real time as projections in a toroidal space. The second piece, *ReactiveText 1.0*, dealt with the possibilities of interaction between code and text by taking fragments from the *Hipercubo* book and scattering them into a shower of letters. The third experiment, *hipercubo/ok/bookviewer 1.0*, was a navigation tool that could be used to access the book's content. Around the same time, I collaborated with Barragán on another experimental project *Typovideo*, for which he developed in Java a server application that could translate streamed video to ASCII code in real time. The application produced a fast, smooth, and stable stream of animated video, implemented in an SGI Octane Unix server machine; it streamed continuously for about a year, broadcasting looped videos and a few online events,[28] and was also exhibited as an artwork within the cycle "Nuevos Nombres" in a show titled *Tecnología de la desilusión* (Technology of disillusion). "Nuevos Nombres" is an ongoing series of curated exhibitions organized by the Biblioteca Luis Ángel Arango in Bogotá to showcase the work of young artists, and the inclusion of *Typovideo* in that context signals the extent to which the city's artistic field was captivated by this area of experimentation.[29] *Typovideo* can be read as a meditation on a topic that clearly interested Barragán at the time, namely the ambiguity of the term "writing" as applied to both text and code, and the problem of the visibility of code as a condition for its creative use. Although these early projects of Barragán's were certainly based on his technical achievements, he did not present them as such but presented them as efforts to bring code into view for the local arts community in order to establish a dialogue in creative and critical terms.

Towards Physical Computing

In 2002, Barragán received a scholarship to pursue graduate studies at the IDII, where he found himself in a challenging atmosphere that immediately drove him to channel his concerns into what would become his thesis project. Barragán's explicit aim in that project was to design a programming framework that would make it easy for users with no background in technology to engage with microcontrollers safely and creatively in order to create prototypes for interactive applications.[30] As he had phrased it in "Software: ¿arte?," he was looking to open up a view of programming as a way of traveling "from the world of bits to the world of atoms" and back; this image now led him to a zone in which the distinction between hardware and software would begin to blur.

At IDII, Barragán came into contact with Casey Reas, who a few years earlier had created the Processing programming language in collaboration with Ben Fry. Fry and Reas were students at the MIT Media Lab at the end of the 1990s, where they worked with John Maeda, who led the Aesthetics + Computation Group. The group had been working on Design by Numbers (DBN), an educational project based on a software toolkit that could be used to conduct code-based design experiments.[31] DBN included a basic programming language and a development environment that aimed to teach design and art students the foundations of coding; it could be downloaded for free, and it could run directly within any Java-enabled web browser. DBN had a small set of instructions based on computer languages ranging from C and Java to Logo, and the team published a book tutorial that explored the basic concepts of coding with expressive purposes. Fry and Reas embarked on the adventure of expanding these methods and tools to initiate designers, artists, and non-experts in coding and enhance computer-programming literacy. Their approach led them to embrace an open-source philosophy that diverged with the Media Lab's perspective, which at the time remained attached to ongoing efforts to apply the logic of intellectual property to code. Processing was their effort to synthesize all these technical and social premises. Accessibility to users was a key concern, and Processing presented itself as a programming sketchbook for pedagogical purposes.[32] The concept and its implementation quickly caught the attention of many users. Although at the time, there were a few other projects seeking to bring coding experience to artists and designers, such as Macromedia's Director and Flash, Processing's open-source distribution under a GPU license made it a distinctively timely alternative. In line with this philosophy, the Processing project was supported by a robust online platform that included examples, a gallery of projects, and a community forum.

As they were at work in the consolidation of Processing and the expansion of its development, Fry enrolled in the doctoral program at the MIT Media Lab, and Reas was appointed as a faculty member at the IDII. Both institutions supported the development of the project, and in 2003, with a

158 *Sidetracking*

boost from a new wave of collaborators, Processing took off, and its influence began to spread among various communities. The reverberations were felt in schools like the IDII, where Processing proved to be an effective tool by which students who were not programmers could gain access to code as a creative tool. At Ivrea, Barragán began to collaborate with Reas, creating examples to illustrate the language's potential and traveling around Europe to conduct Processing workshops.

The Processing team was always interested in creating links between the programming environment and tangible interaction platforms, and one of the project's first libraries allowed Processing to receive input data from external devices like the Basic Stamp or the Basic X using the serial port. There were already a few hardware configurations that lodged a microcontroller within a board designed to allow artists and other creators to develop computing projects, some of which had also been developed with educational purposes, such as the Handy Board, a robotics controller designed by Fred G. Martin at MIT, or the Javelin Stamp board created by Parallax. Although these kits could be said to have successfully bridged the gap that kept non-specialist artists and other creators from a hands-on engagement with coding and physical computing, their boards were programmed each with a different language, which prevented users from creating a code that could be used elsewhere. Moreover, most of the IDEs were proprietary, meaning that users had no access to the code itself. Working with Processing brought these issues into view for Barragán, and he conceived his thesis project as a way to overcome these limitations and enable a truly fluid exchange between a platform for creative programming and a platform for interfaces. In this moment of excitement, the idea of creating a project that would expand the philosophy behind Processing into the domain of hardware began to take shape in his mind and hands.

Wiring

In his 1998 essay "Hardware, the Unknown Being," Friedrich Kittler described the unique status of programmable hardware as condemned to invisibility. Kittler argued that software, which allows us to treat materials as programmable, nonetheless renders its material substrate intangible by presenting itself as "the immateriality of the most material."[33] This circumstance is prejudicial, according to Kittler, for at least one reason: although the programmability of different materials is conditioned by software, advances in the use of matter for storing information take place at a rate of increasing speed that far surpasses advances in the complexity and capacity of software design. For that reason, software acts as a reactionary vector that tends to "project known systems over unknown ones and thereby drastically constrain their degree of freedom."[34] Kittler's philosophical argument could be translated into a practical maxim: we should endeavor to promote platforms that, by visibilizing hardware, can liberate the possibilities of computing as a social practice, in tune with a deeper awareness of the potentialities of programmable matter.

Not soon after Kittler published his essay, platforms built around the idea of accessible microcontrollers gained massive attention from artists, designers, creative technologists, engineers, hackers, and makers of other kinds, and a new kind of culture suddenly converged around the kind of creativity that Kittler had speculatively called for. Read in this context, Wiring can be accurately described as a crucial contribution to a broader process, to the extent that it successfully met three conditions: availability of coding through a user-friendly programming environment, plasticity of interaction through access to an open range of possible hardware-software structures, and community building as an explicit component of the envisioned life of the platform. To meet these ends, Barragán designed from scratch a multi-level framework that included a hardware component (a microcontroller board), a programming language, and software. Since Wiring had to be easy to program and to hook up to a variety of input and output devices, simplicity was the overarching design premise. A wide range of possibilities should be on offer while keeping everything at the same cognitive level so that users could have access to the opportunities and specificities of each component when transitioning from the world of bits to the world of electrons and back around. The aim was to create a tool whose structure was malleable enough to easily cut across hard boundaries inherent to specific media (visual, audible, tactile, time-based) and to operate with them and transform them into one another: from a light sensor to a sound generator, from a microphone to a motor. If in his earlier projects Barragán had been captivated by the duality of code's existence as text, which could convey both semantic meaning and machine instructions, he was now casting a much wider net, as wide as the range of sensors and actuators that could be hooked up to the board. Thus, the project could be described as an extension of his understanding of code as a translation device: a "universal transformer of information" capable of shuttling between the physical and the computational, mediated by electronic circuitry and driven by the concerns and visions of individual designers.

The Wiring Board

The task of designing Wiring's board called for a profound understanding of the different possible architectures of microcontrollers. A set of factors must be carefully weighed against each other in such an architecture: the CPU's capabilities, memory processing, and the programmability of the input and output registers. Barragán had to select an adequate microcontroller, design the board's architecture, and determine how electronic circuits should be implemented to extend the physicality of the board. Once a microcontroller had been selected, Barragán would need to master the language to design the API. For this, he would need to have a very clear structural understanding of

160 *Sidetracking*

the language, the hardware architecture, and the API to make sure that they all communicated efficiently and with enough flexibility. To determine the most appropriate microcontroller, Barragán contacted several semiconductor manufacturing companies to request information about their products: he reviewed visual materials, photographs, and schematics to understand their functioning and suitability.[35] The microcontroller would have to be powerful enough to perform without harsh limitations and spare users the hassle of continuously butting up against the limitations of the technology. After testing several options Barragán settled on the Atmel AVR 128, which had 48 input-output digital pins, 8 analog inputs, and 6 analog outputs (by PWM).[36]

The next step was to design the PCB, the printed circuit board in which the microcontroller would be embedded. The board's overall design should enable it to function as an extension of the microcontroller's architecture and, thus, to mediate between the microscale of the electronic components and the human scale of its users (Figure 5.2). The Wiring board was conceived as a product that could fit ergonomically on a user's hand and present internal processes as open to manipulation in order to function as a pedagogical device through which users could come to understand electronic circuits as extensions of their nervous system, to use McLuhan's turn of phrase.[37] This presented a unique set of challenges determined by Barragán's design premise, which dictated that the board should be an open computer. In terms of hardware, this openness was fairly literal, and it introduced quite a few considerations. For instance, a user with no experience in electronics could accidentally cause the board to overheat by touching two parts of it simultaneously – in fact, this accident is common enough even among experts. The board had to be an open object without being hazardous. Odd as it may sound, another challenge was to find a way of letting users know whether the board was on or off, a feature that was left off of extant boards under the assumption that users would have some training in electrical engineering.

In response to concerns like these, Barragán decided to use LEDs to create a range of visual feedback possibilities between users and the board, letting users know if the board was operational or if there was a transmission process going on between the microprocessor and the board. Barragán also included an LED to be used as a test light and built on this to create the LED blink example, an equivalent of the "Hello World" program that many students use when they are first learning a computer language. In this way, the LED was used to offer immediate feedback on the status of the card, and users could get a sense of how to control the behavior of the LED with an elementary example of code that allowed them to monitor the correct operation of the device.

To offer users access to the board's general architecture, Barragán wanted the distinction between digital and analog pins to be physically inscribed, as it were, in the distribution of the different components across the board.

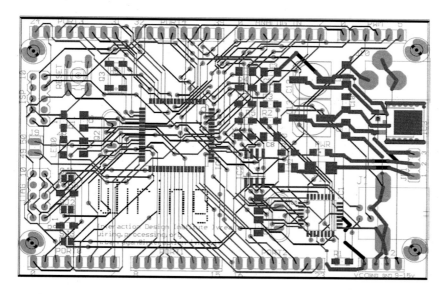

Figure 5.2 PCB schematic of the Wiring input-output board, 2003.
Source: Courtesy of Hernando Barragán.

To achieve this, he had to design the board's silkscreen very carefully. The silkscreen is the layer of ink marks that label the different parts of the PCB, and Barragán took such care in its conception that he designed two versions of a special "Wiring font," a dots version used for the Wiring brand and a line version used on the board itself.[38] In keeping with Warren Sacks's idea that computational practices can be traced back to Enlightenment-era paradigms for the production of structured knowledge,[39] Barragán's PCB silkscreen can be described as a visual index that conveyed a structure of usable resources.

The Wiring Language

Traditionally, computer scientists and engineers have learned to use programming languages like Fortran, Cobol, Lisp, C, or Java in order to acquaint themselves with different paradigms of coding and be able to navigate diverse levels of computational knowledge. The Wiring language was written in C++, a language whose code is directly translated into machine language in the microcontroller, which allows for fast and efficient communication with the board. While developing and implementing the Wiring programming language, Barragán had three concerns in mind, all of which

162   *Sidetracking*

hinged around the different ways in which people could use the platform: he wanted to grant accessibility to complex technical features (such as the registers of a microcontroller), to achieve universality and compatibility across a broad spectrum of technologies, and to hide complex aspects of memory management within the microcontroller. The language was to be responsive to interaction as the key design premise, and for this reason, it could not be wedded to the architecture of a particular microcontroller since the whole point was to establish a way to communicate programming concepts and ideas independently of the technological platform. In that sense, the Wiring language was to be closer to a high-level programming language than to a machine language (Figure 5.3).[40]

Barragán also designed an API (application programming interface), which defines the interactions between software applications, software intermediaries, and the hardware. As in Processing, the original set of commands available in the Wiring language is grouped into sections named "Structure," "Environment," "Data," "Control," "Math," and "Constants." To these, Barragán added a new range of functions included in a section named "Input/Output." These new functions, "digitalRead()," "digitalWrite()," "analogRead()," and "analogWrite()," are by now all too familiar to Arduino users, but at the time, the "Input/Output" section as such was a decisive innovation that crucially modelled the understanding of interaction that Wiring was set to embody. The "analogWrite" instruction, for example, is a metaphorical resource designed to allow users to easily shuttle back and forth between the realm of code and the behavior of different materials. At the technical level, there is no actual analog writing going on, and what the instruction labels as such is actually a pulse-width modulation (PWM) process that, if applied to an LED, will cause the light to change continuously in response to changes in parameter. Its metaphorical representation as an "analog write" allows users to envision an instruction as reflected in the behavior of an LED so that the range of possible outward effects of a coded instruction can be easily grasped. The instruction, in other words, was a way of making Barragán's translatability premise directly visible.

In a similar vein, Barragán altered a typical convention whereby input and output pins are labeled as "registers" in microcontrollers. Typically, microcontroller manufacturers assign individual and unfamiliar names to each of these registers (say, DVAX 01) so that anyone who is hooking up a set of inputs and outputs to a microcontroller will need a clear map for the use of each register. Something described as "pin 1" in a program would thus correspond to different registers in different microprocessors, say, an Atmega 328 and an Atmega 256, which means that programmers need to include these register names in the code, typing in those which are specific to each microprocessor. Barragán instead designed the language so that it could represent inputs and outputs via pin numbers and track the corresponding register in different microcontrollers. Thus, his design hid those aspects that

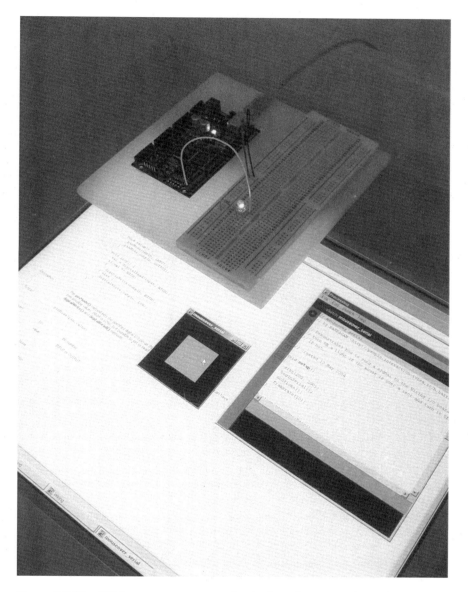

Figure 5.3 The Wiring ecosystem at work: the board connected to a breadboard with an LED, the Wiring code, the website, and the code to interface it with Processing, 2003.

Source: Courtesy of Hernando Barragán

164   *Sidetracking*

would have made communication between the language and the processor inaccessible to those who were not familiar with electrical engineering. Then a basic example of how to turn on and off the LED embedded in the board looks in the following way:

```
int ledpin=13                          // set a variable ledpin #13

void setup()

{
  pinMode(ledpin, OUTPUT); // set pin as output
}

void loop()
{
  digitalWrite(ledpin, HIGH);   // set the LED on
  delay(1000);                  // wait for a second
  digitalWrite(ledpin, LOW);    // set the LED off
  delay(1000);                  // wait for a second

}
```

Wiring's First Users

When all these design concerns were resolved, Barragán manually assembled the first 25 boards, a task that required a great deal of precise labor for which he had to develop and practice a very specific set of fine motor skills. The board itself was scaled in relation to the size of a human hand that would plug things in and out of it, but many of the components were quite small, and heat from the soldering iron could easily affect or damage the microcontroller. Thus, the project was covered with Barragán's fingerprints all over, both literally and metaphorically: he crafted each of its layers, from the most abstract to the most concrete, in the service of a sharply defined vision. Of course, the fact that Wiring was conceived and initially assembled by hand by an individual is consistent with its being a student project, but it can also be said to situate Barragán in the lineage of do-it-yourselfers like Florence, Asuar, and González Camarena. Unlike some of these predecessors, Barragán had access to knowledge and resources through educational institutions, but like all of them, his relation to media technologies was rooted in an awareness of all the work that lies behind the fetish-like presence of an electronic commodity on a store shelf, with its inner components and production history neatly removed from view.

In 2004, Barragán submitted Wiring as his thesis project for the master's degree in Interaction Design, and it was awarded a distinction by a jury that included Bill Mogridge (from IDEO), Fiona Raby, Anthony

Dunne, and Peter Cook (from Archigram). The thesis document, which as of July 2022 can still be accessed online, emphasized the pedagogical nature of the project, which was to be regarded not as a finished product of interaction design but as a flexible tool for designing interactions and for learning how to do so by creating prototypes that could be played with, tested, and modified:

> Design education and practice increasingly rely on digital technology. For designers to successfully enter this domain, they need to understand the inherent qualities in the media they work with, such as electronics and software. Current prototyping tools for electronics and programming are mostly targeted to engineering, robotics, and technical audiences. They are hard to learn, and the programming languages are far from useful in contexts outside a specific technology. Designers need a teaching language and electronics prototyping system that facilitates and encourages the process of learning, that reduces the struggle with electronics design and programming, and that are powerful and flexible enough for the needs of Interaction Design.

Barragán's core idea was that the teaching of design as a creative practice could be enhanced by allowing designers-in-training access to a simplified way of working out prototypes for possible interactive structures. However, the project went beyond the sphere of training and emphasized from the start the importance of fostering a web-based community of creative users that would determine its fate in the future:

> Wiring is both a programming environment and an electronics prototyping input/output board for exploring the electronic arts and tangible media. . . . It illustrates the concept of programming with electronics and the physical realm of hardware control which are necessary to explore physical interaction design and tangible media aspects in the design discipline. The Wiring software and the hardware designs of the Wiring electronic input/output board will be freely available for download on the Web. Users will have access to the Wiring electronic input/output board as well. The site contains a reference, and a number of short prototypical examples that explore the media and illustrate the code and the electronics diagrams allowing users to learn by experimenting with them.

Wiring was put to use straight away as a pedagogical tool in January of 2005, in a class titled "Strangely Familiar: Unusual Objects for Everyday Life," described in the course announcements as a workshop on "applied dreams." IDII students used the Wiring board to transform objects like telephones, alarm clocks, and radios through different approaches to physical interaction. The projects included a radio altered to capture signals from outer space, a table that was capable of receiving and storing messages, and an alarm clock that could physically compel the user to get out of bed. After

Figure 5.4 Myriel Milićević, at that time a graduate student at the IDII, using Wiring for her physical interaction prototypes, 2003.

Source: Courtesy of Hernando Barragán

the workshop, Wiring was embraced by some of Barragán's classmates, like Karmen Franinovic, Michal Rinott, Myriel Milićević, Giorgio Olivero, Víctor Viña, and Nicholas Zambetti (who had also contributed some coding for Wiring). Students from other cohorts went on to use Wiring in their master's thesis projects, such as Milićević's *Neighborhood Satellite*. In this project, the satellite was a handheld device that could sense air quality and light conditions, and it functioned simultaneously as a controller for a video game in which air pollution was visualized as clouds to be navigated by a satellite character (Figure 5.4). When a player's satellite avatar became thoroughly contaminated, they would have to find clean air to replenish and play again. Milićević conceived the game as a tool that could be used to collectively generate a map of local air conditions in particular locations. Ten years later, Zambetti, who by then had moved on to IDEO, emphasized the community-forming capacity of the Wiring project as the key to its success among those who came to use it during those first few years:

> In time, designers and artists become able to reference their familiarity with Wiring to communicate and work with engineers more effectively; this bridge between disciplines has proven to be immeasurably valuable for the design industry. Most importantly, Wiring has established electronics as a medium for art and design by serving as the foundation for a unified community, a common toolset with which to express ourselves, share our knowledge, and work with one another.[41]

Product Displacement

At the end of 2004, Barragán traveled back to Colombia and continued to work on Wiring (Figure 5.5).[42] He assembled a more comprehensive set of examples and tutorials, and created a set of technical diagrams drawn as figurative vector-based representations. In these diagrams, he demonstrated a remarkable capacity to convey the intricacies of circuit design through icons, and it is no exaggeration to say that they are gems of visual semiotics (Figure 5.6). The diagrams teach users how to interact with the hardware by presenting schematics that a non-expert can understand along with the piece of code in the Wiring language that modifies it. This way of visually representing fundamental configurations in electronics was eventually normalized, and at that point, Wiring can be said to have become a complete solution. Barragán approached a few local companies to assess the possibility of producing the board in Colombia, but he found very few that could make the board as a whole and eventually concluded that it would be unrealistic to mass-produce it in South America. He then decided to have the boards made in North America and to assemble them in Colombia. The PCB manufacturing and assembling company Advanced Circuits produced and printed around 10,000 boards in the following years, and Barragán was soon selling and shipping them to various schools and universities. By the

Figure 5.5 Wiring website with the Colombian domain name: www.wiring.org.co, featuring media artist Ana María Montenegro 2005.

Source: http://wiring.org.co

end of 2005, Wiring was being used in all five continents, and the Wiring community was growing by leaps.

Barragán then teamed up with the company Sparkfun to commercially produce a new version of the board. Sparkfun played a crucial role in the open-source hardware revolution by functioning as a marketing platform that allowed users to explore many different ways of using the board. The Sparkfun website presented the Wiring board as illustrating "the concept of programming with electronics and the physical realm of hardware control which are necessary to explore physical interaction design and tangible media aspects" and advised customers to "check out the ever-growing list of related items, most of which have example Wiring code."[43] A vital

Wiring   169

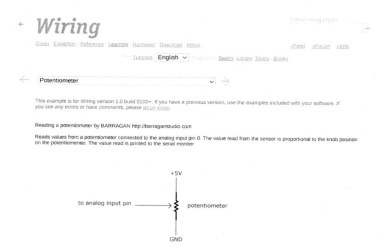

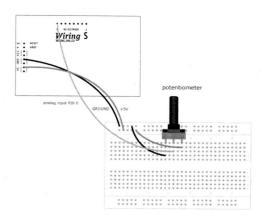

Figure 5.6 Vector-based images visually depicting the electronic components and their interconnections in a Wiring online tutorial, 2005.

Source: http://wiring.org.co

170 Sidetracking

transformation was taking place in the production of electronic components, leading products to be shaped and reshaped to fit the sizes and protocols used by Wiring, Arduino, and other boards. Knowledge was being produced in a networked structure and at many levels, engaging users, language developers, designers, and electronics manufacturing companies. Many such companies created suitable versions of their equipment; Bosch, for example, produced a version of a temperature sensor, made initially for ovens, which could be connected to the board's pins. Other companies also began to produce breakout boards to make their components available to enthusiasts. Technology changed in response to the emergence of a new market for products that before were of interest mostly to industrial concerns or to people with fairly advanced engineering skills. Likewise, the existence of technological families became visible to non-expert users, who could now see that a potentiometer and an air quality sensor could be read by the same code. Many people made sensors out of other sensors: light-measuring sensors, for instance, were adapted into a whole cluster of varieties. It seems fair to say that such a degree of interaction between the production of advanced technologies and its creative users had not been experienced before, and for a while, Wiring was at the heart of it all.

Barragán continued to develop new models of the board, including the Wiring Mini and the Wiring S, but after a few years of development, and many ups and downs, production came to a halt in 2011. For a while, universities and companies in the United States sustained an interest in the project, and some even worked on new versions, including a mutation of the Wiring language called Wiring++, developed by the University of California at Berkeley, Moodkit, and Texas Instruments in 2013.[44] Nonetheless, and in spite of his sustained commitment, Barragán had not been able to turn the board into a viable product, and one of the reasons is undoubtedly the fact that his board was overshadowed by Arduino's phenomenal rise to popularity. By 2013, Wiring seemed to have vanished from view, and it was already being historicized as a mere predecessor to Arduino. In that year's edition of MIT's Open Hardware Summit, a panel titled "Implications of Open Source Business: Forking and Attribution" addressed this particular history. David Mellis, who had written segments of the Arduino software based on Wiring, was a part of the panel and presented the Arduino team's take on the relationship between the two projects, while Barragán explained his own issues with the team's failure to acknowledge his contribution. Although this debate awarded him some much deserved visibility, Barragán's situation did not change considerably, and it seems clear that this is due to the structural inequality that continues to keep the Global South at a remove from commercial outlets for technological innovation.[45] The simple fact that Barragán had returned to Colombia after concluding his studies at IDII could be said to have sealed the fate of his project, which goes to show just how far we still are from a neoliberal meritocracy where good ideas, wherever they may come from, have an equal opportunity to make it in an open market.

Wiring 171

More specifically, the Arduino-Wiring case brings into view two questions that need to be addressed by anyone who is committed to the open-source philosophy as a framework for a democratic unfolding of technological innovation. On the one hand, it illustrates the potentially disruptive role of forking in the context of open-source projects. But is it possible for a forked version of an open-source project to create a splinter community that, for whatever reason, will grow to overshadow and maybe even eliminate the original community? Although this need not be perceived as an intrinsically vicious practice, it can certainly cause us to think twice about what happens when commercial success and failure determine the fate of a design project, especially if they are clearly derived from an unequal access to institutional and financial resources. On the other hand, a project like Wiring has to contend with the limitations to be found in Colombia and other countries of the Global South by anyone who is hoping to mass-produce technological devices (like boards) to be sold at a competitive price. Indeed, Arduino's own internal split was caused by the perceived need to begin producing the boards outside of Italy in order to reduce the cost of production and market value for the sake of a larger client base. The Wiring case shows how even in an age of global connectedness innovators from Latin America and the Global South can easily settle on a perception of themselves as destined to invisibility.

Conclusion

Since the early twentieth century, progressive design academies have been working to configure a robust framework for addressing the implications and potentialities of industrially produced objects. Pioneers like Marcel Breuer, Aleksandr Ródchenko, Varvara Stepanova, Max Bill, and Hans Gugelot are credited for their fundamental contributions to the creation of a new understanding of material objects informed by the philosophy and practice of design. Their approaches paved the way for the development of a novel field of study that turned its attention to the capacity of objects to physically convey their own functionality and to become tools for a better life and for individual and social liberation.[46] A wide range of concepts were coined that sought to capture the complex possibilities for action and forms of life that are embedded in technological artifacts: the new discourses of *Produkt Gestaltung*, *Produktsprache*, *Gut Gemacht – Gute Form*, Semiotics of Design, Form Follows Function, Radical Design, and *Cultura del Progetto* all contributed to creating a rich network of ideas that, by being formulated within a pedagogical framework, could immediately be tested in practice. Although these ideas were at times complementary and at others contradictory – or perhaps because of it – a shared and productive vocabulary emerged by which to explore the nexus between artifacts and their usability.[47]

Although this is an area that is yet to be probed in depth, these conversations were also a point of encounter between voices from the Global North

172 *Sidetracking*

and the Global South, and design academies were and continue to be the sites of a very important form of exchange in this respect. Two notable examples are the intertwined trajectories of Tomás Maldonado (1922–2018) and Gui Bonsiepe (1934), who made their way across the North–South divide in opposite directions. Maldonado started his career as an energetic avant-garde painter in Argentina before moving to Europe, where he became a keen theoretician of the relationship between the arts, technology, and the environment. Throughout the years, Maldonado exerted an important role as director of several international design schools, including the influential Ulm School of Design, and he was a regular lecturer in semiotics, product design, and architectural design. Maldonado forged his way of thinking at the dawn of the computational age and anticipated many of its key concerns. As the Portuguese scholar Isabel Clara Neves has shown, he developed a rigorous approach to the study of visual methodologies, means of representation, and perceptual understanding, inspired by mathematical and topological investigations applied to design processes that Neves describes as "computing without computers."[48] Maldonado predicted and accurately assessed the need to include computational means in design and architecture education, not simply because they could be playfully and productively explored in such pedagogical environments but also because he could presciently assert that it would become a field that designers would be called upon to engage with critically.[49]

In 1963, Maldonado collaborated with Bonsiepe, who was then a student at Ulm, on the design of an international visual language that would allow users to interact with computers using icons meant to be legible by speakers of any language.[50] This graphic language had been commissioned by Olivetti for their Elea computer project, led by the legendary designer Ettore Sottsass, and although it was not implemented it is still acknowledged as one of the earliest examples of a visual design project conceived as an innovative exploration of human-computer interaction – or as Elisabetta Mori has written, as an interface that precedes "the advent of human-computer interaction."[51] At this stage in the development of the theory of design, the ideas of visual semiotics and attention to the scientific turn cultivated by Maldonado clearly informed his understanding of computers as privileged artifacts in which abstract and concrete operations could merge in a way that would irreversibly transform human forms of action. Later on, in the 1990s, he became one of the most articulate analysts of the transformations brought by the consolidation of computational systems and the Internet. In his book *Crítica de la razón informática* (Critique of Computing Reason), he warned against the careless adoption of technologies while sounding a cautionary note as to the potentially damaging effects of blindly refusing to deal with their unstoppable spread.[52]

In the meantime, Bonsiepe relocated to Latin America after concluding his studies at Ulm and became part of the team that conceived Chile's first school of design. In the early 1970s, in the context of Allende's socialist experiment, Bonsiepe also joined the Cybersyn project, led by Stafford Beer and Fernando Flores, which aimed to build what can be described as a proto-internet system designed to generate a model of Chile's economy based on the principles of cybernetics management.[53] As a theoretician, Bonsiepe made significant contributions to our understanding of physical objects and interfaces, which he summarized in one of the most important books on design published in the 1990s, *Del objeto a la interfase* (From the Object to the Interface), where he explored the cultural and ontological implications of the transition from the object to the interface as paradigms for the object-hood of artifacts.[54] After a brief spell working for a software company in Silicon Valley, Bonsiepe had quickly grasped the potential restructuring of human experience enabled by the personal computer, and in a daring theo-retical move, he argued for an expansion of the concept of interface beyond the confines of computer science. In his view, a generalized concept of inter-face could be the keystone for an updated framework for understanding the aims of design as a practice:

> I interpret design as interface design. Design is located in an area where the interaction between users and artifacts (objects) is structured, both with physical objects in the form of products and semiotic objects in the form of signs. Each physical artifact is assumed to have a semiotic facet, but the instrumental value is the core for effective action. The interface is the backbone of design activities. I consider the old thought of deem-ing designers as generators of forms totally obsolete. In new media, we can observe a change that refers to the concern for the form, replacing it with the concern for the structure. The designers thus structure the spaces of action for the users through their interventions in the uni-verses of materiality and semiotics.[55]

Barragán's work in Wiring could be framed within this tradition, and this is not only because he also shuttled between the South and the North while looking for a new direction for design as a practice. Like Maldonado, Barragán was interested in redefining our relationship with technological objects by working out of the interstice between computer engineering and design. Like Bonsiepe, he was interested in yet another interstitial space, between object and interface. Twenty years after the appearance of the first commercial computer equipped with a graphical user interface, Barragán could sense that the meaning of the transition that Bonsiepe had theorized was due for reevaluation. The consolidation of the desktop and the port-able computer as design standards had actually been based on a limited understanding of what interfaces could be and do as objects. The question now was how the open and fluid understanding of objecthood explored by design and computational thinking could be applied to an electronically mediated and programmable interface as something that could be touched and manually operated.

174 *Sidetracking*

At IDII, Barragán actually discussed his project with Sottsass, who in the 1960s and 1970s pioneered an approach to object design inspired by a desire for radical cultural transformation, creating an exciting visual vocabulary of smooth textures, saturated colors, and shapes that trod the line between the organic and the technofantastic.[56] In its own way, although somewhat paradoxically, Barragán's aesthetically austere project is part of this lineage as well: the Wiring board, as an object, should be able to explain itself and its technological qualities but also to evoke possibilities and incite the imagination. For Barragán, this led to the notion that he would have to work against the traditional idea of casing or skin within product design. His challenge was to design a piece of *naked* hardware that could also communicate its operability with efficiency and elegance, and signal freedom of use by showing what streamlined PC design intended to hide. In a way, the nakedness of the Wiring board is not simply an effort to make form into a mere vehicle for functionality; more dramatically, it could be described as an overcoming of the dialectic of form and function, where each of them is open for the sake of the other.

The Wiring board's contribution to the field of programmable product design is twofold. First, the Wiring software (comprising the language, the API, and the IDE) was designed to make the programmability of hardware into something accessible. In relation to this, Barragán's use of the principles of visual communication to illustrate the operability of electronic circuits is a testimony to Maldonado's legacy. Second, Barragán traveled the reverse of Bonsiepe's conceptual route, from the interface back to the object. He did this, we could argue, because he saw that the interface could now be a way of bringing programmability to a wider variety of objects and spaces, beyond the office and into the house, the artist's studio, the science lab, and the workshop. In other words, Barragán applied the logic of the interface to hardware design, and in so doing, he arguably outlined, if only projectively, a new understanding of what a *user* can be. Even before the Internet of Things (IoT) had become a market compulsion, Barragán had grasped its most promising component: a widespread and open programmability that could allow us to build objects that can talk, move, and even learn. Arguably, the IoT is an industrial and commercial appropriation of what Wiring and Arduino first brought to communities of makers, hackers, and creators, but this should not lead us to regard them as mere steps in a ladder.

Following Kittler, we may say that hardware is no longer an unknown being. Wiring and Arduino are clear precursors to the rise of an open hardware community that has recently been enlivened by the success of the Raspberry Pi. Bearing in mind that these artifacts have all been linked to educational processes and institutions, we could read them as concrete responses to Kittler's urges. In "There is no Software," another of his radical attempts to create a critical philosophy of technology, Kittler targeted the foundations of the distinction between software and hardware, between the realm of immaterial bits and bytes and the world of atoms. Kittler's claim in that essay is that everything that happens at the computational level happens at the hardware level, even if it is not visible to our eyes.[57] This emphasis on the agency of the physical substrate of programming ignited intense discussions about the definition of hardware and software as separate components of computational processes, and this is a discussion that we should continue to engage in as cloud computing and similar notions gain a hold on the public imagination. If only by the imagery that they evoke, these notions seem to easily lean back on the idea that computational processes are immaterial and happen in no place. In fact, we know full well that these new computational processes rely on physical components and large-scale hardware infrastructures. Kittler's ideas allow us to challenge the widespread misperception of the internet as an immaterial realm removed from the specificities of time and space, and to be rid of the uncritical association of freedom with immateriality. As we enter into conversation with new generations who have been connected to the Internet through wireless means for their entire lives, these questions gain in poignancy. Now that experiments in biocomputation and quantum computing are beginning to creep into our reality – as the realm of hardware spreads into the textures of living cells and atoms – the need to deconstruct the distinction between software and hardware is more urgent than ever, and we need tools like Wiring to allow the perspectives of non-experts and non-academics to inform the discussion.

Notes

1 Friedrich Kittler, *Aufschreibesysteme 1800/1900* (Munich: Editorial, 2003); *Discourse Networks, 1800/1900*, translated by Michael Metteer, with Chris Cullens (Stanford: Stanford University Press, 1992).
2 Chris Wiltz, "COVID-19 Has Makers Building Their Own Ventilators," *Design News*, April 8, 2020, www.designnews.com/gadget-freak/covid-19-has-makers-building-their-own-ventilators.
3 Circuits Today, "Story and Development of Arduino." *Circuits Today*, www.circuitstoday.com/story-and-history-of-development-of-arduino, accessed June 4, 2021.
4 Bauhaus was operational for 14 years, Vkhutemas for 10 years, and Ulm for 15 years.
5 Bruno Latour and Peter Weibel (eds.), *Making Things Public: Atmospheres of Democracy* (Cambridge; Karlsruhe: MIT Press; ZKM, 2005).
6 Valerio Ochetto, *Adriano Olivetti: La biografia* (Rome: Edizioni di Comunita, 2015).
7 Alexandra Deschamps-Sonsino, *The Airport & the Convent: Life at the Interaction Design Intitute Ivrea* (n.p.: Blurb Books, 2021).
8 Ricardo Meggiato, "Che succede in Arduino?" *Wired.it*, February 12, 2015, www.wired.it/gadget/computer/2015/02/12/arduino-nel-caos-situazione/?refresh_ce=.
9 Arduino Team, "Two Arduinos Become One." *Arduino Blog*, October 1, 2016, https://blog.arduino.cc/2016/10/01/two-arduinos-become-one-2/.
10 Hernando Barragán, "The Untold History of Arduino." *The Untold History of Arduino*, 2016. https://arduinohistory.github.io/.
11 David Morgan (ed.), *Religion and Material Culture: The Matter of Belief* (London; New York: Routledge, 2009).

176 Sidetracking

12 Dan Hicks and Mary C. Beaudry (eds.), *The Oxford Handbook of Material Culture Studies* (Oxford: Oxford University Press, 2018).

13 Raúl Rojas and Ulf Hashagen (eds.), *The First Computers: History and Architectures* (Cambridge: MIT Press, 2002).

14 Nancy Forbes and Basil Mahon, *Faraday, Maxwell, and the Electromagnetic Field: How Two Men Revolutionized Physics* (Amherst: Prometheus, 2019).

15 David Laws, "Who Invented the Transistor?," *Computer History Museum Blog*, December 4, 2013, https://computerhistory.org/blog/who-invented-the-transistor/.

16 Bernhard E. Burdek, *Design: The History, Theory and Practice of Product Design* (Boston: Birkhäuser, 2005).

17 Bruno Latour, *Reassembling the Social: An Introduction to Actor-Network-Theory* (Oxford: Oxford University Press, 2007).

18 Tony Freeth, "Decoding an Ancient Computer." *Scientific American* 301, no. 6 (December 2009): 76–83.

19 Donald R. Hill, *The Book of Ingenious Devices (Kitáb al-Hiyal) by The Banú (sons of) Músà bin Shákir*, Translated and Annonated by Donald R. Hill (Dordrecht: Reidel, 1979).

20 Computer History Museum, "The Engines," *Computer History Museum*, Accessed July 19, 2021, www.computerhistory.org/babbage/engines/.

21 Steve Wozniak and Gina Smith, *iWoz: Computer Geek to Cult Icon. How I Invented the Personal Computer, Co-Founded Apple, and Had Fun Doing It* (New York: W. W. Norton, 2007).

22 José Vicente Asuar, "Música con computadores, ¿cómo hacerlo?" *Revista Musical Chilena* 26, no. 118 (January 1, 1972): 36–66.

23 Dan O'Sullivan and Tom Igoe, *Physical Computing: Sensing and Controlling the Physical World with Computers* (Boston: Course Technology Press, 2004).

24 Marco Palacios, *Between Legitimacy and Violence: A History of Colombia, 1875–2002*, translated by Richard Stoller (Durham: Duke University Press, 2006).

25 Fabian Prieto Ñañez, *Ingeniería de sistemas y computación, 1968–2010: Los pequeños números que hemos visto cambiar* (Bogotá: Universidad de los Andes, 2015).

26 Originally, Java had been designed to explore the emerging field of digital interactive television, but in the absence of sufficient conditions, it eventually became a general-purpose, object-oriented programming language with a WORA approach (write once, run anywhere). The Java code can be executed on all operating systems with a Java virtual machine, something that was relatively new at that moment. See: Federico Biancuzzi and Shane Warden, *Masterminds of Programming: Conversations with the Creators of Major Programming Languages* (Sebastopol: O'Reilly Media, 2009).

27 Hernando Barragán, "Software: ¿arte?," in *Hipercubo/ok: Arte, ciencia y tecnología en contextos próximos*, edited by Andrés Burbano and Hernando Barragán (Bogotá: Ediciones Uniandes, 2001), 187–195.

28 Images of the project are used as illustrations in Barragán, "Software: ¿Arte?"

29 Fernando Ramírez, *Nuevos nombres: Tecnología de la desilusión* (Bogotá: Banco de la República, 2003).

30 Hernando Barragán, *Wiring: Prototyping Physical Interaction Design* (Ivrea: Interaction Design Institute, 2004).

31 John Maeda and Paola Antonelli, *Design by Numbers* (Cambridge: MIT Press, 2001).

32 Casey Reas and Ben Fry, *Getting Started with Processing: A Hands-On Introduction to Making Interactive Graphics* (Sebastopol: Maker Media, 2015).

Wiring 177

33 Friedrich Kittler, "Hardware, das unbekannte Wesen," in *Medien, Computer, Realität: Wirklichkeitsvorstellungen und neue Medien*, edited by Sybille Kramer (Frankfurt: Suhrkamp, 1998), 124.
34 Kittler, "Hardware," 131.
35 "Wiring," accessed June 22, 2022, http://wiring.org.co/.
36 Atmel was an American manufacturer founded by Greek American George Perlegos in the 1980s; the AVR family of microcontrollers was created in 1996 and had on-chip flash memory for program storage. The AVR 128 are single-chip, reduced instruction set computers (RISCs) using a compact and highly optimized set of instructions.
37 Marshall McLuhan and Quentin Fiore, *The Medium Is the Massage* (Berkeley: Gingko Press, 2001).
38 Barragán, *Wiring*.
39 Warren Sack, *The Software Arts* (Cambridge: MIT Press, 2019).
40 Barragán, *Wiring*.
41 Nicholas Zambetti, discussing the new Wiring board in 2011, quoted in "Wiring," *Barraganstudio*, accessed July 31, 2021, http://barraganstudio.com/b/?p=185.
42 The Wiring website has a Colombian. co domain.
43 Sparkfun, "Wiring Board," *SparkFun Electronics*, accessed July 26, 2021, www.sparkfun.com/products/retired/9663.
44 The guiding thought behind Wiring++ was to apply an object-oriented programming logic to the Wiring language to be able to support parallel Processing through the use of threads by using the pins as objects. Although the project is on hold, its premise is undoubtedly worth developing.
45 In 2007, Barragán was invited to co-author a chapter on hardware for Reas and Fry's book *Processing: A Programming Handbook for Visual Designers and Artists* (Cambridge: MIT Press, 2007). In his contribution, Barragán traced the roots of his project back to Processing, arguing that the Processing software and API had from their inception been geared towards reading data through serial communication in order to connect with microcontrollers, sensors, and actuators, and went on to offer technical advice on the ways in which Processing and Wiring could be interfaced.
46 Burdek, *Design*.
47 Beatriz Colomina and Mark Wigley, *Are We Human? Notes on an Archaeology of Design* (Zürich: Lars Müller Publishers, 2017).
48 Isabel Clara Neves and João Rocha, "The Contribution of Tomás Maldonado to the Scientific Approach to Design at the Beginning of the Computational Era: The Case of the HfG of Ulm," paper presented at *Future Traditions: 1st eCAADe Regional International Workshop*, Porto, April 4, 2013.
49 Tomás Maldonado, María García, and Gabriel Pérez-Barreiro, *Tomás Maldonado in Conversation with/en conversación con María Amalia García* (New York: Fundación Cisneros, 2011).
50 Tomás Maldonado, *Vanguardia y racionalidad: artículos, ensayos y otros escritos, 1946–1974* (Buenos Aires: Gustavo Gili, 1977), 109–111.
51 Elisabetta Mori, "Olivetti ELEA Sign System: Interfaces Before the Advent of HCI." *IEEE Annals of the History of Computing* 42 (2020): 24–38.
52 Tomás Maldonado, *Crítica de la razón informática* (Barcelona: Paidós, 1998).
53 Eden Medina, *Cybernetic Revolutionaries: Technology and Politics in Allende's Chile* (Cambridge: MIT Press, 2011).
54 Gui Bonsiepe, *Del objeto a la interfase* (Buenos Aires: Infinito, 1999).
55 Bonsiepe, *Del objeto a la interfase*, 174–175.

178 Sidetracking

56 Deyan Sudjic, *Ettore Sottsass and the Poetry of Things* (London: Phaidon, 2019).
57 Friedrich Kittler, *No hay software y otros ensayos sobre filosofía de la tecnología* (Manizales: Universidad de Caldas, 2017), 39–48.

Bibliography

Arduino Team. "Two Arduinos Become One," *Arduino Blog*, October 1, 2016, https://blog.arduino.cc/2016/10/01/two-arduinos-become-one-2/.

Asuar, José Vicente. "Música con computadores, ¿cómo hacerlo?" *Revista musical chilena* 26, no. 118 (January 1, 1972): 36–66.

Barragán, Hernando. "Software: ¿arte?." In *Hipercubo/ok: Arte, ciencia y tecnología en contextos próximos*, edited by Andrés Burbano and Hernando Barragán. Bogotá: Ediciones Uniandes, 2001, 187–195.

———. *Wiring: Prototyping Physical Interaction Design*. Ivrea: Interaction Design Institute, 2004.

———. "The Untold History of Arduino," *The Untold History of Arduino*, 2016, https://arduinohistory.github.io/.

Biancuzzi, Federico and Shane Warden. *Masterminds of Programming: Conversations with the Creators of Major Programming Languages*. Sebastopol: O'Reilly Media, 2009.

Bonsiepe, Giu. *Del objeto a la interfase*. Buenos Aires: Infinito, 1999.

Burdek, Bernhard E. *Design: The History, Theory and Practice of Product Design*. Boston: Birkhäuser, 2005.

Circuits Today. "Story and Development of Arduino," *Circuits Today*, www.circuitstoday.com/story-and-history-of-development-of-arduino, accessed June 4, 2021.

Colomina, Beatriz and Mark Wigley, *Are We Human?: Notes on an Archaeology of Design*. Zürich: Lars Müller Publishers, 2017.

Computer History Museum. "The Engines," *Computer History Museum*, Accessed July 19, 2021, www.computerhistory.org/babbage/engines/.

Deschamps-Sonsino, Alexandra. *The Airport & the Convent: Life at the Interaction Design Institute Ivrea*. N.p.: Blurb Books, 2021.

Forbes, Nancy and Basil Mahon. *Faraday, Maxwell, and the Electromagnetic Field: How Two Men Revolutionized Physics*. Amherst: Prometheus, 2019.

Freeth, Tony. "Decoding an Ancient Computer." *Scientific American* 301, no. 6 (December 2009): 76–83.

Hicks, Dan and Mary C. Beaudry (eds.). *The Oxford Handbook of Material Culture Studies*. Oxford: Oxford University Press, 2018.

Hill, Donald R. *The Book of Ingenious Devices (Kitáb al-Hiyal) by The Banú (sons of) Músà bin Shákir, Translated and Annonated by Donald R. Hill*. Dordrecht: Reidel, 1979.

Kittler, Friedrich. *Discourse Networks, 1800/1900*, translated by Michael Metteer, with Chris Cullens. Stanford: Stanford University Press, 1992.

———. "Hardware, das unbekannte Wesen." In *Medien, Computer, Realität: Wirklichkeitsvorstellungen und neue Medien*, edited by Sybille Kramer. Frankfurt: Suhrkamp, 1998, 119–132.

———. *Aufschreibesysteme 1800/1900*. Munich: Fink, 2003.

———. *No hay software y otros ensayos sobre filosofía de la tecnología*. Manizales: Universidad de Caldas, 2017.

Latour, Bruno. *Reassembling the Social: An Introduction to Actor-Network-Theory.* Oxford: Oxford University Press, 2007.

Latour, Bruno and Peter Weibel (eds.). *Making Things Public: Atmospheres of Democracy.* Cambridge; Karlsruhe: MIT Press; ZKM, 2005.

Laws, David. "Who Invented the Transistor?" *Computer History Museum Blog,* December 4, 2013, https://computerhistory.org/blog/who-invented-the-transistor/.

Maeda, John and Paola Antonelli. *Design by Numbers.* Cambridge: MIT Press, 2001.

Maldonado, Tomás. *Vanguardia y racionalidad: artículos, ensayos y otros escritos, 1946–1974.* Buenos Aires: Gustavo Gili, 1977.

———. *Crítica de la razón informática.* Barcelona: Paidós, 1998.

Maldonado, Tomás, María Amalia García, and Gabriel Pérez-Barreiro. *Tomás Maldonado in Conversation with/en conversación con María Amalia García.* New York: Fundación Cisneros, 2011.

McLuhan, Marshall and Quentin Fiore. *The Medium Is the Massage.* Berkeley: Gingko Press, 2001.

Medina, Eden. *Cybernetic Revolutionaries: Technology and Politics in Allende's Chile.* Cambridge: MIT Press, 2011.

Meggiato, Ricardo. "Che succede in Arduino?," *Wired.it,* February 12, 2015, www.wired.it/gadget/computer/2015/02/12/arduino-nel-caos-situazione/?refresh_ce=.

Morgan, David (ed.). *Religion and Material Culture: The Matter of Belief.* London; New York: Routledge, 2009.

Mori, Elisabetta. "Olivetti ELEA Sign System: Interfaces Before the Advent of HCI." *IEEE Annals of the History of Computing* 42 (2020): 24–38.

Neves, Isabel Clara and João Rocha. "The Contribution of Tomás Maldonado to the Scientific Approach to Design at the Beginning of the Computational Era: The Case of the HfG of Ulm." Paper presented at *Future Traditions: 1st eCAADe Regional International Workshop,* Porto, April 4, 2013.

Ochetto, Valerio. *Adriano Olivetti: La biografia.* Rome: Edizioni di Comunita, 2015.

O'Sullivan, Dan and Tom Igoe. *Physical Computing: Sensing and Controlling the Physical World with Computers.* Boston: Course Technology Press, 2004.

Palacios, Marco. *Between Legitimacy and Violence: A History of Colombia, 1875–2002,* translated by Richard Stoller. Durham: Duke University Press, 2006.

Prieto Ñañez, Fabian. *Ingeniería de sistemas y computación, 1968–2010: Los pequeños números que hemos visto cambiar.* Bogotá: Universidad de los Andes, 2015.

Ramírez, Fernando. *Nuevos nombres: Tecnología de la desilusión.* Bogotá: Banco de la República, 2003.

Reas, Casey and Ben Fry. *Processing: A Programming Handbook for Visual Designers and Artists.* Cambridge: MIT Press, 2007.

———. *Getting Started with Processing: A Hands-On Introduction to Making Interactive Graphics.* Sebastopol: Maker Media, 2015.

Rojas, Raul and Ulf Hashagen (eds.). *The First Computers: History and Architectures.* Cambridge: MIT Press, 2002.

Sack, Warren. *The Software Arts.* Cambridge: MIT Press, 2019.

Sudjic, Deyan. *Ettore Sottsass and the Poetry of Things.* London: Phaidon, 2019.

180 *Sidetracking*

Wiltz, Chris. "COVID-19 Has Makers Building Their Own Ventilators," *Design News*, April 8, 2020, www.designnews.com/gadget-freak/covid-19-has-makers-building-their-own-ventilators.

Wozniak, Steve and Gina Smith. *iWoz: Computer Geek to Cult Icon. How I Invented the Personal Computer, Co-Founded Apple, and Had Fun Doing It.* New York: W. W. Norton, 2007.

Conclusions

In this book, I have engaged in a multifaceted research strategy based on historical studies, the technical analysis of media, the exploration of geo-cultural particularities, and the symbolic and practical reenactment of earlier technologies. Accordingly, the conclusions to this complex process reveal numerous layers of understanding of media technologies from Latin America. This has been possible thanks to the use of resignification as a key interpretive device, in the historical case studies, and a focus on the locally differentiated emergence of technological design, in the contemporary case studies. In this concluding chapter, I would like to offer some broad reflections based on the insights of this research project, which kept me busy for well over a decade.

The Goddess Technology

I have described my case studies as media technologies from the margins of history, and by now, it should be clear that I do not mean to imply that these technologies come from regions that are irrelevant to the stream of technological development. What I call the margins of history are rather locations whose technological histories have not been the object of a properly structured research program, which has led to the invisibilization of remarkable projects. These margins are underrepresented regions of the technological landscape – both of its history and of its present. I hope to have established that a detailed and creative study of the technical experiments generated in one of these marginal regions – Latin America – can contribute greatly to our understanding of media technologies.

In "Creole Technologies and Global Histories," David Edgerton argues that technology in the poor world cannot be explained on the basis of a simple-minded inventory of technologies imported from elsewhere, or of traditional or local technologies, or as a combination of both.[1] Although Edgerton's perspective certainly broadens the conventional point of view concerning technology in places like Latin America, one possibility that is absent from his sharp analysis is that of taking stock of technological invention in the poor world. It is my opinion that, on the contrary, a historical

DOI: 10.4324/9781003172789-9

182 Conclusions

discourse centered on the role of technological invention in places like Latin America is not only possible but necessary. In this text, I have attempted to move forward in this direction through the study of five case studies, singling out three historical and two contemporary media technological inventions as worthy subjects of scholarly scrutiny. I am convinced that we will not be able to establish an accurate account of what technology is in our world unless we continue to explore cases like these. I have argued, moreover, that the theoretical framework that could allow us to establish a proper analytical framework to make sense of processes of technological invention in the Global South must itself be crafted through the informed study of phenomena that have taken place there.

If we are to develop an accurate account of technological change in Latin America, we must certainly take into consideration and work through a variety of contemporary scholarly approaches: recent studies of traditional technologies,[2] the exploration of technology transfer from other latitudes,[3] the description of how technologies are shaped by use,[4] and the study of adaptation and modification as innovation processes.[5] In this book, however, I aimed to outline a path that does not necessarily fit any of these academic projects and to put forward a different and complementary point of view based on the historical study of invention (with a focus on media technologies). Although the argument of this book could be seen as leaning too emphatically on the kind of innovation-centric perspective that is characteristic of now-debated directions in technological historiography, I hope it has been clear that my aim is actually to contribute to developing a different appreciation of the problem of heuristics informed by the specific challenges that the Latin American context poses for that discursive framework.[6]

In his influential 1971 book *The Open Veins of Latin America*, the Uruguayan cultural critic Eduardo Galeano famously claimed that "the Goddess Technology does not speak Spanish."[7] This book means to suggest otherwise: in fact, technology can speak Spanish and has done so historically, although this speech has not been heard in the past. What this entails is that we must endeavor not to ignore it in the present. Technology can speak Spanish, technology has spoken Portuguese, and technology can speak and has spoken indigenous languages; technology can speak Maya, Kichwa, or Navajo, and to dispel any doubts, one need only refer to examples like that of the Code Talkers from the Navajo Nations.[8] The question is, then, why is it that when technology speaks Spanish, Portuguese, or Kichwa, our ears are unable to hear it, even when we know those languages well?

The experience that I wanted to share with the reader of this book is one that I myself lived through as my research progressed: an experience of surprise at finding myself traversing unknown routes that led me to a highly significant constellation of phenomena and to the complex history of performative technical imagination of media technologies in Latin America. I also wanted to show that this experience of surprise is also heavily loaded with ideological implications. The fact is that the invisibility of these

Conclusions 183

inventions is itself the result of a multiplicity of constructs: not only are they not regarded as part of "the history of technology" in a global sense, but they have also been excluded from the historical narratives created to ground the consolidation of Latin America's postcolonial states. In Latin America, the notion of technical invention has little place in canonical histories of media, technology, or its nation states, and this fact is indisputably related to the subcontinent's historical position in the shifting global map of power relations during the nineteenth and twentieth centuries.[9] This is why I understand my task as an inquiry into the borders of history, and it is also my reason for invoking technical invention as a key concept. Technical invention is usually regarded as having its natural place in wealthy and developed environments, and it is even applied as a criterion to differentiate societies that are referred to as educated from those that are not or that are only in the process of becoming so. To offer a different account of invention and its political, economic, and epistemic context is one of the steps that we need to take in order to topple these hegemonic assumptions.

Performative Technical Imagination

In her 2007 book *The Technical Imagination*, Argentinean critic Beatriz Sarlo explored early references to science and technology in the Argentinean literature of the first half of the twentieth century.[10] Sarlo advances a highly original reading of the way in which a Latin American society used storytelling as a vehicle to anticipate, imagine, and configure technological worlds, and she goes on to explain how a unique vision of modernity took shape through the literary work of authors like Horacio Quiroga and, in particular, Roberto Arlt. Arlt was a poet, novelist, and inventor from Argentina who used the inventor persona in many of his writings, and as Sarlo shows, he used literature in order to fine-tune the winds of modernity and to stage the appearance of technology in modern Latin America. Inspired by Sarlo's approach, I have chosen to travel the same route in the opposite direction: I decided to start with specific artifacts and their inventors and attempted to then track and outline the connections between their work and particular conceptions of artistic creativity – indeed, it is no coincidence that a few of the characters that are present in this book read very much like literary figures. I have tried to analyze the relationship between technical and artistic creativity from two different angles: on the one hand, the historical case studies bring into view a mixture of technical and artistic creativity in the way in which they were conceived and implemented by their makers; on the other, I have introduced an experimental approach of my own by undertaking creative projects in order to explore the symbolic meaning of these media technologies by way of reenactment.

It seems fair to say that, in general, the way in which an inventor develops a particular technology has many affinities with processes of creation found in the arts in general and in media arts in particular. Undoubtedly,

184 *Conclusions*

the kind of creativity required by an inventor is not necessarily the same as that of a painter or writer; nonetheless, I argue that historical research on media technologies is a privileged place to explore the relationship between technical and artistic creativity. The inventors discussed in the chapters of this book were working and experimenting with novel technical ways of producing, transmitting, or manipulating images, sounds, and interactions, and in doing so, they were unquestionably able to bring to light crucial issues and dimensions of aesthetics. Surely, an inventor who is just looking for an innovative way to produce or reproduce images is likely to become immersed in aesthetic concerns, and I have found myself time and again surprised by the double role that inventors often play as technical innovators and practitioners of an artistic discipline at the same time. Although it does not concern media technologies as such, a notable example from the Latinx context is the case of Mexican American Victor L. Ochoa, a fiction writer who also patented several flying machines at the beginning of the twentieth century in the United States.[11]

In the three historical cases that make up the first part of this book, I have found substantial evidence of the subtle forms of interaction between technical creativity – manifested in the inventions themselves – and artistic imagination – embodied in the artistic uses of the technologies invented or in the very process of creation. Hércules Florence was both an inventor and a professional visual artist;[12] José Vicente Asuar was an engineer and a composer, and he developed his engineering skills to create a computer with the explicit goal of using it to explore new compositional principles.[13] Although the case of Guillermo González Camarena is somewhat different, it is worth noting that he started out as a successful composer of popular music and that he developed his first color television system in a studio that he shared with the revered Mexican muralist Jorge González Camarena, who was in fact his elder brother.[14] This connection between technical and artistic creativity is also true for the contemporary cases: the Lua programming language was widely embraced by an industrial technological art form, computer games, which has become a second home for it, and the Wiring board was conceived from the beginning as a platform to foster interactive creative projects involving software and hardware. Wiring's creator, Hernando Barragán, is rightly considered as a professional in the fields of engineering, design, and art, and his work has been exhibited and celebrated in all three contexts. This is probably the most important contribution that this book hopes to make to the field of Latin American studies: to situate art, comprising all forms of cultural creativity, as a critical component of processes of technical invention, and thus to expose it as a legitimate vector driving technical change. This is a perspective that has not been explored in depth in studies of technological development in the Global South, and I hope that other scholars will feel inspired to improve on my efforts.

One reason for my interest in the interactions between technical and artistic creativity might be that my original background is in cinema – to

Conclusions 185

paraphrase Mark Twain, to a man with a hammer, everything looks like a nail. However, and as Friedrich Kittler has pointed out, it is also the case that the nature of technology cannot be fully disentangled from the field of art at the conceptual level. We must take into account the fact that the etymological root from which the Western concept of technology stems is the Greek term τέχνη, meaning both "art" and "technology," among other things.[15] Indeed, the twentieth century produced deep philosophical inquiries that sought to shed light on the imbrications of art and technology – to mention only one key example, John Sallis has argued that two of Martin Heidegger's influential essays, "The Question Regarding Technology" and "The Origin of the Work of Art," should actually be read as complementary components of a single intellectual endeavor.[16] For my part, I have chosen a path that is more practical than philosophical, and I would venture to say that, to some extent, reflection on these issues cannot be complete without a practical engagement.

When I developed the creative projects that built upon my experimental explorations based on historical research, I also found that there is room to explore phenomena that have thus far been neglected by traditionally construed historical research. One such phenomenon is the construction of mythical narratives about these forgotten technologies. Although my historical examination in the case of González Camarena allowed me to ascertain that the widespread belief in Mexico that the cameras used in NASA's Apollo and Voyager missions were based on his design was unfounded, it was almost impossible for me to disregard the poetic implications of this fabrication when I set out to conceptualize my own creative reenactment of his design. Something similar happened in the case of my creative project inspired by Florence; after he returned from a scientific expedition to the Amazon, Florence wanted to publish his notes on *zoophonie* in a book, and this is what led him to experiment with different printing techniques, including those using photosensitive chemicals. I found it essential to give completion to his vision and to explore how the *zoophonie* scores could be represented with the technology that he invented but was unable to use for such a purpose. In the case of Asuar, the situation is somewhat different, for here, the project was inspired by my discovery of his design's suitability for a form of music that would not have been a part of his mindset: techno music. The idea was then to create a contemporary adaptation of his COMDASUAR reconceptualized as a machine for creating loops to be used in other compositions and software packages. In spite of the differences, the three historical studies share a common denominator: in each case, the creative projects led me to engage with the symbolic and poetic worlds evoked by these three technologies and their histories.

Experimental Media Archaeology

The detailed description of technical devices has been a central element of my argumentative strategy, and my reason for this is that I find it extremely

186 *Conclusions*

important to ward off potential misunderstandings of the nature of the kind of technologies in which I am interested. In that regard, my project means to draw from media archaeology, a project that has done much to bring the concrete and singular aspects of technological artifacts into consideration.[17] The value of such an approach is particularly visible in the case of Florence's invention of *photographie* in 1833. In the previous literature, Florence's work has been consistently interpreted as an early instance of photography based on contemporary assumptions about what photography is as a technology. Boris Kossoy and other authors who have analyzed Florence's photographic experiments agree on the value of his work as an inventor of photography, but they also understand the camera obscura as a key structural component of photography as a technology and thereby fail to perceive the unique technological profile of his system.[18] For that reason, these authors read Florence' s design in light of artifacts like the Daguerreotype,[19] whereas a careful analysis of the sources and descriptions, and of the actual techniques used by Florence, have led me to conclude that his experiments are actually closer to a printing system based on photochemical means, that is to say, a photographic process that is not built around the camera obscura. Once my research led me to probe into this aspect of his project, the contact copies and the chemicals used to produce these copies emerged as the central problem. In this case, then, it was essential to present and establish a novel perspective by which to approach Florence's work and to clarify just what kind of photography he actually invented.

In the case of González Camarena's color television system, my in-depth study of the technical details of his patents allowed me to determine the precise place of his designs in their historical context. By comparing the technical description of his first patent with similar patents, most prominently Peter Goldmark's, I could show that González Camarena's work was not necessarily unique, although it was highly advanced. González Camarena obtained a US patent for a color television system just a couple of months before Goldmark, but it seems clear that both systems were built around the same premise of using a color wheel to create field-sequential color images. Going further, I compared González Camarena's Chromoscopic Adapter and Bi-color Simplified System with technical descriptions of the color cameras used in NASA's Apollo and Voyager missions, which allowed me to ascertain the absence of any evidence of a direct relationship between them. That conclusion was only possible after analyzing the documentation about the device carefully.

As for Asuar, the process of describing the COMDASUAR allowed me to understand its unique method for achieving synthetically produced sound. Asuar's use of the timers as sound generators entails a unique approach, quite different from that of others based on pulse-code modulation. In fact, I originally assumed that the COMDASUAR produced sound through analog means, or else by using a simplified version of a system like pulse-code modulation, and it was only by taking the time to work through his schematics and written descriptions that I was able to determine just how inventive his design was.

Of course, there are limits to what can be established on the basis of such detailed attention to the technical apparatus. In my efforts to fully understand the technologies described in the first part of this book, I was consistently constrained by the fact that I could only interact with them indirectly by way of historical documents, patents, and archives. Even if I was able to describe the technical device as accurately as possible, the absence of existing operational exemplars prevented me from a real direct experience of what it might be like to interact with them. To that extent, there is an unbridgeable gap that separates the most accurate of descriptions from an actually embodied encounter with these devices; the most that I could achieve would be to work with a model, not with the original thing.

Despite these limitations, when we examine the legacy of media archaeology, and in particular the direction in which the field has advanced through the work of Siegfried Zielinski and Erkki Huhtamo, we see that this is a field to which there is still much to contribute and that this cannot be achieved without a kind of relocation. This is why I have based my own approach on two ideas that can be used to redefine the tenets of media archaeology. Firstly, I have argued for the usefulness of undertaking practical and creative projects based on historical case studies. Secondly, I have argued for an expansion of the scope of media archaeological research by exploring a different geo-cultural area and finding examples that are not part of the corpus of the field. Of course, this is in line with the fact that both Zielienki and Huhtamo have taken their work in similar directions. After the introduction of Variantology Zielinski has overseen the production of five monumental edited volumes that, however, do not engage with Latin American case studies, in spite of the stated desire to do so in the last chapter of the last published volume in the series. For his part, Huhtamo has also called for an expansion of the media archaeological framework and stated that he refuses to believe that the history of media like the panorama or the magic lantern has no instances outside of the Western canon. This shift in direction led to a collaborative panel in ISEA 2019 in Gwangju, South Korea, where I joined Huhtamo and Machiko Kusahara to examine three instances of the magic lantern and unveil the different historical variants of that influential device in Europe, Japan, and Mexico.

In my own research, the decision to use practical projects to explore the nature and potentialities of historical media technologies has also allowed me to clarify elusive aspects in the documentation and opened a door to developing artistic projects derived from the outcomes. This is something that developed gradually as my work took shape. Originally, the aim of this practical approach was to validate by experiment the information found in some of the literature. My first experiments based on Florence's *photographie*, for example, were conceived as a way to clear some doubts about the possibility of using gold chloride in a photographic process. I was aware

188 *Conclusions*

that the Rochester Institute of Technology had conducted its own experiments to that end and that they had concluded that such chemical processes were indeed technologically plausible,[20] but many questions remained, so I decided to conduct my own experiments with gold chloride in order to better understand and clarify several aspects of the story. In the first of these experiments, I found out that the images kept getting darker and darker when they were being developed, including areas that were supposed to be white. As I later established, one reason for this was that I had not adequately cleaned the gold chloride and that water was not enough. I then double-checked the literature searching for information on how to stop the chemical reaction to light, and I came to identify with the way in which Florence himself described the problems that he had to deal with until he discovered the properties of ammonia.

When it came to González Camarena's color television system, there was no need for experimental validation since I had no doubts that the system worked. What drew me to attempt a reenactment in this case was rather an interest in the visual characteristics and aesthetic qualities of those color television images. The fact that the visual or sonic elements of old media have been lost with time is a matter of deep concern for the kind of study that I am engaged in. Therefore, and at the risk of sounding nostalgic, one of the most critical operations of my exploration of past media technologies was to try to recover and bring into view the qualitative peculiarities of my case studies. The practical project based on González Camarena's design allowed me to see just how different the color produced by a filter wheel system was from that of full electronic color equipment; most importantly, I could directly see how the qualities of the physical filters would modify the final visual results. A complete reconstruction of González Camarena's color process was not achieved since I was using the filters in the camera but not in the monitor, and in that sense, my project only covered half of the process. However, it was still enough to show exciting and distinctive visual qualities; the colors produced with filters are not crisp and tend to have a more pastel-like appearance, which is due to the interrelation of the elements, including the density of the filters. This feature of the system determined some of its historical mutations, as in the decision to replace the red filter by an orange filter in the Voyager cameras to compensate for the low sensibility of the Vidicon camera, which accounts for the orange tint seen in images of Jupiter captured by Voyager.[21]

In turn, the experimental project based on the COMDASUAR had other characteristics. Asuar created his sounds digitally and manipulated them in the analog domain. I found that the most interesting component of his system was the software, particularly his heuristic program. In his own presentation of the COMDASUAR, the Chilean inventor clearly described the operations that could be used to generate and produce musical ideas with this program, and this drove me to create a simplified model of the COMDASUAR that would allow to focus on and explore the functionalities of

Conclusions   189

this software, without reconstructing the analogue part of the system. The goal was to create a model that would combine aspects of old and new technologies, an odd but handy compositional device or, better yet, a personal computer in the sense in which Asuar understood it. The Raspberry Pi board offered a unique platform to develop this project because of its technical configuration and the fact that it shares many of the characteristics that Asuar was looking for in his own design, like versatility and affordability. From a structural point of view, the software applications designed in Csound can be described as new software versions of the ideas developed by Asuar in 1978, and the experience of using it has much to tell us about the possibilities and limitations of the COMDASUAR as a tool for composition.[22]

Although I devoted a great deal of effort to finding ways of reenacting the creative experience enabled by the media technologies created by Florence, González Camarena, and Asuar, it is clear that the results of my work cannot be described as proper reconstructions. At best, we can regard them as models or experiments that allow us to better understand different aspects of these historical artifacts. However, I must acknowledge the importance of earlier efforts to reconstruct historical media technologies, like Paul Doornbusch's admirable work on the early computer music system at CSIRAC, which were essential sources of inspiration for my project.[23]

In addition to all this, the experimental approach allowed me to inflect the notion of the resignification of media technologies in a new way, and I believe that the theoretical implications of this decision are worth elaborating. In case studies like my own, in which the inventor is no longer present, only a creative user who is also a retrospective user – a *retroactive* user, then – can be a proper agent of resignification. The concept of resignification was coined by professor Hernán Thomas to account for socio-technical processes in which original technologies are deeply transformed by use. As Thomas argues, this is not simply a process of adaptation or transfer since resignified technologies typically come to find a novel meaning, even for purposes that are totally different from the ones that they were originally created to serve.[24] In my own approach, I argue that historical media technologies can only be fully understood by being resignified through creative experimentation.

In my two contemporary case studies, Lua and Wiring, I was of course able to explore the tools directly as a user, so there was no need for me to engage with them retroactively. Nonetheless, here, too, my interest in their history was motivated by my experiences of these technologies as platforms for creativity. I first came across Lua through two of my fellow colleagues at UCSB's Media Arts and Technology program, Wesley Smith and Graham Wakefield, who were developing the project LuaAV, a framework for creative computing somewhat similar to Processing but based on the Brazilian programming language. Their work introduced me to the general framework of Lua, which I found fascinating, and this in turn made me want to

190   *Conclusions*

dig into its structure and its history. In the case of Wiring, I was lucky to be aware of the project since Barragán started working on it. At the time I had been following his work and for a few years, during which we occasionally collaborated, and I first perceived Wiring as a natural turn in his work; however, I was unable to anticipate how influential it would become. While I was still a graduate student, I was in fact able to contribute to the first efforts to interface the Wiring board with C++ code, and later on, I used the Wiring Mini board on some of my own projects, the most visible of which was *Two Cycles*, a platform for nomadic electronic sound based on two bicycles in motion, each of which was equipped with a GPS, accelerometers, and small weather station based on Wiring that could sense air quality (CO, CO_2, and alcohol). The parameters captured by these sensors and meters were transformed into sound in real time, and a portable Wi-Fi system shuttled the data back and forth from one bike to the other according to acceleration and proximity.

Invention, Innovation, and the Narratives of Unsuccess

One of the most challenging theoretical problems that I encountered in my research was that of conceptualizing my case studies as examples of invention while challenging the assumption that technological change is a function of success. My research suggests that the function of success as a core category must be debated, although it is not my intention to undermine the historical relevance of priority. On the contrary, in my research, I have relied on the idea that it is essential to establish a chronology that is as detailed as possible, to determine what happened before and what happened after, and to highlight the importance of events that happened in parallel. Nonetheless, chronological accuracy does not substitute for conceptual rigor.

Narratives around technological change often present invention and innovation as elements of a single two-step process.[25] The economist Joseph Schumpeter famously argued for a fundamental distinction between invention, understood as a novel creation, and innovation, understood as an economically successful invention.[26] Schumpeter's vision of innovation has been influential in many fields, from economics to innovation policy design, and similar accounts of the problem have been outlined by William Middendorf and others.[27] It must be noted that these authors do not frame this distinction from an ontological point of view but rather as a methodological resource that allows them to explain historical dynamics in their respective fields of interest. In my own field of interest, however, such a clear-cut distinction fails to capture much of what is at stake.

Time and again, my case studies led me to question the narrative of an implicit teleology that leads from invention to innovation. There are certainly many reasons to be suspicious of this teleology and to argue that innovation must be understood as a possible development but not necessarily as the final aim of an invention. A question to be asked in this regard is whether it is possible to think about invention, and about networks of interwoven inventions, without reading them in light of a presupposed drive to fulfillment in the form of a prosperous life as commodities. My sense is that this is indeed possible and that one way of achieving it is by developing a perspective that focuses on the localized creative process and the meaning of a particular technology in a specific moment, bearing in mind that, from a historical point of view, it is often the case that inventions and technical concerns come to acquire a renewed meaning years, decades, or even centuries after their creation.

In his book *How Invention Begins*, John Lienhard focuses on the problem of priority, which he understands as the consensus that leads to the acceptance of a canonical inventor as the author of a particular technology. Lienhard outlines the daunting difficulties that arise when the achievements of such canonical inventors are compared with those of other inventors who came up with similar proposals at more or less the same time.[28] A detailed study of the problem of priority in several different media technologies may lead us to a sad conclusion: in most cases, only one or two inventors have been credited with the invention of particular media technologies like photography, although careful examination often suggests that there were many key creative technologists who contributed to or even invented the same technology in parallel. As a result of this entrenchment of established narratives, most of those inventors are simply forgotten and, what is perhaps more dramatic, alternative versions of established technologies are forgotten.

In this text, I have turned my attention to creators who, for the most part, have not been credited as the canonical inventors of specific media technologies and who are better described as nodes in an interwoven network of technological invention. For this reason, historiography plays an important role in my research. The answer to the problem of priority is often elusive, but it may also be the case that it is not crucial. Given the amount of evidence regarding synchronous or multiple inventions, it comes as no surprise that this is particularly true in the case of media technologies. More generally, the same point can be made about several key inventions, including the computer: the best answer to the question of priority is arguably to say that, in fact, priority is just not the most appropriate concept for understanding the genesis of a technology. This should come as no surprise if we regard technologies as cultural products, and yet there is a tenacious resistance to deal with the consequences of this conceptual shift. Lately, a new way of articulating the task at hand has been put forward, and some authors have sought to account for the origins of media technologies by attending to the climates that characteristically determine the development of innovative solutions to technological problems.[29] If, along these lines, we regard the priority problem as secondary, we will no longer be simply concerned with individual inventions, but our attention will be directed towards what Lienhard calls the filigreed fabric of interwoven invention,[30] and it is my hope that my case studies will be useful in that regard.

192 *Conclusions*

There is a lot to learn from the study of constellated processes of invention that configure various attempts to find technical solutions, most of which did not consolidate into commodities. Of course, if we recognize today the historical importance of the impact that photography, color television, musical computing, computer games, and platforms for digital interaction have had on a wide variety of social spaces, it is interesting to explore the processes underlying the configuration of such technologies in a broad sense. The three historical cases studied in the first part of this book are inventions that did not lead to innovation processes as Schumpeter understands them, even though they can certainly be described as highly innovative. The value of these case studies relies on the creative proposal, the new trait, rather than on the commercial impact of the inventions. The two contemporary case studies in the second part of the book are stories of a different sort. Lua has had and continues to have an important impact on several areas of computing, from video games to embedded systems, although this impact has not translated into economic success for the Lua team, all of whom have consolidated academic careers. Wiring, however, has been very influential, and its legacy and profound contribution to the open hardware community have gained increasing recognition through time, although the project was unsustainable and inevitably came to a halt.

When we think today about media technologies like photography, color television, musical hardware and software, computer games, and platforms for physical interaction, we know that they have introduced remarkable shifts in the histories of image, sound, storytelling, and programming. Since canonical historical accounts of these transformations have interpreted the technologies involved as the result of innovation processes, attention to success has been a significant factor motivating the description.[31] To better understand invention, it is essential to take a closer look at the creative process, and this is a task that may be addressed in different ways: by analyzing the interactions between invention and knowledge; by exploring the inventor's relationship to their social environment; by determining the effectiveness and potentialities of the technologies, exploring the motivations, the concern for profit, and the exercise of freedom that underlie the act of inventing; and last but not least, by examining the role that failure can play in this creative landscape.[32]

We must not forget that there are reasons why invention and innovation have been presented as closely connected processes. One such reason is the historical importance of figures like Thomas Alva Edison in the United States, who was at the same time a creative inventor and an extremely ambitious businessman.[33] The unquestionable impact of Edison's achievements as a designer and entrepreneur provides a solid foundation for the standard interpretation of processes of invention. Indeed, we may recall what Friedrich Kittler once said about him: "Edison . . . is an important figure for American culture, like Goethe for German culture. But between Goethe and myself there is Edison."[34] Nonetheless, a deeper understanding of particular media technologies and their significance can be enriched by studying the different versions of that technology that coexisted at the time of its emergence. In doing so, we are confronted with the problem of accounting for how, from out of these different versions, a divergent path came to separate what the technology became from what it might have become.

Decolonial Technologies and the Question of Open-Source

The recent wave of new discursive and critical frameworks for interpreting and analyzing Latin American reality has much to gain from a confrontation with the question concerning technology, and this book is a modest attempt to formulate some thoughts around the role of media and technology in Latin American societies and histories. It is my hope that these examinations can be used to challenge the linkages between modernity and colonialism, which have led some to define coloniality as "the dark side of the modern project."[35] As the ongoing renewal in the study of the history of science in Latin America has shown, a critical approach leading to new perspectives for the study of technology, and of media technologies in particular, will allow us to find different ways of understanding and reframing inherited discursive assumptions.[36] Nevertheless, and although decolonial discourses command our attention and respect, we must be careful not to use them recklessly. In their manifesto of sorts, *On Decoloniality*, Walter Mignolo and Catherine Walsh argue that "decoloniality" should be understood as a fundamental concept, like Freud's "the unconscious" or Marx's "surplus value."[37] This ambitious characterization has fostered a tendency to bring decolonial practices into play wherever critical theory is needed, which might lead to their misuse and even abuse. It could be said that for a field like decolonial studies to move forward it must make room within itself for cases and topics that can lead it to question its own assumptions.

From my own standpoint, there are two important questions to raise in this regard. Firstly, when our field of study reaches into deep time, it becomes clear that the concept of decoloniality is enriched by further historical inquiries into the colonial period. There are, for instance, experts in colonial culture who are not aware of decolonial discourse, and vice versa, and there is certainly a need for cross-pollination between these academic communities. Since not all colonial histories unfold in the same way, the instruments that we use to make sense of them should be versatile and adaptable. Secondly, until now, decolonial studies have only dealt tangentially with technological topics, and I believe that this is an area where there is important work to be done. The discipline should come to terms with the concepts and ideas being developed by disciplines like science and technology studies, for instance, and it should work towards developing ways of addressing specific topics of concern, like the pervasive role of surveillance in contemporary societies, the uses of AI, new developments in biotechnology, and of course, the

194   *Conclusions*

contemporary transformation of media technologies that are reshaping the world and even altering the ways in which capitalism works through the emergence of new modalities like cognitive capitalism or surveillance capitalism. In my view, we can find important guidelines on how to confront both of these questions in the work of Silvia Rivera Cusicanqui. Firstly, because she has shown us how important it is to revisit historical figures from the colonial period, like the Inca writer Felipe Guamán Poma de Ayala (1534–1615), whose contexts were determined by the interaction of colonial and decolonial assemblages. Secondly, because she has outlined a keen approach to the sociology of the image, which she understands as an "art of doing," a practice that is simultaneously and inextricably "theoretical, aesthetic, and ethical" and that "sees no boundaries between artistic creation and conceptual and political reflection."[38] If, following these guidelines, we can set the terms for a sociology of technical invention through the arts, our field of study would be clearly defined.

Books can often be defined as performing a particular operation, and in that regard, *Different Engines* is a question book: a book that seeks to voice a question about the interactions between technical invention and the arts through findings that may contribute to expanding decolonial and postdevelopment lines of thought and inquiry. Among the thinkers who are currently pushing the envelope in these intellectual projects, my work has been strongly influenced by that of Arturo Escobar, and this is for several reasons. Escobar engaged in an exploration of the anthropology of cyberculture in his 1994 essay "Welcome to Cyberia: notes on the anthropology of cyberculture," which remains highly influential to this day;[39] he has contributed enormously to our efforts to rethink the idea of development; he has put forward a suggestive account of the relationship between the ideas of territory and difference grounded on judicious field work; and he has recently turned his attention to design by linking two presumably antithetical concepts: autonomy and interdependence, which appear time and again throughout my argument, sometimes in the foreground and sometimes in the background. The theme of autonomy was directly addressed in my study of the Lua programming language, with reference to Emanuel Adler's analyses of Brazil's search for technological autonomy; but it has also been present, indirectly, as a thread that takes on different guises throughout the book. The sense that Escobar's recent work on design can be elaborated from a technologically informed perspective is not foreign to what the author himself proposes, and it is worth remembering that he was greatly influenced by the concepts developed by Terry Winograd and Fernando Flores, and most significantly by their 1984 work *Understanding Computers and Cognition: A New Foundation for Design*, where they argue for a new reading of the principles of design based on an ontological perspective through a lucid reading of computing and programming as representational processes. This leads us to conclude that Escobar's search for the Pluriverse can certainly be regarded as infused by reflections coming from computer science and

Conclusions 195

computing theory, and I understand my own work as a contribution to this line of search.

In 2022, with the influence that digital media have in all aspects of life, it is more important than ever for us to reflect on the grounds and criteria by which we make decisions about technology. It is a common assumption that technology has reached a level of complexity that far surpasses the layperson's capacity for understanding and that only experts are in any position to make adequate decisions on our behalf. Much to the contrary, this book aims to show that, on many levels, technological invention is constantly at play in many different locations and social spaces. As my case studies suggest, there are individuals and communities in Latin America, as elsewhere, who have developed a deep understanding of what became influential media technologies, to the point of venturing new systems and premises, which clearly suggests that these societies could well be in a position to make their own technological decisions if they ceased to regard their own technological creators as outliers. In any case, it should be noted that an interest in technological autonomy does not entail a call for disconnection. It would be unrealistic and pointless to insist on isolation, and this book's historical case studies have clearly shown that Latin American realities have long been shaped by shifting relational networks among local and foreign locations and cultures: everything happened somewhere between nodes, along lines connecting places like Brazil and France, Mexico and the United States, Chile and other Latin American countries, Brazil and the United States, Colombia and Italy, at different moments and embedded within broader complex networks and assemblages. This means that we must always be able to take notions of cultural, national, and regional identity with a twist, and that we should strive to fully and rigorously embrace the implications of relationality as a master concept, which is certainly not the same as simplifying or side-stepping the inequalities and asymmetries that continue to frame the way in which such networks come into being and develop. As my case studies have shown, these inequalities have not prevented technological creators from moving back and forth along the threads that connect individual nodes, and for them, this has been a space of agency, self-assertion, and creativity. In that regard, this book can be broadly construed as a call for self-criticism on the part of Latin American societies. It has taken us much too long to address these issues, and the historical lack of understanding and support for technical innovators is a clear indication of the systematic disinterest in these topics among us. If we are to be equipped to face the challenges that the contemporary world presents to our ways of life, we will have to earnestly commit to dealing with these questions and avoid easy exits.

Readers may have noticed that the open-source philosophy and practical framework play an important role in my last two case studies. Both Lua and Wiring were developed in conversation with the principles of open-source, and this is something that tremendously facilitated their development. In

196   *Conclusions*

the case of Lua, which I have described as the only success story in the book, the team became fully aware of the open-source culture once the project was underway, but they were quick to grasp its relevance and keen to use it in their favor. As I have shown, Lua would probably not have spread as it did if the team had not decided to release new versions of the language under the MIT license. In broad terms, it is fair to say that open-source, open hardware, open culture, and open knowledge are vital concepts that can undoubtedly promote the further evolution of technology, science, and the arts in Latin America and elsewhere in the Global South. However, a closer look at the Lua example also shows that the team was able to maintain control over the evolution of the programming language by taking on a studied approach to open-source and by limiting development to the work of a closed group. This goes to show that there are many possible ways to implement the principles of open-source based on a clear understanding of the implications, and it is crucial to be aware of the latter in order to avoid the misperception of open-source culture as a deus ex machina or a panacea. As the case of Wiring shows, the open-source philosophy can just as easily lead creators from the Global South down a path that places their innovations at risk of being co-opted. Wiring had all the components of a project that could have been widely adopted, but an unjustified decision to fork the project away from its founder without a proper attribution process at a time when a community was just beginning to consolidate around it, along with the difficulties that came with trying to handle the production aspects of the project from Colombia, made it unsustainable in the long term.

As I reach the end of this brief overview of the insights produced by my research for this book, I can hardly fail to mention the absence of women in my case studies, which poses a critical problem. At the onset of my research, I set out to look for artifacts, and as I delved into the stories behind those artifacts, I found that they were overwhelmingly the work of male subjects, perhaps a feminist reading of these same case studies might have put into question the idea that these artifacts were solely created by single male individuals and sought instead to unveil the more diverse social contexts and networks of innovation and care that enabled them. I could not presume to be able to fully outline the historical reasons behind this contingency, but I must stress that this is certainly one more area of our historical and social reality where the narrative of male dominance must be thoroughly and rigorously denaturalized. In a field of study such as my own, where information and adequate documentation are incredibly hard to obtain, the absence of evidence as to the work of women technical creators cannot be accepted as a bottom line. If I had the opportunity to start over with this project, I would decisively question my decision to regard the artifacts themselves as my gateway into social and geopolitical realities, and I would place feminist lines of questioning at the very heart of my research methodology. There are important topics to be addressed here, which go beyond

Conclusions 197

the obvious difficulties that many modern societies in the Global South have had, and continue to have, when it comes to perceiving women as agents of technological creativity. This is certainly not the case in the contemporary scholarship on these subjects, and it is clear that my intellectual influences and theoretical sources are decisively framed by the contributions of female colleagues like Eden Medina, María Fernández, Gabriela Aceves, Beatriz Sarlo, Anita Say Chan, Alejandra Bronfman, and Joanna Page, to mention only a few of the outstanding scholars and practitioners whose works have been published in English, which is the language of this book. To complete this list, we could add an equally outstanding list of publications in Spanish and Portuguese by authors like Jazmin Adler or Simone Osthoff. These bibliographical considerations lead to another important observation: about 15 years ago, when I started to work on the research whose results I have compiled in this book, there was a very small number of academic works on Latin America that engaged with topics like STS studies of media technologies and the history of media arts, computing, science, or technical invention regarding media technologies. The recent surge of works by the scholars that I have just mentioned, and the many that are currently under preparation, can certainly be said to signal the consolidation of a promising interdisciplinary dialogue. Today, I am convinced that a book like this will be sown in a fertile ground because the growing number of remarkable publications will be just as many nodes in a network that will soon come to be acknowledged as an established, crucial, and lively field of study.

Notes

1 David Edgerton, "Creole Technologies and Global Histories: Rethinking How Things Travel in Space and Time." *Journal of History of Science and Technology* 1 (2007): 75.
2 Alexander Herrera, *La recuperación de tecnologías indígenas: Arqueología, tecnología y desarrollo en los Andes* (Bogotá: Universidad de los Andes, 2011).
3 Jonathan D. Hagood, "Why Does Technology Transfer Fail? Two Technology Transfer Projects from Peronist Argentina." *Comparative Technology Transfer and Society* 4 (2006): 73–98.
4 Andres F. Valderrama, "The Map of Transmilenio: Representation, System and City." *STS Encounters* 4, no. 2 (2011): 69–110.
5 Hernán Thomas, *Social Studies of Technology in Latin America* (Quito: FLACSO, 2010), 35–53.
6 David Edgerton, *The Shock of the Old: Technology and the Global History Since 1900* (Oxford: Oxford University Press, 2007), 184–205.
7 Eduardo Galeano, *Las venas abiertas de América Latina* (Mexico City: Siglo XXI, 1994), 315.
8 Judith S. Avila, *Code Talker: The First and Only Memoir by One of the Original Navajo Code Talkers of WWII* (New York: Berkley Trade, 2011).
9 Oscar Guardiola, *What if Latin America Ruled the World?* (London: Bloomsbury, 2010), 286–322.
10 Beatriz Sarlo, *The Technical Imagination: Argentine Culture's Modern Dreams* (Stanford: Stanford University Press, 2007).

198 Conclusions

11 David D. Romo, *Ringside Seat to a Revolution: An Underground Cultural History of El Paso and Juarez: 1893–1923* (El Paso: Cinco Puntos Press, 2005), 45–51.

12 Boris Kossoy, *Hércules Florence: A descoberta isolada da fotografia no Brasil* (São Paulo: Edusp, 1980), 190.

13 Federico Schumacher, "50 años de música electroacústica en Chile." *Revista Musical Chilena* 61, no. 208 (2007): 66–81.

14 Guillermo González Camarena Jr. and Arturo González Camarena, interview with author, 2010.

15 Martin Heidegger, "The Origin of the Work of Art," in *Poetry, Language, Thought* (New York: Harper Perennial Modern Classics, 2001), 15–86.

16 María del Rosario Acosta and Andrés Burbano, "Entrevista con John Sallis," in *La mirada de las cosas: El arte como provocación* (Bogotá: Universidad de los Andes, 2008), 97–113.

17 Siegfried Zielinski, *Deep Time of the Media* (Cambridge: MIT Press, 2006), 255.

18 Boris Kossoy, "Hercule Florence, l'inventeur en exil," in *Les Multiples inventions de la photographie* (Cerisy-la-Salle: Ministère de la Culture de la Communication des Grands Travaux et du Bicentenaire, 1988) 73–80.

19 Rosana Monteiro, "Brasil, 1833: A descoberta da fotografia revisitada" (Masters thesis, Unicamp, 1997), 50–54.

20 Kossoy, *Hercules Florence*, 237.

21 Bradford Smith, interview with author, 2012.

22 The help and orientation of UCSB researcher Andrés Cabrera was fundamental in the COMDASUAR understanding and recontruction.

23 Paul Doornbusch, *The Music of CSIRAC, Australia's First Computer Music* (Melbourne: Common Ground Publishing, 2005).

24 Hernán Thomas, "Estructuras cerradas vs. procesos dinámicos: Trayectorias y estilos de innovación y cambio tecnológico," in *Actos, actores y artefactos: Sociología de la Tecnología* (Bernal: Editorial de la Universidad Nacional de Quilmes, 2008), 217–262.

25 Michael J. O'Brien and Stephen J. Shennan, "Issues in Anthropological Studies of Innovation," in *Innovation in Cultural Systems: Contributions from Evolutionary Anthropology*, edited by Michael J. O'Brien and Stephen J. Shennan (Cambridge: MIT Press, 2010), 3–18.

26 Joseph Schumpeter, *Essays: On Entrepreneurs, Innovations, Business Cycles, and the Evolution of Capitalism* (New Jersey: Transaction Publishers, 1989), 47–63.

27 William H. Middendorf, *What Every Engineer Should Know about Inventing* (New York: CRC Press, 1981), 9–28.

28 John Lienhard, *How Invention Begins: Echoes of Old Voices in the Rise of New Machines* (Oxford: Oxford University Press, 2006), 19–36.

29 Norbert Wiener, *Invention. The Care and the Feeding of Ideas* (Cambridge: MIT Press, 1994), 11–76.

30 Lienhard, *How Invention Begins*, 233.

31 Pierre Bonhomme, "Le patrimoine au present," in *Les multiples inventions de la photographie*, 19.

32 Emanuel Adler, "Argentina's Aborted Venture into Computers in the Mid-1970s," in *The Power of Ideology: The Quest for Technological Autonomy in Argentina and Brazil* (Berkeley: University of California Press, 1987), 223–238.

33 Lisa Gitelman, *Scripts, Grooves, and Writing Machines: Representing Technology in the Edison Era* (Stanford: Stanford University Press, 1997), 97–146.

34 Matthew Griffin and Susanne Herrmann, "Technologies of Writing: Interview with Friedrich A. Kittler." *New Literary History* 27, no. 4 (1996): 735.

Conclusions 199

35 Santiago Castro-Gomez, *La hybris del punto cero: Ciencia, raza e ilustración en la Nueva Granada (1750–1816)* (Bogotá: Pontificia Universidad Javeriana, 2006), 21–65.
36 Arturo Escobar, *Encountering Development: The Making and Unmaking of the Third World* (New York: Princeton University Press, 2011), 208.
37 Walter D. Mignolo and Catherine E. Walsh, *On Decoloniality: Concepts, Analytics, Praxis* (Durham: Duke University Press, 2018).
38 Silvia Rivera Cusicanqui, *Sociología d la imagen: miradas ch'ixi desde la historia andina* (Buenos Aires): 13–34.
39 Arturo Escobar et al., "Welcome to Cyberia: Notes on the Anthropology of Cyberculture [and Comments and Reply]," *Current Anthropology* 35, no. 3 (1994): 211–231.

Bibliography

Acosta, María del Rosario and Andrés Burbano. "Entrevista con John Sallis." In *La mirada de las cosas: El arte como provocación*. Bogotá: Universidad de los Andes, 2008, 97–113.

Adler, Emanuel. *The Power of Ideology: The Quest for Technological Autonomy in Argentina and Brazil*. Berkeley: University of California Press, 1987.

Avila, Judith S. *Code Talker: The First and Only Memoir by One of the Original Navajo Code Talkers of WWII*. New York: Berkley Trade, 2011.

Castro-Gomez, Santiago. *La hybris del punto cero: Ciencia, raza e ilustración en la Nueva Granada (1750–1816)*. Bogotá: Pontificia Universidad Javeriana, 2006.

Doornbusch, Paul. *The Music of CSIRAC, Australia's First Computer Music*. Melbourne: Common Ground Publishing, 2005.

Edgerton, David. "Creole Technologies and Global Histories: Rethinking How Things Travel in Space and Time." *Journal of History of Science and Technology* 1 (2007): 75–112.

———. *The Shock of the Old: Technology and Global History Since 1900*. Oxford: Oxford University Press, 2007.

Escobar, Arturo. *Encountering Development: The Making and Unmaking of the Third World*. New York: Princeton University Press, 2011.

———. *Designs for the Pluriverse: Radical Interdependence, Autonomy, and the Making of Worlds*. Durham: Duke University Press, 2018.

Escobar, Arturo, David Hess, Isabel Licha, Will Sibley, Marilyn Strathern, and Judith Sutz. "Welcome to Cyberia: Notes on the Anthropology of Cyberculture [and Comments and Reply]." *Current Anthropology* 35, no. 3 (1994): 211–231.

Galeano, Eduardo. *Las venas abiertas de América Latina*. Mexico City: Siglo XXI, 1994.

Gitelman, Lisa. *Scripts, Grooves, and Writing Machines: Representing Technology in the Edison Era*. Stanford: Stanford University Press, 1997.

Griffin, Matthew and Susanne Herrmann. "Technologies of Writing: Interview with Friedrich A. Kittler." *New Literary History* 27, no. 4 (1996): 731–742.

Guardiola, Oscar. *What if Latin America Ruled the World?* London: Bloomsbury, 2010.

Hagood, Jonathan D. "Why Does Technology Transfer Fail? Two Technology Transfer Projects from Peronist Argentina." *Comparative Technology Transfer and Society* 4 (2006): 73–98.

200 Conclusions

Heidegger, Martin. "The Origin of the Work of Art." In *Poetry, Language, Thought*. New York: Harper Perennial Modern Classics, 2001, 15–86.

Herrera, Alexander. *La recuperación de tecnologías indígenas: Arqueología, tecnología y desarrollo en los Andes*. Bogotá: Universidad de los Andes, 2011.

Kossoy, Boris. *Hércules Florence: A descoberta isolada da fotografia no Brasil*. São Paulo: Edusp, 1980.

———. "Hercule Florence, l'inventeur en exil." In *Les Multiples inventions de la photographie*. Cerisy-la-Salle: Ministère de la Culture de la Communication des Grands Travaux et du Bicentenaire, 1988, 73–80.

Lienhard, John. *How Invention Begins: Echoes of Old Voices in the Rise of New Machines*. Oxford: Oxford University Press, 2006.

Middendorf, William H. *What Every Engineer Should Know about Inventing*. New York: CRC Press, 1981.

Mignolo, Walter D. and Catherine E. Walsh. *On Decoloniality: Concepts, Analytics, Praxis*. Durham: Duke University Press, 2018.

Monteiro, Rosana. "Brasil, 1833: A descoberta da fotografia revisitada." Master's thesis, Unicamp, 1997.

O'Brien, Michael J. and Stephen J. Shennan. "Issues in Anthropological Studies of Innovation." In *Innovation in Cultural Systems: Contributions from Evolutionary Anthropology*, edited by Michael J. O'Brien and Stephen J. Shennan. Cambridge: MIT Press, 2010, 3–18.

Rivera Cusicanqui, Silvia. *Sociología de la imagen: Miradas ch'ixi desde la historia andina*. Buenos Aires: Tinta Limón, 2015.

Romo, David D. *Ringside Seat to a Revolution: An Underground Cultural History of El Paso and Juarez: 1893–1923*. El Paso: Cinco Puntos Press, 2005.

Sarlo, Beatriz. *The Technical Imagination: Argentine Culture's Modern Dreams*. Stanford: Stanford University Press, 2007.

Schumacher, Federico. "50 años de música electroacústica en Chile." *Revista musical chilena* 61, no. 208 (2007): 66–81.

Schumpeter, Joseph. *Essays: On Entrepreneurs, Innovations, Business Cycles, and the Evolution of Capitalism*. New Jersey: Transaction Publishers, 1989.

Thomas, Hernán. "Estructuras cerradas vs. procesos dinámicos: Trayectorias y estilos de innovación y cambio tecnológico." In *Actos, actores y artefactos: Sociología de la Tecnología*. Bernal: Editorial de la Universidad Nacional de Quilmes, 2008, 217–262.

———. *Social Studies of Technology in Latin America*. Quito: FLACSO, 2010.

Valderrama, Andrés F. "The Map of Transmilenio: Representation, System and City." *STS Encounters* 4, no. 2 (2011): 69–110.

Wiener, Norbert. *Invention. The Care and the Feeding of Ideas*. Cambridge: MIT Press, 1994.

Zielinski, Siegfried. *Deep Time of the Media*. Cambridge: MIT Press, 2006.

Index

Note: *Italic* page references indicate figures.

Aceves, Gabriela 12, 197
Adler, Emanuel 12, 71, 128–131, 194
Adler, Jazmin 197
Algol programming language 121–122
Altair 8800 microcomputer 98
analog-to-digital converter (ADC) 89
Analytical Engine 87–88, 152
anthropology of cyberculture 194
Antikythera mechanism 151
API (application programming
 interface) 124–125
Apollo mission and color television 7,
 43–44, 63, 185
Arab Renaissance and automation
 151–152
Arduino (electronics prototyping kit)
 11, 147–149, 170
Argentina's geopolitics 107n16
Arlt, Roberto 183
ARP synthesizer 93–94, 98, 101
artifact, understanding 37
artistic creativity 4, 183–185
Asuar Digital Analog Computer *see*
 COMDASUAR
Asuar, José Vicente: computer music
 and 78–79, *79*, 83, *83*, 103–106,
 152; creativity of, artistic and
 technological 184–185; hardware
 design of 100–101, 103; impact of
 7–8; innovation of 82, 91; *Preludio*
 of 91; software design by 96,
 98, 101, 103; writings of 90–93,
 96–103; *see also* COMDASUAR
Atmega 328/256 microprocessors 163
Atmel AVR 128 microcontroller 160,
 177n36

Babbage, Charles 87
Banzi, Massimo 148–149
Barragán, Hernando: API design by
 162; circuit design and 167; code
 writing by 156; creativity of, artistic
 and technological 154, 184; at IDII
 157–158, 174; microcontroller
 selected by 159–160; in New York
 City 155; open-source philosophy
 and 174; physical computing and 11;
 political context of student years of
 154; programming language designed
 by 162–164; software design by
 157–159, 162; teaching design
 and 165; Wiring and 11, 149–150,
 154–157, 159–160, 162–165,
 167–168, 170–171, 173–174
Basic Stamp microcontroller 154–155,
 158
Bayard, Hippolyte 6, 30
BEABÁ (ABCs) computer art project
 133, *134*
Bi-color television system 70, 186
bioacoustics 22–23
Bonsiepe, Gui 11, 172–174
Brazil: CAPRE in 128, 130; computer
 history in 127–131; computer
 policies in 130–131; Executive
 Group for the Application of
 Electronic Computers in 128; FINEP
 in 129; Florence's relocation to 20;
 industrial development in 128–130;
 Langsdorff expeditions in 21–25, 29;
 Lua support and 116; Petrobras in
 116, 123; photography in 18, 38n3;
 postcolonial 6, 20–21; printing press

202 *Index*

in 23–25; technological autonomy and 194–195

Bronfman, Alejandra 197

Cabrera, Andrés 104

CAPRE (Brazilian agency) 128, 130

Carlos, Wendy 94

case studies *see* software studies

Celes, Waldemar 10, 116, 141

Chan, Anita Say 197

Channel 5 60–63, *62*, 69

Chile: computer history/systems in 84–85; computer music in 84, 84–85; coup d'état in 7, 85; media technologies in 7; Pinochet and 84–85; political changes in 85; restructuring of society in 84

Chowning, John 89, 97, 100

Chromoscopic Adapter for Television Equipment 46, *47*, 48, 54, *55*, *56*, 65, 69–71, 186

Coan, Paul 43–44, 48–50

Cobol programming language 121

Cobra (computer production company) 128–129

code: art and 155–157; Barragán's writing of 156; COMDASUAR 104–105, *105*; hardware and 116; Lua and 131–137; visibility of 131–137; Wiring and 154–156

Colombia: artistic experimentation in 154–155; code-art relationship in 155–156; gold chloride experiments in 33; "opening" of 154; political changes in 154; Wiring board production in 167–168; Wiring project and limitations of 171, 196

colonization/colonial studies 4, 12

color filter wheel 44–45, *47*, 64

color television: Apollo mission and 7, 43–44, 63, 185; background information 43–46; bi-color television system and 70, 186; Channel 5 and 60–63, *62*, 69; Chromoscopic Adapter for Television Equipment and 46, *47*, 48, 54, *55*, *56*, 65, 69–71, 186; Coan and 43–44, 48–50; color filter wheel and 44–45, *47*, 64; development of 43–46; equipment 59–63, 60–63, *61*; in Europe 69; Goldmark and 45–46, 48–49, 186; GonCam and 60; González (Guillermo) and

development of 46, *47*, 48–54, *55*, *56*, 57–60, 185–186; impact of 75n61; invention and 3; media technologies as natural resource and 50–54; in Mexico 46, 48, 50–63, 68; NTSC and 45–46, 68; overview 6–7, 68–71; PAL color system and 69; patent applications and, 54–59, 72n19; reconstructions 65–67, *68*, 188; SECAM color system and 69; in United States 45–46; Voyager mission and 7, 63–64, 185; World's Fair display 70

COMDASUAR: analog controls of 100–101; ARP synthesizer and 93–94, 98, 101; Asuar's written account of 96–103; code 104–105, *105*; composition and 86–90, 101, *102*, 103; development/design of 80–81, 90–96; drawings of 95, 95; geopolitical circumstances and 84–85, 107n16; limitations of 100; microprocessor for 98; open-source version of 106; operating system 101; overview 7, 103–106; PDP-8 computer and 94, 98, 101; as personal computer 81–82, 85; programs 101, *102*, 103, 110n64; public use and 83–86; purpose of 81, 96; reconstruction of 10–106, *105*, 110n69, 185, 188–189; software 96, 98, 101, 103–106, 188–189; sound generation system of 99, *99*, 93, 109n43, 186–187; Wiring board and, 104, 110n69

computer art: BEABÁ 133, *134*; *Derivadas de uma imagem* (Derivatives of an image) 133, *135*, 136; *Fotoformas* 132–133, *132*; invention and 3; overview 3; *see also* computer music; photography

computer history: in Brazil 127–131; in Chile 84–85

computer music: Analytical Engine and 87–88; *Así habló el computador* (Thus Spoke the Computer) LP and 78–79, *79*, 83; Asuar and 78–79, *79*, 83, *83*, 103–106, 152; background information 78–82; in Chile 84–85; Chowing and 89; composition 86–90, 92–93; *El computador virtuoso* (The Virtuoso Computer) LP and 81, 94; FM synthesis and

89–90; Hiller and Isaacson's *Iliac Suite* and 89; history of 106; invention and 3; mathematic models and 88–89; Mathews and 89; music concrete and 88, 90; overview 3, 6, 103–106; Pulse-Code Modulation and 89, 99–100, 108n30; software 88; *Switched on Bach* LP and 94; Xenakis and 89; Z3 computer and 87–88; *see also* COMDASUAR

Cope, David 107–108n19

Cordeiro, Waldemar 133, 136

creation process 183–184

creative user 189

creativity *see* artistic creativity; technological creativity

Csound programming language 104, 110n67, 189

CSS programming language 156

culture and media technologies 3

cyberculture, anthropology of 194

Cybersyn project 173

da Costa Marques, Ivan 129–130

Daguerre, Louis 25, 30

daguerreotype 25, 37, 186

De Barros, Geraldo 131–133, *132*, 136

decoloniality 193

decolonial studies 12

decolonial technologies 193–197

DEL (Delta Entry Language) programming language 123–124

Derivadas de uma imagem (Derivatives of an image) 133, *135*, 136

Design by Numbers (DBN) 157

dichroic color filters 65–66

digital-to-analog converter (DAC) 89

discourse networks 150

Duque, Alejandro 155

Edgerton, David 181

Edison, Thomas Alva 192

Escobar, Arturo 12, 194

Estridentismo (avant-garde movement) 52

Europe and color television 69

exile and technological creativity 30

experimental media archaeology 185–190

experimental reconstructions *see* reconstructions of technology

Experiments in Musical Intelligence (EMI) 107–108n19

Fernández, Maria 12, 197

Figueiredo, Luiz Henrique de 10, 116, 123–124, *138*

FINEP (Brazilian agency) 129

Florence, Hércules: bioacoustics and 22–23; biographical sketch of 20; creativity of, artistic and technological 184–185; glass negatives and 36–37, *36*; gold chloride experimentation and 31–35, *34*, *35*, 187–188; impact of 6–8; Langsdorff expedition and 21–25, 29; natural soundscape and 22–23, 31; *photographie* and 18–25, 33, 35, *36*, 37, 186–188; photography development and 25–29, *28*, *34*, 35–37; printing of work and 23–25, *24*, 33; reconstructions of apparatus of 33–37, *34*, *35*, *36*, 187–188; relocation to Brazil 20; *zoophonie* and 18–25, *19*, 35, *36*, 37, 186

Flores, Fernando 194

Flusser, Vilém 17, 29–30

FM synthesis 89–90

Folkman, Benjamin 94

Fortran programming language 93, 121

Fotoformas 132–133, *132*

Fox Talbot, Henry 36

Frege, Gottlob 115, 142n2

Fritzing (electronics prototyping kit) 11

Fry, Ben 157–158

G-10 minicomputer 129

Galeano, Eduardo 182

game studies 126, 137, 139–140

General Public License (GPL) 126

glass negatives 35–37, *36*

Global North: Global South linkages/ dialogues and 150, 153, 155; Latin America and 1–2; technology transfer to 48; television as global medium and 69; *see also specific country*

Global South: Global North linkages/ dialogues and 150, 153, 155; innovation and 170, 196; invention in 181–182; media technologies in 4; paradox working in 118; technology and, relationship with 71; technology transfer from 48; technoscape of 142; women and technological creativity in 197; *see also specific country*

Goddess technology 181–183

204 *Index*

gold chloride experimentation 31–35, *34, 35*, 187–188
Goldmark, Peter 45–46, 48–49, 186
GonCam (company) 60
González Camarena, Guillermo: bi-color television system and 70, 186; Channel 5 and 60–63, *62*, 69; color television development and 46, 47, 48–54, *55, 56*, 57–60, 69–71, 185–186; creativity of, artistic and technological 184–185; death of 71; impact of 7–9; Subjective Color Television system and 70; technological autonomy in Latin America and 71; Telesistema Mexicano and 61–63
González Camarena, Jorge 54, 60, 63, 184
Gost 10859 standard 122
Grim Fandango computer game 126
Gusmão, Bartolomeu de 29

Handy Board (robotics controller) 158
hardware: Asuar's design of 100–101, 103; Barragán's design of 174; capabilities of 141; code and 116; G-10 minicomputer 129; hybrid 131; invisibility of 158; locally produced 130–131; Lua 125, 141–142; naked 174; open-source 168, 170, 192, 196; reconstruction of COMDASUAR and 104; software blending with 175; software as separate from 175; visibility of 158–159; Wiring 157–158, 160, 165, 168, *169*; *see also specific type*
Heidegger, Martin 185
Helmholtz, Hermann von 44
Herrera de la Fuente, Luis 51
Hiller, Lejaren 89
hipercubo/ok/ 156; bookviewer 1.0 navigation tool 156
Hiperlook (experimental browser) 156
history: of computer music 106; of computers, in Brazil 127–131; of computers in Chile 84–85; of Lua 138; media 1, 12, 181; media art 4; of science in Latin America 193
HTML programming language 156
Huhtamo, Erkki 187
Hurtado, Xavier 154

Ierusalimschy, Roberto 10, 116, 119, 125, 137, *138*
innovation: alternative markets for 60; of Asuar 82, 91; globally explosive 149–150, 153; Global South and 170, 196; invention and 190–193; media technologies and 10; musical 89–90, 92; open-source philosophy and 171; of personal computer 152; Petrobras and oil 123; Schumpeter's vision of 190, 192; software studies and 5–6; technological historiography and 182; unsuccess narratives and 190–193
integrated circuit 151
Interaction Design Institute (IDII) 11, 148–149, 157–158, 174
interface 150–153
invention: color television and 3; computer art and 3; computer music and 3; creation process and 183–184; in Global South 181–182; innovation and 190–193; invisibility of 182–183; in Latin America 3, 183; learning from processes of 192; outside centers of techno-scientific discourse 29; physical computing and 3; programming language and 3; software studies and 5–6; term of 3; unsuccess narratives and 190–193
Isaacson, Leonard 89
Italy 147, 149

JavaScript programming language 122, 125, 137, 176n26
Javelin Stamp board 158

Kac, Eduardo 12, 155
Kittler, Friedrich 31, 147, 150, 158–159, 174–175, 185, 192
Kossoy, Boris 21–22, 26, 30, 32, 186
Kubitscheck, Juscelino 128
Kubota, Shigeko 1

Langsdorff, Gregory 21–25, 29
language and media technologies 182
Latin America: colonization in 4; Global North and 1–2; invention in 3, 183; media archaeology and 12; media history and 1, 12; media technologies in 1–2, 4, 9, 193; oppression/exploitation in 4–5; postcolonial 183; science history

in 193; technological autonomy in 71; technological change in 182; technological creativity in 6; *see also* South America; *specific country*
Latour, Bruno 68, 85, 148
Lienhard, John 191
Lisp programming language 121–122
Lovelace, Ada 87
Lozano Hemmer, Rafael 155
Lua (programming language): Brazil's computer history and 127–131; Brazil's support of 116; code and 131–137; community 139; conference presentation of 138, *138*; development/design of 116, 122–125, 130–131, 139, 142; embeddedness of 125; evolution of 138–139; experience of, direct 189–190; functionality of 137; hardware 125, 141–142; history of 138; impact of 192; Internet of Things and 116; Latin script used in 120; licensing framework 126; logo *117*; new versions of 137; open-source philosophy and 11, 116, 126, 139, 195–196; overview 10–11, 137–142; Petrobras's use of 116, 123–125; place of origin and 118–120, 141–142; political context of 130–131; portability of 124–125, 131, 137; Robolox game platform and 139, *140*; scripting languages and 125–126, 137; socio-cultural context of 131; software 126, 131; success of, global 116–117, 126, 196; suitability of 137; syntax of 125; Takhteyev's study of 118–120; Tecgraf's use of 116, 123–125, 142; users of, 118, 140–141, 142n5; video games and 126, 139–140, *140*
Luasoftware 126, 131
LuaAV project 189–190

Macintosh computer 152
Maldonado, Tomás 172–173
Maples Arce, Manuel 52
margins of history 181
Martino, Gianluca 149
mathematic models 88–89
Mathews, Max 89, 97, 99–100
media archaeology: contributions to, room for 187; experimental 185–190; Latin America and 12;

resignification of 9; shift in 1; software studies and 4–5
media art histories 4
media arts *see* computer music; photography
media history 1, 12, 181; *see also* software studies
media studies *see* software studies
media technologies: attention to 37; in Chile 7; computer as 10; contemporary 2, 192–193; culture and 3; as designs 8; framework 5; in Global South 4; hybridity of 121; innovation and 10; interdisciplinary dialogues and 197; language and 182; in Latin America 1–2, 4, 9, 193; in Mexico 7, 50–51; narratives 3; as natural resource 50–54; in 1990s 1; resignification 64–65; storytelling and 183–185; technological mainstream and 3; unique development of 4; *see also* software studies
Medina, Eden 84, 197
Mexico: color television in 46, 48, 50–63, 68; Estridentismo in 52; media as natural resource in 50–54; media technologies in 7, 50–51; patent application in 54–59; postcolonial 7; technological revolution in 50; United States and, relationship with 53–54; wireless media in 51–52
Milićević, Myriel *166*, 167
minicomputers 129–130
Mogilefsky, Bret 126
moon landing and color television 7, 43–44, 63, 185
Moscati, Giorgio 133, *134*, *135*, 136
music composition *see* computer music

National Television System Committee (NTSC) 45–46, 68
natural soundscape 22–23, 31
Niño, Patricia 155
Nmap 141–142

Ochoa, Victor L. 184
Olivetti 147–148
Olivetti, Camilo 147
open-source philosophy/culture: Arduino and 147–148; Barragán and 174; COMDASUAR and 106;

206   *Index*

as design condition 153; hardware
168, 170, 192, 196; innovation and
171; interaction among societies and
9–10; Lua and 11, 116, 126, 139,
195–196; software and 153; software
studies and 193–197; Sparkfun and
168; Wiring and 157, 171, 195–196
Osthoff, Simone 197

Page, Joanna 12, 197
Paik, Nam June, 1
patent applications 54–59, 72n19
PDP-8 computer 94, 98, 101
Penix-Tadsen, Phillip 140
personal computers 82, 152
Petrobras 116, 123–125, 131, 142
Phase Alternating Line (PAL) color
system 69
photographie 18–25, 33, 35, 36, 37,
186–188
photography: background information
17–20; Bayard and 30; in Brazil 18,
38n3; camera obscura and 26–27,
29–35; current practices 37–38;
emergence of 17; equipment 27–28,
28; Florence and development of
25–29, *28*, *34*, 35–37; Fox Talbot
and 36; glass negatives and 35–37,
36; gold chloride experimentation
and 31–35, *34*, *35*, 187–188; image
types in 17, 35–36; invention and 3;
overview 3, 6, 35–38; *photographie*
and 18–25, 33, 35, *36*, 37, 186–188;
polygraphie and 25; as technology
31; zone of indetermination and
17–18; *zoophonie* and 18–25, *19*,
35, *36*, 37, 186
physical computing: Barragán and 11;
invention and 3; overview 9–11;
Processing programming language
and 11; *see also* Wiring
Pluriverse 194–195
polygraphie 25
portability 124–125, 131, 137, 152
primitive distribution of possibilities 17
printing press 6, 23–25, 39n25
problem of priority 191
Processing programming language:
creation of 157–158; function of
13n5, 157; physical computing and
11; Wiring and 11, 110n69, *153*,
157–158, 162, *163*, 177n45, 189
programming languages: API and
124–125; background information

115–118; Barragán's design of
162–164; describing 115–116;
development of, 122, 126, 115–116,
142n2; emergence of 120–122;
examples of 122–123; invention and
3; overview 9–11, 137–142; pillars
of 121; place of origin and 118–120,
141–142; recent 122–123; in United
States 121; Wiring 162–164, 170,
177n44, 190; Zuse and 127; *see also
specific name*
prospective archaeology 65, 71
Pulse-Code Modulation (PCM) 89,
99–100, 108n30
Python programming language 125

Quiroga, Horacio 183

Raspberry Pi board 104–105, *105*,
110n68, 174, 189
ReactiveT-ext 1.0 156
Reas, Casey 157–158
reconstructions of technology:
color television 65–67, *68*, 188;
COMDASUAR 104–106, *105*,
110n69, 188–189; defining 13n4;
of Florence's apparatus 33–37, *34*,
35, *36*, 187–188; limitations of 187;
prospective archaeology and 65;
software studies and 9; Z3 computer
88
resignification of technology 8–9,
64–65, 71, 74n52 181, 189
retroactive user 189
retrospective user 189
Rivera Cusicanqui, Silvia 194
Roblox game platform 139, *140*
robotics 151–152
Ruiz, Tania 155
Rutishauser, Heinz 121

Sack, Warren 121, 162
Sallis, John 185
Sammet, Jean E. 121
Santos, Guillermo *19*, 33, *36*
Sarlo, Beatriz 12, 182, 197
Schreyer, Helmut 127–128
Schulze, Johann Heinrich 31
Schumacher, Federico 84
Schumpeter, Joseph 190, 192
scripting languages 125–126, 137,
141
Sequential Color with Memory
(SECAM) color system 69

Index 207

Simondon, Gilbert 17
Smith, Wesley 189
software: Arduino 170; as art 155–157; Asuar's design of 96, 98, 101, 103; Barragán's design of 157–159, 162; COMDASUAR 96, 98, 101, 103–106, 188–189; computer music 88; G-10 minicomputer 129; hardware blending with 175; hardware as separate from 175; Kittler's view of 158–159, 174–175; Lua 126, 131; open-source philosophy and 153; place of origin and 118–120, 139, 141–142; reconstruction of COMDASUAR and 104; roots of 121; Wiring 157–159, 165, 174; *see also specific name*
software studies: alternative conceptual models and, search for 8; artistic projects derived from 187–188; chronology of 5; contemporary 9–10; decolonial technologies and 193–197; experimental media archaeology and 185–190; fields in dialogue with 4, 12; framework developed via 11–12; Goddess technology and 181–183; innovation and 5–6; insights from 181–197; invention and 5–6; lessons from 2; media archaeology and 4–5; media art histories and 4; media art history and 4; media history and 4; open-source philosophy and 193–197; organization of 5–6; overview 2–3; reconstructions of technology and 9; resignification of technology and 8–9; selecting 2; storytelling and 183–185; technological creativity and 3, 5–6; technological creativity versus artistic creativity and 4; unsuccess narratives and 190–193; women's absence in 196–197; *see also* color television; computer music; Lua; photography; Wiring
SOL (Simple Object Language) programming language 123–125
Solomon, Leslie 70
Sottsass, Ettore 172, 174
South America 20, 39n25, 107n16, 167; *see also* Latin America; *specific country*
Sparkfun (company) 168

storytelling and media technologies 183–185
subvocal imagination 119
Superplan programming language 121

Takhteyev, Yury 118–120, 124–125, 130, 139, 141
Tecgraf 116, 123–125, 142
technical images 17–18, 35–36
technical innovation *see* innovation
technical invention *see* invention
technical objects 17, 38n2
technological autonomy 71, 194–195
technological change 3, 182, 190
technological creativity: artistic creativity and 183–185; exile and 30; software studies and 3, 5–6; women as agents of 197
technological decisions 195
technology transfer 48, 65
Thomas, Hernán 8–9, 64, 74n52 189
Toledo, Raimundo 84
traditional images 17–18, 29, 35–36
Transmediale festival (2001) 156
transmission of technology 48, 65
Typovideo project 156

Ulm School of Design 11, 131, 148, 172
United States: color television development in 45–46; Mexico and, relationship with 53–54; programming languages in 121
unsuccess narratives 190–193

Varela, Francisco 155
video games and Lua 126, 139–140, *140*
Vielliard, Jacques 23
Voyager mission and color television 7, 63–64, 185

Wakefield, Graham 189
Winograd, Terry 194
wireless media 51–52
Wiring (platform): Arduino and 149; background information 147–150; Barragán and development of 11, 149–150, 154–157, 159–160, 162–165, 167–168, 170–171, 173–174; Basic Stamp microcontroller and 154–155, 158;

208 *Index*

board 104, 110n69, 149–150, *153*, 159–160, *161*, 162, 174, 190; code and 154–156; creation of 157; design of 159; displacement of 167–171; ecosystem 162, *163*; experience of, direct 189–190; hardware 157–158, 160, 165, 168, *169*; interface and 150–153; open-source philosophy and 157, 171, 195–196; overview 11, 171–175; physical computing and 11, 157–158; Processing programming language and 11, 110n69, 153, 157–158, 162, *163*, 177n45, 189; programming language 162–164, 170, 177n44, 190; questions raised by case study 171; reasoning behind 154; software 157–159, 165, 174; tutorial, online *169*; users, first 164–165, *166*, 167; website 167, *168*

women as agents of technological creativity 197

World of Warcraft (WoW) video game 139

writing systems 150

Xenakis, Iannis 89

Z1/Z2 computers 127, 150
Z3 computer 87–88
Zielinski, Siegfried 1, 65, 187
zone of indetermination 17–18
zoophonie 18–25, *19*, 35, *36*, 37, 186
Zuse, Konrad 87–88, 121, 127, 150